CALVERT
MATH

Calvert Math is based upon a previously published textbook series. Calvert School has customized the textbooks using the mathematical principles developed by the original authors. Calvert School wishes to thank the authors for their cooperation. They are:

Audrey V. Buffington
Mathematics Teacher
Wayland Public Schools
Wayland, Massachusetts

Alice R. Garr
Mathematics Department Chairperson
Herricks Middle School
Albertson, New York

Jay Graening
Professor of Mathematics
    and Secondary Education
University of Arkansas
Fayetteville, Arkansas

Philip P. Halloran
Professor, Mathematical Sciences
Central Connecticut State University
New Britain, Connecticut

Michael Mahaffey
Associate Professor,
    Mathematics Education
University of Georgia
Athens, Georgia

Mary A. O'Neal
Mathematics Laboratory Teacher
Brentwood Unified Science
    Magnet School
Los Angeles, California

John H. Stoeckinger
Mathematics Department Chairperson
Carmel High School
Carmel, Indiana

Glen Vannatta
Former Mathematics Supervisor
Special Mathematics Consultant
Indianapolis Public Schools
Indianapolis, Indiana

ISBN-13: 978-1-888287-53-0
ISBN-10: 1-888287-53-5

1 2 3 4 5 6 7 8 9 10   12 11 10 09 08

SENIOR CONSULTANT/PROJECT COORDINATOR

Jessie C. Sweeley, Manager of Curriculum Development

PROJECT FACILITATOR/LEAD RESEARCHER

Nicole M. Henry, Math Curriculum Specialist

FIELD TEST TEACHERS

The following Calvert teachers used the Calvert Math prototype in their classrooms and added materials and teaching techniques based on Calvert philosophy and methodology.

Andrew S. Bowers	Brian J. Mascuch	Patricia G. Scott
James O. Coady Jr.	John M. McLaughlin	E. Michael Shawen
Roman A. Doss	Mary Ellen Nessler	Ada M. Stankard
Shannon C. Frederick	Margaret B. Nicolls	Virginia P.B. White
Julia T. Holt	Michael E. Paul	Jennifer A. Yapsuga
Willie T. Little III	Diane E. Proctor	Andrea L. Zavitz

CALVERT EDUCATION SERVICES (CES) CONSULTANTS

The following CES staff worked with the Day School faculty in developing the mathematical principles for Calvert Math.

Eileen M. Byrnes	Christina L. Mohs	Mary-Louise Stenchly
Nicole M. Henry	Kelly W. Painter	Ruth W. Williams
Linda D. Hummel		

REVISION AUTHORS

The following Day School faculty and CES staff contributed to the correlation of the math materials to national standards and to the authoring of revisions based on the correlations.

Nicole M. Henry	Willie T. Little III	Mary Ethel Vinje
Julia T. Holt	Mary Ellen Nessler	Jennifer A. Yapsuga
Barbara B. Kirby		

COPY EDITORS

Bernadette Burger, Senior Editor

Sarah E. Hedges	Mary Pfeiffer
Maria R. Kerner	Megan L. Snyder

GRAPHIC DESIGNERS

Vickie M. Johnson, Senior Designer
Vanessa Ann Panzarino

To the Student
This book was made for you. It will teach you many
new things about mathematics. Your math book is
a tool to help you discover and master the skills
you will need to become powerful in math.

About the Art in this Book
Calvert homeschooling students from all over the world
and Calvert Day School students have contributed
their original art for this book. We hope you enjoy
looking at their drawings as you study mathematics.

Contents

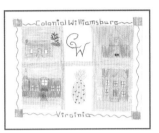

1 Number Theory and Integers

2 Decimals

3 Fractions, Decimals, and Percents

4 Computing Fractions

5 Linear Equations and Inequalities

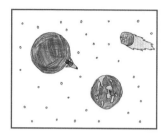

6 Ratios, Rates, Proportions, and Percents

7 Geometry and Plane Figures

8 Geometry and Measurement

9 Three-Dimensional Figures

10 Probability

11 Displaying and Analyzing Data

12 Functions and Coordinate Graphing

Diagnosing Readiness

In this preliminary chapter, you will take a diagnostic skills pretest, practice skills that you need to work on, and take a diagnostic skills posttest. This preliminary chapter will assure you have the skills necessary to begin Chapter 1.

Diagnostic Skills Pretest

Complete the diagnostic skills pretest below. If you get one or more problems in a section incorrect, please refer to the section number in parenthesis for review. After reviewing this chapter, take the diagnostic skills posttest at the end of the chapter.

Round to the underlined place-value position. (Section 1)

1. 4̲9

2. 8̲33

3. 9,6̲05

4. 1̲5,821

Round to the greatest place-value position. (Section 1)

5. 283

6. 7,582

7. 4,802

8. 342,528

Write in standard form. (Section 2)

9. seventeen thousandths

10. twenty and three hundredths

Write in expanded form. (Section 2)

11. 5.28

12. 16.821

13. 6.5211

Replace each ■ with <, >, or = to make a true statement. (Section 3)

14. 2,480 ■ 2,840

15. 19,811 ■ 19,802

16. 52,258 ■ 52,258

Order the numbers from least to greatest. (Section 3)

17. 125, 250, 111, 258, 115

18. 32,405; 33,551; 31,529; 32,452

Estimate. (Section 4)

19. $85 − $42

20. 19,916 + 2,661 + 1,485

21. 890 × 4

22. 28 × 76

23. 1,408 ÷ 8

24. 3,776 ÷ 59

Add. (Section 5)

25. $943 + $863

26. 3,528 + 6,444

27. $52,046 + $41,388

28. 76,360 + 35,640

29. $42,075 + $9,825

30. 1,256 + 3,524 + 2,325

Subtract. (Section 6)

31. 600 − 234

32. $6,791 − $899

33. 3,406 − 4,108

34. 64,700 − 899

35. 24,406 − 15,507

36. 314,500 − 64,601

Multiply. (Section 7)

37. $\$68 \times 17$ **38.** $9{,}653 \times 14$ **39.** 749×30

40. 567×802 **41.** 673×56 **42.** $800 \times \$307$

Divide. (Section 8)

43. $5\overline{)340}$ **44.** $8\overline{)2{,}460}$ **45.** $37\overline{)259}$ **46.** $204\overline{)3{,}264}$

47. $\$19{,}076 \div 3$ **48.** $17{,}830 \div 65$ **49.** $\$56{,}000 \div 700$

1 Place Value and Rounding

In a recent presidential election, 92,652,842 people voted. A newspaper reporter may express this as about 92,653,000, about 93,000,000, or about 90 million. In each case, the reporter rounded the number.

Trillions			Billions			Millions			Thousands			Ones		
hundred trillions	ten trillions	trillions	hundred billions	ten billions	billions	hundred millions	ten millions	millions	hundred thousands	ten thousands	thousands	hundreds	tens	ones
						9	2	6	5	2	8	4	2

The chart above shows the place-value position of each digit in 92,652,842. To round a number, look at the digit to the right of the place being rounded. Round 92,652,842 to the nearest million.

Round up if the digit to the right is 5, 6, 7, 8, or 9.

To the nearest *million*, 92,652,842 rounds to 93,000,000.

The underlined digit remains the same if the digit to the right is 0, 1, 2, 3, or 4.

Try THESE

Name the digit in each place-value position in 1,509,786.

1. hundreds
2. millions
3. thousands
4. ten thousands

Round to the nearest ten.

5. 286
6. 21
7. $555
8. 4,306

Round to the nearest hundred.

9. 240
10. 650
11. $964
12. 2,480

Round to the underlined place-value position.

1. 6<u>8</u>9
2. <u>1</u>,324
3. 1,6<u>3</u>5
4. $2,9<u>8</u>2
5. 8,<u>0</u>20
6. 20,<u>6</u>91
7. 10,<u>4</u>26
★8. <u>9</u>,560

Round to the greatest place-value position.

9. 15
10. 465
11. 39,806
12. 18,017
13. 2,164,518
14. 350,407
★15. 9,850
★16. 995,111

Each number has been rounded to a certain place-value position. Name that place-value position.

17. 4,385 ➡ 4,390
18. 8,245 ➡ 8,000
19. 3,115 ➡ 3,100
20. 589 ➡ 600
★21. 6,965 ➡ 7,000
★22. 106,500 ➡ 110,000

Problem SOLVING ··

23. Rank the areas of the states in the chart from 1 through 6. The state with the largest area gets a rank of 1.

24. Round each state's area to the nearest ten thousand square miles.

25. Why may the population of a large city be reported to the nearest thousand, while that of a small town is reported to the nearest hundred?

State	Area (in square miles)
New York	47,224
Texas	261,914
Alaska	570,374
Maine	30,865
Washington	66,581
Nebraska	76,878

2 Decimals and Place Value

Florence Griffith Joyner holds the Olympic record for the 100-meter track-and-field event. Her time was ten and fifty-four hundredths seconds. The number can be written as the **decimal** 10.54.

The place-value chart used for whole numbers can be extended to the right of the ones place to name numbers less than one. The decimal point is used to separate the ones and the tenths places.

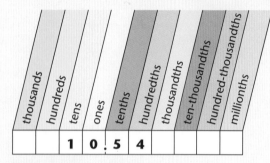

Write: 10.54
 Say: ten and fifty-four hundredths

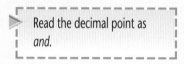

Read the decimal point as *and*.

More Examples

A. Write: 0.6
   Say: six tenths

B. Write: 0.43
   Say: forty-three hundredths

C. Write: 5.036
   Say: five and thirty-six thousandths

The place-value chart can help you write decimals in standard form or expanded form. In the number 10.76, the digit 6 is in the hundredths position. This digit and its place-value position name the number six hundredths, 0.06.

Standard Form: 2.146

Expanded Form: 2 + 0.1 + 0.04 + 0.006

two   one tenth   four hundredths   six thousandths

Try THESE

Write in words.

1. 0.8
2. 0.04
3. 0.017
4. 7.2
5. 1.29
6. 0.0526
7. 0.000006
8. 9.00057

• •

Write in standard form.

1. seven tenths

2. three hundredths

3. three hundred

4. five and nine tenths

5. forty-six hundredths

6. twelve thousandths

7. 0.2 + 0.03

8. 40 + 5 + 0.8

9. 0.5 + 0.002

10. four and six ten-thousandths

11. sixty ten-thousandths

12. nine hundred-thousandths

13. two millionths

14. 0.5 + 0.02 + 0.07 + 0.009

15. 0.2 + 0.0003 + 0.00008

Write in expanded form.

16. 3.16

17. 10.257

18. 2.2964

Problem SOLVING •

19. In 0.33, how does the value of the 3 on the left compare with the 3 on the right?

20. Brian scored 9.675 in a gymnastic event. Write 9.675 in expanded form.

21. A train travels 436.8 miles a day. Write this distance in words.

3 Comparing and Ordering Whole Numbers

Camp Hill Middle School has 421 students, and Valley Middle School has 389 students. The number line below can be used to compare 421 and 389.

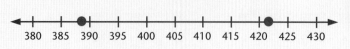

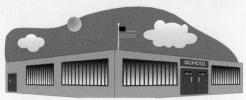

389 is to the left of 421	421 is to the right of 389
389 is less than 421 ← **Say** →	421 is greater than 389
389 < 421 ← **Write** →	421 > 389

The symbols < and > always point toward the lesser number. Compare numbers by starting at the left and comparing the digits in each place-value position.

More Examples

A. 7,857 and 7,832

same
digits

7,857 > 7,832

In the tens place, 5 > 3.

B. 5,647 and 5,648

same
digits

5,647 < 5,648

In the ones place, 7 < 8.

C. Order 657, 585, 857, 664, and 458 from least to greatest.

Think about a number line, and put the numbers in order from least to greatest.

458, 585, 657, 664, 857

Try **THESE** ....

Replace each ■ with <, >, or = to make a true statement.

1. 9 ■ 0

2. 54 ■ 74

3. $38 ■ $51

4. 940 ■ 904

5. 2,076 ■ 2,096

6. 649 ■ 906

....

Replace each ■ with <, >, or = to make a true statement.

1. 6 ■ 5

2. 8 ■ 18

3. 15 ■ 12

4. 24 ■ 30

5. 52 ■ 52

6. 21 ■ 20

7. $7 ■ $9

8. 800 ■ 600

9. $700 ■ $700

10. 72 ■ 719

11. 89¢ ■ 90¢

12. $46 ■ $64

13. 8,650 ■ 8,650

14. 4,763 ■ 4,789

15. 237 ■ 2,036

16. 1,269 ■ 1,369

17. 2,370 ■ 2,360

18. 7,320 ■ 7,322

19. 10,040 ■ 10,404

20. 171,234 ■ 171,243

21. 28,303 ■ 27,303

22. 361,076 ■ 351,298

23. 888,547 ■ 888,544

24. 616,723 ■ 267,114

25. 4,278,632 ■ 4,228,326

26. 8,475,598 ■ 8,475,987

27. 16,401,543 ■ 16,411,621

28. 278,329,643 ■ 279,210,332

Problem SOLVING ....

Order the numbers in each list from least to greatest.

29. 42, 9, 24, 16, 41, 20

30. 69, 142, 71, 75, 51, 15

31. 106, 100, 160, 109, 116, 121

32. 2,302; 2,320; 2,303; 2,139; 2,330

33. 10,045; 11,000; 10,000; 11,412; 10,898; 11,141

34. 347; 1,001; 842; 88, 990; 633; 57; 784; 556; 642

35. The chart below lists the golf scores of each team. Rank the team names in order from 1 through 8. The team with the least score gets a rank of 1.

Team	Blue	Red	Gold	Gray	Fox	Cubs	Irons	Tee
Score	400	419	398	457	416	395	408	420

4 Estimation: Using Rounding

Last year, 3,141,027 people visited the San Diego Zoo. About how many people visited each day? Since you only need to know about how many people, you can estimate to find the answer.

Follow these steps to estimate 3,141,027 ÷ 365.

Step 1	Step 2	Step 3
Round the divisor. 365 rounds to 400. $400\overline{)3{,}141{,}027}$	Find the number of digits in the quotient. $\overset{\text{x x x x}}{400\overline{)3{,}141{,}027}}$	Find the multiple of the rounded divisor that is close to the dividend. **THINK** $4 \times 7 = 28$ $\overset{8{,}000}{400\overline{)3{,}200{,}000}}$

About 8,000 people visited the San Diego Zoo each day.

More Examples

To estimate sums, differences, or products, round each number. Then add, subtract, or multiply.

A.
$$\begin{array}{r} 3{,}794 \\ 12{,}376 \\ +\ 1{,}021 \\ \hline \end{array} \longrightarrow \begin{array}{r} 4{,}000 \\ 12{,}000 \\ +\ 1{,}000 \\ \hline 17{,}000 \end{array}$$
Round to the same place-value position.

B.
$$\begin{array}{r} 2{,}300 \\ -\ 980 \\ \hline \end{array} \longrightarrow \begin{array}{r} 2{,}300 \\ -\ 1{,}000 \\ \hline 1{,}300 \end{array}$$
980 rounded to the nearest hundred is 1,000.

C.
$$\begin{array}{r} 876 \\ \times\ 7 \\ \hline \end{array} \longrightarrow \begin{array}{r} 900 \\ \times\ 7 \\ \hline 6{,}300 \end{array}$$
Do not change 1-digit factors.

D.
$$\begin{array}{r} 506 \\ \times\ 27 \\ \hline \end{array} \longrightarrow \begin{array}{r} 500 \\ \times\ 30 \\ \hline 15{,}000 \end{array}$$

Try THESE

Estimate.

1.
$$\begin{array}{r} 306 \\ +\ 622 \\ \hline \end{array} \quad \begin{array}{r} 300 \\ +\ 600 \\ \hline \end{array}$$

2.
$$\begin{array}{r} 4{,}565 \\ -\ 1{,}104 \\ \hline \end{array} \quad \begin{array}{r} 5{,}000 \\ -\ 1{,}000 \\ \hline \end{array}$$

3.
$$\begin{array}{r} 629 \\ \times\ 75 \\ \hline \end{array} \quad \begin{array}{r} 600 \\ \times\ 80 \\ \hline \end{array}$$

4. $6\overline{)504}$ $\overset{\text{xx}}{6\overline{)504}} \longrightarrow 6\overline{)480}$

5. $52\overline{)1{,}037}$ $50\overline{)1{,}037} \longrightarrow \overset{\text{xx}}{50\overline{)1{,}000}}$

Estimate.

1. 458
    − 90

2. 1,002
    + 365

3. 6,591
    − 710

4. $3,211
    +   695

5. 4,723
    − 805

6. 58
    × 12

7. $82
    × 27

8. 124
    × 56

9. 24
    × 6

10. 9)436

11. 8)478

12. 6)$608

13. 7)5,647

14. 78)572

15. 46)368

16. 415 + 8,137

17. 875 − 95

★18. 3,432 ÷ 788

★19. 64,296 ÷ 893

Problem SOLVING

20. Three garden hoses are joined together to reach a flower bed. The hoses are about 23 feet, 47 feet, and 82 feet long. Will their combined length reach 150 feet?

21. Lui An fills her car's tank with 19 gallons of gasoline after driving 558 miles. About how many miles did her car get per gallon?

5 Adding Whole Numbers

The textbook warehouse has 275 history books and 187 science books. To find the total number of books in the warehouse, add 275 and 187.

Estimate:
$$\begin{array}{r} 300 \\ + 200 \\ \hline 500 \end{array}$$

Add in each place-value position as follows.

Step 1	Step 2	Step 3
Add the ones.	Add the tens.	Add the hundreds.
$\begin{array}{r} {\scriptstyle 1} \\ 275 \\ + 187 \\ \hline 2 \end{array}$	$\begin{array}{r} {\scriptstyle 1\ 1} \\ 275 \\ + 187 \\ \hline 62 \end{array}$	$\begin{array}{r} {\scriptstyle 1\ 1} \\ 275 \\ + 187 \\ \hline 462 \end{array}$

There are 462 instruments in the warehouse.

The answer 462 is reasonable, since it is close to the estimate of 500.

More Examples

A.
$$\begin{array}{r} {\scriptstyle 1\ 1\ 2} \\ 1{,}837 \\ 78 \\ + \ \ 209 \\ \hline 2{,}124 \end{array}$$

$$\begin{array}{r} 1{,}800 \\ 100 \\ + \ 200 \\ \hline 2{,}100 \end{array}$$

B.
$$\begin{array}{r} {\scriptstyle 1\ \ 1\ 1} \\ 2{,}561 \\ 4{,}387 \\ + \ 3{,}942 \\ \hline 10{,}890 \end{array}$$

$$\begin{array}{r} 3{,}000 \\ 4{,}000 \\ + \ 4{,}000 \\ \hline 11{,}000 \end{array}$$

Add.

1. $800 + 80$

2. $27 + 38$

3. $\$706 + 101$

4. $4{,}792 + 5{,}006$

5. $69{,}916 + 55{,}107$

6. $25{,}628 + 14{,}968$

Add.

1. $86
   + 94

2. 241
   + 65

3. 265
   + 467

4. 858
   + 625

5. 1,427
   + 462

6. 1,594
   + 166

7. $4,982
   + 2,652

8. 5,280
   + 4,895

9. 10,684
   + 9,565

10. 65,862
    + 31,789

11. 226 + 72

12. $2,016 + $382

13. 72 + 28

14. $37 + $95

15. $687 + $48

16. 706 + 945

17. 2,807 + 406

18. 3,642 + 899

19. 5,736 + 1,296

20. $9,886 + $6,227

21. 12,795 + 8,646

22. 28,664 + 4,702

23. 19,685 + 7,868

24. 32,847 + 5,628

25. 15,265 + 27,799

26. 24,637 + 18,962

27. 44,778 + 56,428

28. 125,580 + 45,927

29. 68
    72
    + 65

30. $35
    93
    + 75

31. 210
    86
    + 198

32. 19
    234
    49
    + 106

33. $389
    524
    603
    + 942

34. 9,489
    6,339
    2,174
    + 13,816

35. 886
    227
    + 794

36. 6,381 + 89 + 462

37. 9,276 + 77,478 + 32,287

38. 28,726 + 4,903 + 16,196 + 80,041

39. 18,046 + 25,681 + 43,752 + 64,658

Problem SOLVING

40. A newspaper deliveryman drives 1,938 miles one week and 793 miles another week. What is his total mileage?

41. A company makes deposits of $7,328, $10,942, and $8,499. How much money is deposited?

6 Subtracting Whole Numbers

A small music hall seats 829 people. There are 698 people at one show. To find the number of empty seats, subtract the number of people from the number of seats. Subtract 698 from 829. An estimate is 800 – 700 or 100.

Step 1	Step 2	Step 3
Subtract the ones.	Rename 82 tens as 7 hundreds and 12 tens.	Subtract the tens and hundreds.
829 – 698 1	7 12 8̸2̸9 – 698 1	7 12 8̸2̸9 – 698 131

The answer 131 is reasonable, because it is close to the estimate of 100.

Use addition to check the subtraction.

$$\begin{array}{r} 698 \\ + 131 \\ \hline 829 \end{array}$$

More Examples

A.
$$\begin{array}{r} \overset{1\ 1}{\underset{}{}}\overset{19\ 17}{1,2\cancel{0}\cancel{7}} \\ - 548 \\ \hline 659 \end{array}$$
$$\begin{array}{r} 1,200 \\ - 500 \\ \hline 700 \end{array}$$

B.
$$\begin{array}{r} \overset{3\ 9\ 9\ 16}{4,\cancel{0}\cancel{0}\cancel{6}} \\ - 457 \\ \hline 3,549 \end{array}$$
$$\begin{array}{r} 4,000 \\ - 500 \\ \hline 3,500 \end{array}$$

Try THESE

1. 55 – 23

2. $749 – 235

3. 2,526 – 167

4. 32,128 – 31,234

• •

Subtract.

1. 656
   − 598

2. 888
   − 298

3. 4,837
   − 482

4. $1,326
   − 138

5. 8,469
   − 6,735

6. 6,275
   − 2,186

7. 2,937
   − 1,939

8. 57,382
   − 6,469

9. 62,474
   − 2,239

10. 660
    − 45

11. 520
    − 107

12. 460
    − 188

13. 300
    − 128

14. 108
    − 49

15. $717
    − 388

16. 206
    − 167

17. 416
    − 88

18. 610
    − 95

19. 515
    − 408

20. $717
    − 388

21. 206
    − 167

22. 416
    − 88

23. 610
    − 95

24. 515
    − 408

25. 2,064
    − 823

26. 6,403
    − 796

27. $4,005
    − 84

28. 2,001
    − 1,623

29. 8,006
    − 7,928

30. 2,716
    − 1,947

31. 40,106
    − 7,838

32. 11,411
    − 1,596

33. $11,010
    − 2,786

34. 51,110
    − 23,861

35. $661 − $453

36. 945 − 559

37. 1,568 − 1,177

38. 2,431 − 1,654

39. 45,832 − 9,843

40. $83,649 − $56,728

41. 93,584 − 73,464

42. 236,423 − 87,937

43. 327,365 − 128,776

44. 910 − 259

45. 6,000 − 1,287

46. 26,679 − 8,582

47. 10,054 − 6,075

48. 43,111 − 18,456

49. 61,053 − 58,476

Problem SOLVING •

50. Lee sells 245 raffle tickets, and Joe sells 168. How many more tickets does Lee sell than Joe?

51. Carla saves $1,067 for a used car. The car costs $4,022. How much more money does Carla need to save to buy a car?

7 Multiplying Whole Numbers

In one week, a campground rented 257 campsites at $14.
To find the total amount of money the campground made,
multiply 257 by $14.

Estimate: $300 × $10 = $3,000

Step 1	Step 2	Step 3
Multiply by the ones.	Multiply by the tens.	Add.
4 × 257	1 ten × 257	
257 × 14 ——— 1028	257 × 14 ——— 1028 257	257 × 14 ——— 1028 257 ——— $3,598

The total amount is $3,598. Compared to the estimate, this answer is reasonable.

You can also multiply 3-digit numbers.

Multiply 325 × 165.

Step 1	Step 2	Step 3	Step 4
Multiply by the ones.	Multiply by the tens.	Multiply by the hundreds.	Add.
5 × 325	6 tens × 325	1 hundred × 325	
325 × 165 ——— 1625	325 × 165 ——— 1625 1950	325 × 165 ——— 1625 1950 325	325 × 165 ——— 1625 1950 325 ——— 53,625

More Examples

A.
```
    43
  × 36
  ————
   258
   129
  ————
 1,548
```

B.
```
     932
   × 580
  ———————
   74560
    4660
  ———————
 540,560
```

C.
```
     7,561
   ×   544
  —————————
     30244
     30244
     37805
  —————————
 4,113,184
```

Multiply.

1. 34 × 21	2. 56 × 90	3. 562 × 120	4. 212 × 967

Exercises

Multiply.

1. 63 × 12	2. 231 × 32	3. 402 × 21	4. 72 × 43
5. 37 × 16	6. 700 × 25	7. 208 × 43	8. 2,198 × 42
9. $2,164 × 40	10. 3,265 × 72	11. 2,605 × 42	12. 7,903 × 33
13. 216 × 814	14. $448 × 692	15. 593 × 197	16. 234 × 432
17. 247 × 800	18. 7,148 × 501	19. 1,267 × 304	20. 5,237 × 109

21. $68 × 35
22. 75 × 46
23. 39 × 87
24. 216 × 68
25. 50 × $423
26. 677 × 29
27. 9,284 × 71
28. 8,740 × 12
29. 90 × 11,200
30. 6,255 × 43
31. 35,009 × 92
32. $700 × 792
33. 264 × 573
34. 460 × 1,480
35. 2,466 × 767
36. 9,044 × 2,020

Problem SOLVING

37. There are 42 rows of seats in the theater. Each row has 36 seats. How many seats are in the theater?

38. A truck carries 278 crates. Each crate contains 45 pounds of fruit. How many pounds of fruit does the truck carry?

8 Dividing Whole Numbers

The park service has 257 evergreens to plant in 9 equal-sized areas. To find the number of evergreens to plant in each area divide 257 by 9.

You can estimate $270 \div 9 = 30$.

Step 1	Step 2	Step 3
Divide the hundreds.	Divide the tens.	Divide the ones.
2 hundreds ÷ 9	25 tens ÷ 9	77 ÷ 9
$$9\overline{)257}$$	$$\begin{array}{r} 2 \\ 9\overline{)257} \\ -18 \\ \hline 7 \end{array}$$ 9×2 tens $= 18$ tens	$$\begin{array}{r} 28\ R5 \\ 9\overline{)257} \\ -18\downarrow \\ \hline 77 \\ -72 \\ \hline 5 \end{array}$$ 9×8 tens $= 72$ tens
There are not enough hundreds to divide without renaming. Why is 0 not written in the hundreds place of the quotient?		

You can use multiplication to check the division.

Remember to add the remainder.

$$\begin{array}{r} 7 \\ 28 \\ \times 9 \\ \hline 252 \end{array} \qquad \begin{array}{r} 252 \\ +5 \\ \hline 257 \end{array}$$

Compared to the estimate of 30, the answer is reasonable.

You can also divide by 2- or 3-digit numbers.

Divide 270 by 38.

Step 1	Step 2
There are not enough hundreds or tens in the quotient. $$38\overline{)270}$$	Divide the ones. $$\begin{array}{r} 7\ R4 \\ 38\overline{)270} \\ -266 \\ \hline 4 \end{array}$$

Divide 8,000 by 144.

Step 1	Step 2
Divide the tens. Estimate 800 tens ÷ 144 as 6 tens. $$\begin{array}{r} 5 \\ 144\overline{)8,000} \\ -720\downarrow \\ \hline 80 \end{array}$$	Divide the ones. $$\begin{array}{r} 55\ R80 \\ 144\overline{)8,000} \\ -720 \\ \hline 800 \\ -720 \\ \hline 80 \end{array}$$

Divide.

1. $8)\overline{82}$ 2. $7)\overline{7,217}$ 3. $42)\overline{210}$ 4. $354)\overline{900}$

Exercises ···

Divide.

1. $9)\overline{729}$ 2. $7)\overline{2,667}$ 3. $4)\overline{78}$ 4. $9)\overline{316}$

5. $8)\overline{4,275}$ 6. $5)\overline{718}$ 7. $8)\overline{1,408}$ 8. $3)\overline{4.615}$

9. $2)\overline{11,220}$ 10. $6)\overline{18,922}$ 11. $4)\overline{41,886}$ 12. $32)\overline{241}$

13. $39)\overline{244}$ 14. $68)\overline{496}$ 15. $20)\overline{216}$ 16. $40)\overline{431}$

17. $65)\overline{1,300}$ 18. $23)\overline{1,187}$ 19. $59)\overline{3,776}$ 20. $50)\overline{2,500}$

21. $46)\overline{1,676}$ 22. $42)\overline{2,480}$ 23. $86)\overline{3,440}$ 24. $62)\overline{1,858}$

25. $316)\overline{1,581}$ 26. $592)\overline{3,552}$ 27. $262)\overline{2,005}$ 28. $216)\overline{2,808}$

29. $142)\overline{3,124}$ 30. $289)\overline{8,959}$ 31. $588)\overline{4,550}$ 32. $486)\overline{15,600}$

33. $\$3,255 \div 5$ 34. $422 \div 3$ 35. $\$42,972 \div 9$

36. $3,389 \div 59$ 37. $\$4,757 \div 67$ 38. $\$43,704 \div 72$

39. $\$39,293 \div 893$ 40. $\$17,604 \div 652$ 41. $125,250 \div 408$

Problem SOLVING ··

42. A car travels 3,375 miles on 125 gallons of gasoline. How many miles does it travel on each gallon of gasoline?

43. There are about 2,000 pumpkins in a field. How many trips does a wagon make if it carries 175 pumpkins each trip?

Diagnostic Skills Posttest

Round to the underlined place-value position. (Section 1)

1. 6̲81

2. 1,6̲85

3. 14̲,852

4. 2̲9,544

Round to the greatest place-value position. (Section 1)

5. 31,015

6. 2,310

7. 152,486

8. 997,568

Write in standard form. (Section 2)

9. forty-seven hundredths

10. one and ninety thousandths

Write in expanded form. (Section 2)

11. 6.25

12. 8.524

13. 25.84

Replace each ■ with <, >, or = to make a true statement. (Section 3)

14. 2,310 ■ 2,311

15. 10,308 ■ 10,306

16. 528,416 ■ 528,641

Order the numbers from least to greatest. (Section 3)

17. 951, 867, 999, 672, 987

18. 625; 1,125; 526; 418; 982

Estimate. (Section 4)

19. 425 + 817

20. 6,512 − 847

21. $259\overline{)17,674}$

22. 2,472 × 5

23. 741 × 317

24. $42\overline{)8,421}$

Add. (Section 5)

25. $263 + 88$

26. $\$948 + \$235$

27. $2,167 + 5,998$

28. $125,421 + 635,805$

29. $\$1,268 + \$14,431 + \$8,892$

Subtract. (Section 6)

30. $\$469 - \$276$

31. $2,743 - 195$

32. $12,127 - 2,746$

33. $1,900 - 179$

34. $52,824 - 46,809$

35. $31,015 - 26,519$

Multiply. (Section 7)

36. 26×11

37. $\$72 \times 14$

38. 817×18

39. 273×46

40. $9,042 \times 85$

41. $1,607 \times 916$

Divide. (Section 8)

42. $6\overline{)642}$

43. $12\overline{)132}$

44. $20\overline{)145}$

45. $57\overline{)1,046}$

46. $86\overline{)5,442}$

47. $612\overline{)17,748}$

Number Theory
and Integers

Jamie Mesrobian
Williamsburg, VA

Objective: to compare and order integers

Positive and negative numbers are used to describe many situations.

The average January overnight temperature in Nome, Alaska, is 20° *below* zero Fahrenheit. **-20°F**

The average June daytime temperature in Anchorage, Alaska, is 60° *above* zero Fahrenheit. **60°F**

Numbers, such as +60 and -20, are called integers. An **integer** is a number from the set
. . . , -5, -4, -3, -2, -1, 0, +1, +2, +3, +4, +5, ... Integers can be graphed on a number line.

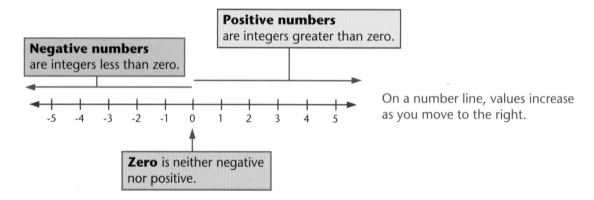

On a number line, values increase as you move to the right.

Each **positive integer** is a whole number. For example, +4 and 4 name the same number. So, the positive symbol may be omitted.

Each **negative integer** is the opposite of a whole number. On the number line, two numbers that are **opposites** are the same distance from 0. For example, -2 and 2 are opposites.

The distance a number is from 0 on the number line is called its **absolute value**.

Say: The absolute value of -2 is 2.　　　　**Say:** The absolute value of 2 is 2.

Write: |-2| = 2　　　　**Write: |2| = 2**

We can also compare and order integers. A number line makes it easy to determine which of two numbers is greater.

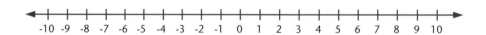

Examples

A. -2 is to the left of 4,
so -2 < 4.

B. -3 is to the right of -5,
so -3 > -5.

Try THESE

Replace each ____ with an integer that describes the situation.

1. 15 ft below street level, -15 ft
   20 ft above street level, ____

2. stock value up $4, 4
   stock value down $2, ____

Exercises

Name the opposite of each integer.

1. -1   2. 8   3. 0   4. -4   5. -52   6. 41

Name the absolute value of each integer.

7. -7   8. 6   9. -4   10. -24   11. 0   12. 9

13. What integer is neither positive nor negative?

14. What integer is its own opposite?

15. What is true about the absolute value of opposites?

Replace each ■ with >, <, or = to make a true statement.

16. 2 ■ 4   17. -3 ■ -4   18. 4 ■ -4

19. 2 ■ 0   20. 9 ■ -5   21. -8 ■ 9

22. |-3| ■ 0   23. |-6| ■ |-10|

Use the number line on p. 3 to order the numbers in each list from least to greatest.

24. 5, 0, 3   25. 8, -9, -3   26. -4, 1, -6, 2   27. -5, -7, 0, -1

28. -8, 9, 3, -7, 5, -9   29. 1, 4, 0, -2, 3, -5   ★ 30. 0, |-14| 13, -12, |-16|, 17

Problem SOLVING

31. If +8 stands for 8 steps forward, what integer stands for 4 steps backward?

32. If +12 stands for 12 miles east, what does -5 stand for?

33. At 6:00 P.M. the temperature was 1°. By midnight it was 10° colder. What was the temperature at midnight?

Objective: to add and subtract integers

A Chinook is a warm, dry wind on the east side of the Rocky Mountains that causes a rapid rise in temperature. For example, a Chinook causes the temperature in Rapid City, SD, to increase 25°C in 15 minutes. If the original temperature was -10°C, what was the final temperature?

It is not convenient to use a number line to solve a problem like this. Study the patterns in the following examples so that you can add integers without a number line.

Adding Integers

A. $3 + 4 = 7$
$8 + 7 = 15$

> The sum of two positive numbers is positive.

B. $-3 + -4 = -7$
$-8 + -7 = -15$

> The sum of two negative numbers is negative.

> **Rule:** To add integers with the same sign, add their absolute values. Give the result the same sign as the addends.

C. $-5 + 2 = -3$
$5 + -2 = 3$

> The difference between 5 and 2 is 3.

D. $1 + -7 = -6$
$-1 + 7 = 6$

> The difference between 1 and 7 is 6.

> **Rule:** To add integers with different signs, find the difference of their absolute values. The sum is positive if the positive integer has the greater absolute value and negative if the negative integer has a greater absolute value.

To find the final temperature, add $-10 + 25$. The final temperature is 15°C.

Subtracting Integers

For every subtraction sentence, there is a corresponding addition sentence.

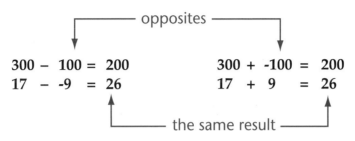

Subtraction	**Addition**

opposites

$$300 - 100 = 200$$
$$17 - {-9} = 26$$

$$300 + {-100} = 200$$
$$17 + 9 = 26$$

the same result

> **Rule:** To subtract an integer, add its opposite.

Try THESE ....

Add or subtract. Rewrite each subtraction problem as an addition problem.

1. $6 + 5$
2. $-7 + 9$
3. $-4 + -2$
4. $5 - 8$
5. $6 + -9$
6. $-5 + -1$
7. $-3 + 3$
8. $6 - 7$

Exercises ....

Add or subtract.

1. $-7 + -5$
2. $-4 + 16$
3. $1 - -3$
4. $-9 - 2$ $= 2 - -9 = -11$ ⁻⁹ +
5. $-48 + 16$
6. $-3 - 0$
7. $-8 + -14$
8. $-9 - -5$ $-2 + 9 =$
9. $-10 - 1$
10. $7 - -8$
11. $-183 + 289$
12. $-64 - -83$
13. $-4 + 2 - 1$
14. $5 - 6 + 7$
15. $-6 - 3 + 1$
16. $12 + 3 - 9$

Evaluate each expression if $x = -3$, $y = -2$, and $z = 4$.

17. $5 + x$
18. $x + x$
19. $x + y$
★20. $|y| + |z|$

Evaluate each expression if $n = -4$, $p = -2$, and $r = 5$.

21. $n - -2$
22. $n - r$
23. $r - p$
★24. $|n - p|$

25. A submarine at 1,300 m *below* sea level *descends* an additional 1,150 m. Write a number sentence for this problem. Then find how far below sea level the submarine is now.

26. At night the average surface temperature on the planet Saturn is -150°C. During the day the temperature rises 27°C. Write an addition sentence for this problem. Then find the temperature on the planet's surface during the day.

27. A weather balloon rises 200 feet from the ground, drops 150 feet, and then rises 300 feet. Write a number sentence for this problem. Then find the height of the balloon.

28. At 7:00 P.M. the temperature was 8°C. What was the temperature at midnight if the temperature was 10° lower?

29. The temperature rose about 3°F each hour for 12 hours. If the final temperature was -5°F, what was the original temperature?

★**30.** Place the digits 3, 4, 7, 8, and 9 in the boxes to make a true sentence.

__ __ + - __ = __ __

Mind BUILDER

Rational Numbers

Any number that can be expressed as a quotient of two integers, where the divisor is not 0, is called a **rational number**. The following numbers are rational.

$$\frac{2}{3} \qquad 3\frac{1}{2} = \frac{7}{2} \qquad -\frac{1}{8} \qquad 2.1 = \frac{21}{10} \qquad 0 = \frac{0}{1}$$

The graph of a rational number is a point on the number line.

Replace each ● with >, <, or = to make a true statement.

1. $-\frac{1}{2}$ ● $\frac{3}{4}$

2. $-1\frac{1}{4}$ ● $-1\frac{1}{2}$

3. $-1\frac{3}{4}$ ● $\frac{3}{4}$

4. $\left|1\frac{1}{2}\right|$ ● $-\left|1\frac{1}{2}\right|$

Cumulative Review

Compute.

1. $91 - 55$ 2. $\$265 + \$93$ 3. 77×4 4. $\$714 \div 7$

5. $-4 + 9$ 6. $5 - 7$ 7. $4 + -3$ 8. $2 - 8$

Round to the underlined place-value position.

9. 1,520   10. 628   11. 24,625   12. 925

13. 5,426   14. 36,584   15. 114,585   16. 2,258,426

Estimate.

17. $645 + 862$ 18. $70.85 - 3.96$ 19. $\$88 \times 9$ 20. 24×76

Replace each ■ with >, <, or = to make a true statement.

21. 51 ■ 50   22. 616 ■ 661   23. -5 ■ 5   24. 0 ■ -2

25. 563 ■ 536   26. -6 ■ 5   27. 9 ■ -7   28. -2 ■ 1

Solve.

29. Felicia drives her car 18,243 miles in a year. The car averages 24 miles per gallon. About how many gallons of gasoline are used during the year?

30. Davis bought toothpaste for $2, shampoo for $3, and conditioner for $3. How much change did he receive from $10?

31. Lynette ran 12 miles on Monday, 8 miles on Wednesday, and 15 miles on Friday. How many miles did she run that week?

32. James planted 5 rose bushes last week. This week he planted twice as many. How many rose bushes did he plant altogether?

Objective: to multiply and divide integers

Glaciers are thick masses of ice that move slowly across land. Cold temperatures cause the glacier front to advance. Warmer temperatures cause the glacier to melt, and it appears to retreat. The movement of a glacier can range from a few centimeters to a meter a day.

Suppose a glacier melts at a rate of 7 centimeters per day. By how much will the glacier melt in 3 days?

The integer -7 represents melting 7 centimeters per day. $-7 + -7 + -7 = -21$

> *Remember:* 3×7, $3 \bullet 7$, and $3(7)$ all represent multiplication.

$3 \bullet -7 = -21$

> *Think:* Multiplication is repeated addition.

In 3 days, the glacier melted 21 centimeters. This is represented by the integer -21.

Suppose the glacier melts 7 centimeters per day. What was its position 3 days ago?

$-3 \bullet -7 = ?$ The integer -3 represents 3 days ago.

THINK Three days ago the glacier was 21 centimeters forward.

This means that $-3 \bullet -7 = 21$. These sentences suggest the following rule.

> **Rule:** The product of two integers with the **same** sign is positive.
> The product of two integers with **different** signs is negative.

In mathematics, multiplication and division are inverse operations. In the examples below, each division sentence is related to a multiplication sentence.

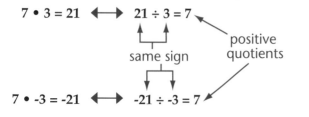

$7 \bullet 3 = 21 \longleftrightarrow 21 \div 3 = 7$

same sign → positive quotients

$7 \bullet -3 = -21 \longleftrightarrow -21 \div -3 = 7$

$-7 \bullet 3 = -21 \longleftrightarrow -21 \div 3 = -7$

different signs → negative quotients

$-7 \bullet -3 = 21 \longleftrightarrow 21 \div -3 = -7$

> **Rule:** The quotient of two integers with the **same** sign is positive. The quotient of two integers with **different** signs is negative.

Choose the correct value for each multiplication or division expression.

1. $-3 \cdot -4$ a. -12   b. 12
2. $9 \cdot -6$ a. -54   b. 54
3. $-18 \div 3$ a. -6   b. 6
4. $48 \div 6$ a. -8   b. 8
5. $-14 \div -7$ a. -2   b. 2
6. $-8 \cdot -4$ a. -32   b. 32
7. $7 \cdot -8$ a. -56   b. 56
8. $-45 \div 5$ a. -9   b. 9

Exercises

Multiply or divide.

1. $7 \cdot 3$
2. $-6 \cdot -4$
3. $7 \cdot -5$
4. $0 \cdot -8$
5. $72 \div -8$
6. $0 \div 16$
7. $-63 \div -7$
8. $-15 \div 3$
9. $8 \cdot 6$
10. $12 \cdot -8$
11. $-16 \cdot 9$
12. $-7 \cdot -9$
13. $85 \div -17$
14. $75 \div 15$
15. $-55 \div 11$
16. $-175 \div -25$
17. $-144 \div 24$
18. $105 \div -15$
19. $7 \cdot -18$
20. $-14 \cdot -12$

Evaluate each expression if $x = -12$ and $y = -5$.

21. $3y$
22. $x \div -3$
23. $-2y$
24. $-24 \div x$

Problem SOLVING

25. If you multiply three negative factors, is the product positive or negative? Explain.
26. Complete the tables using multiplication.

-4	3	-12
3	-1	-3
-12	-3	36

-5	4	-20
4	-1	-4
-20	-4	80

27. From noon until 6:00 P.M. the temperature change was -12°F. Find the average change per hour.

28. Several cliffs on Cape Cod recede 3.3 feet each year. How much do the cliffs recede in 5 years?

29. At 8:00 P.M. the temperature is 9°C. It drops 2 degrees each hour. What is the temperature at 1:00 A.M.?

Constructed RESPONSE

30. In the last step of a problem, Dean multiplied by 0.2 instead of dividing by 0.2. His answer was 34.8. What is the correct answer? Explain.

MiXeD REVIEW

Estimate the sum or difference.

31.	763	32.	342	33.	5,392	34.	2,615
	+ 78		+ 581		− 2,119		− 759

Mind BUILDER

Integer Game

Here is a game for two to four players. It requires 13 cards marked as shown.

| -6 | -5 | -4 | -3 | -2 | -1 | 0 | 1 | 2 | 3 | 4 | 5 | 6 |

One player (the dealer) shuffles the cards and gives each player two cards. Then each player finds the sum and the product of the numbers on the two cards and decides which number is greater.

> For example, if Player 1 received the -3 card and the 4 card, his sum would be 1 (-3 + 4), and his product would be -12 (-3 × 4). Since 1 is greater than -12, his score is 1.

The players take turns showing their cards and announcing their scores. After they record their scores, the cards are returned to the dealer.

Repeat the process four more times. At the end of the game, each player adds his five scores. The player with the highest total wins.

Those Interesting Integers

Which three consecutive integers have a product that is 800 times their sum?

Extension

Which three consecutive odd integers have a product that is less than a perfect square?

1.4 Exponents

Objective: to understand and use powers and exponents

In a meeting room, there are 10 rows of 10 chairs. To find the total number of chairs, multiply 10×10. Another way to express 10×10 is 10^2. In 10^2, the exponent is 2 and the base is 10. The **exponent** tells how many times the **base** number is used as a factor.

$100 = \underbrace{10 \times 10}_{\text{factors}} = 10\underset{\text{base}}{^2} \longleftarrow$ exponent

> We say "ten squared" or "ten to the second power."

$10^2 = 100 \longleftarrow$ The product is the standard form.

We can write a power as a product of its factors. When we evaluate the product of the factors, the answer is in **standard form**, numbers written without exponents. $10^2 = 100$

A variable can also be raised to a power. $x^3 = x \cdot x \cdot x$

Say "x cubed" or "x to the third power."

We can evaluate expressions with variables and exponents.

x^2 when $x = 6$ $\qquad x^2 = x \cdot x$, so $x^2 = 6 \cdot 6 = 36$

Examples

A. Write 7^3 as a product of factors.

$7^3 = 7 \cdot 7 \cdot 7$

B. Write 5^3 in standard form.

$5^3 = 5 \cdot 5 \cdot 5 = 125$

Say "five cubed" or "five to the third power."

C. Write 6^4 in standard form.

$6^4 = 6 \cdot 6 \cdot 6 \cdot 6 = 1,296$

Say "six to the fourth power."

D. Write using exponents.

$h \cdot h \cdot h \cdot h = h^4$

Name the base and exponent for each problem.

1. 10^3
2. 10^4
3. x^6
4. 2^6
5. m^5

6. 7 squared
7. 3 cubed
8. 4^5
9. 8^1
10. 1^6

Complete.

1. $7^\blacksquare = 7 \times 7 \times 7$
2. $125^\blacksquare = 125 \times 125$
3. $\blacksquare^3 = 4 \times 4 \times 4$
4. $\blacksquare^1 = 2$
5. $\blacksquare^2 = 64$
6. $\blacksquare^3 = 27$

Write, using exponents.

7. $8 \times 8 \times 8$
8. 2×2
9. $7 \times 7 \times 7 \times 7 \times 7$
10. $m \times m \times m$
11. $3 \times 3 \times 3 \times 3$
12. $y \times y \times y \times y$

Write in standard form.

13. 9 squared
14. 10^3
15. 16^1
16. 1^8
17. 3^4
18. 2^5
19. 35 squared
20. 6^3

Write the power in words.

21. 4^2
22. 5^3
23. 2^5
24. x^4

Evaluate each expression for the given value of the variable.

25. x^2 when $x = -7$
26. y^3 when $y = 4$
27. n^4 when $n = 2$

28. Use a calculator to compare 10^4 and 4^{10}. Are they equal? If not, which is greater?

29. The graph at the right shows the ones digits for powers of 4. Use the information from the graph to predict the ones digit for 4^{11}. Check you answer with your calculator.

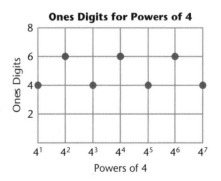

Ones Digits for Powers of 4

Ones Digits

Powers of 4

30. Evaluate 2^1, 2^2, 2^3, and 2^4. What happens to the answer each time the exponent is increased? Based on your answer, what do you think is the value of 2^5?

Objective: to evaluate variable expressions

Suppose you are an astronaut who travels to the Moon to collect rock samples. When you get there, you find that you weigh more on Earth than you do on the Moon. In fact, objects on Earth weigh 6 times more than they do on the Moon.

Weight on Moon (in pounds)	10	30	50	n
Weight on Earth (in pounds)	60	180	300	$6 \times n$

The value of an expression, such as $6 \cdot n$ or $6n$, may be changed by replacing n with different numbers. The letter n is called a **variable**. A variable is used to stand for some number.

> An expression that contains at least one variable is called an **algebraic expression**.

Examples

Evaluate each expression if $a = 4$.

Expression	Replace a with 4.	Value
$a + 5$	$4 + 5$	9
$10 - a$	$10 - 4$	6
$3a$	$3 \cdot 4$	12
$\frac{a}{2}$	$\frac{4}{2}$	2
a^3	4^3	64
$2a^3$	$2 \cdot 4^3$	128
$6a - 4$	$6 \cdot 4 - 4$	20

> $3a$ is the same as $3 \cdot a$.
> $\frac{4}{2}$ means "$4 \div 2$."

$2a^3$ → First use exponent. Then multiply.

$6a - 4$ → First multiply, and then subtract.

Another Example

An expression may have more than one variable.

Evaluate $3c + 4m$ if $c = 8$ and $m = 10$.

$3c + 4m = 3 \cdot 8 + 4 \cdot 10$ Replace c with 8 and m with 10.

$= 24 + 40$ Use the order of operations. First multiply.

$= 64$ Then add.

Try THESE

Evaluate each expression if $n = 9$.

1. $n + 9$
2. $8 + n$
3. $n + 7$
4. $2.9 + n$
5. $n^2 + 4$
6. $15 - n$
7. n^3
8. $3n^2$
9. $11.9 - n$
10. $n^2 - 25$

Evaluate each expression if $s = 9$ and $t = 12$.

1. $s + t$
2. $2s - t$
3. $9s + 5t$
4. $s^2 + t$
5. $3(t + s)$
6. $t + 12s + 7$
7. $t^2 - (s^2 + 1)$
8. $2s + 4t - 3^3$
9. $\frac{st}{4}$
10. $\frac{12t}{s}$

Evaluate each expression if $a = 6$, $b = 8$, $c = 5$, and $d = 0.5$.

11. $a + b + c$
12. $a + b - d$
13. $ad(a \bullet d)$
14. $bd - 1.5$
15. $c^2 + d^2$
16. $b^2 - a^2$
17. $6b - 8c$
18. $2c^2 - 4b$

Copy and complete each table by evaluating the expression.

19.

x	$x + 1$
0	?
1	?
2	?
3	?

20.

y	$5 - y$
0	?
1	?
2	?
3	?

21.

a	$3a^2$
0	?
1	?
2	?
3	?

22.

b	$5b + 4$
0	?
0.5	?
1.0	?
1.5	?

Problem SOLVING

23. The expression $15 + 0.10c$ is used to find the monthly telephone bill for c local calls. If Ralph makes 42 local calls in July, what is his bill?

24. U-Rent rents cars and charges by the day with a base price. The expression $22d + 40$ represents how much it would cost to rent a car for d days. If Carlos rents a car for 8 days, how much will it cost him?

25. What is the difference between a number and a variable?

Constructed RESPONSE

26. Look at the problem in the box that Isabella completed. Is the problem correct? If not, explain her error.

> $4c$ when $c = 7$
>
> $4c = 47$

Objective: to solve problems using the four-step plan

To solve problems, it is helpful to follow this four-step plan.

- Read the problem carefully.
- Ask yourself questions like "What facts do I know?" and "What do I need to find?"

- See how the facts relate to each other.
- Decide how to solve the problem.
- Choose the method of computation.
- Write an equation.
- Make an estimate of the answer.

- Carry out your plan.
- Do the computation.
- Answer the problem.

- Reread the problem.
- Is your answer close to the estimate?
- Ask yourself "Does the answer make sense for the problem?"
- If not, try another way to solve the problem.

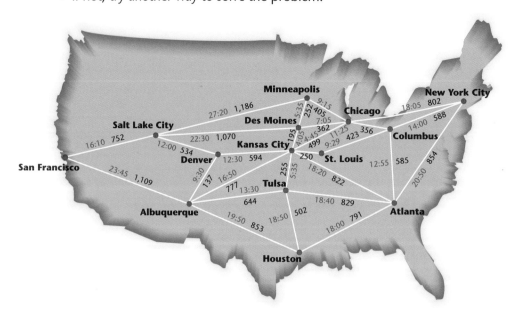

Example

The Robinson family is planning a trip from New York City to St. Louis. Use the information from the map on p. 16 to find the distance they will drive.

 READ   You need to find the distance from New York City to St. Louis. The map gives the driving distance and the driving time. The driving time is not needed.

 PLAN   The most direct route from New York City to St. Louis is through Columbus. Use the map and addition to find the driving distance. Write an equation. $588 + 423 = n$. Estimate $588 + 423$ as $600 + 400$, or $1,000$.

 SOLVE $588 + 423 = n$
$n = 1,011$

The driving distance from New York City to St. Louis is 1,011 miles.

 CHECK   The solution is close to the estimate. The solution is reasonable.

Solve

Use the map if necessary.

1. The Robinsons drive from St. Louis to Denver. It takes them 17 hours and 15 minutes (17:15). How far do they drive?

2. The Robinsons drive from Denver to Kansas City to Des Moines in 2 days. How far do they drive?

3. James Farber drives 498 miles in 11 hours. The total length of his trip is 826 miles. How much farther does he have to drive?

4. A trip from Houston to Atlanta takes 18 hours. Estimate the average speed in miles per hour.

5. Use the map to find 3 different routes from Denver to Columbus. Find the distance for each route. Which is the shortest distance?

6. The trans-Alaska pipeline can deliver about 2 million barrels of oil a day. The 810-mile trip takes about 5 days. How many miles a day is this?

Mid-Chapter REVIEW

Add, subtract, multiply, or divide.

1. $-3 + 5$ 2. $6 \cdot -5$ 3. $-81 \div -9$ 4. $7 - 10$

Write using exponents.

5. $8 \cdot 8 \cdot 8 \cdot 8$ 6. $10 \cdot 10 \cdot 10$ 7. $p \cdot p \cdot p \cdot p \cdot p$

Objective: to evaluate expressions using the order of operations

Pat and Monica are helping to plan a class trip to the local Science Center. They want to find the total cost of thirty $4 tickets and eight $6 tickets.

Pat thinks the total cost is $168, but Monica believes the tickets will cost $768. Who is correct?

$$30 \cdot 4 + 8 \cdot 6$$

The order of operations is important to solve this problem.

Pat   30 • 4 + 8 • 6
   120 + 48
    168

Monica   30 • 4 + 8 • 6
    120 + 8 • 6
     128 • 6
      768

In order for the expression $30 \times 4 + 8 \times 6$ to have only one correct value, the operations must be completed in the correct order. The correct order of operations is as follows:

> 1. Do all operations within parentheses or brackets. Work inside to outside.
>
> 2. Evaluate (find the value of) all **powers**.
>
> 3. Do all multiplication and/or division from left to right.
>
> 4. Do all addition and/or subtraction from left to right.

Pat is correct.

More Examples

A. $14 - 8 \div 2^3$

 $14 - 8 \div 8$ Evaluate the power 2^3.
  $14 - 1$ Divide 8 by 8.
   13 Subtract 1 from 14.

B. $4 \cdot [(10 + 8) \div 6]$

 $4 \cdot [18 \div 6]$ Do the operations in the innermost parenthesis first.
  $4 \cdot 3$
   12

Try THESE ·

Name the operation that you should do first to evaluate each expression.

1. $5 - 3 + 1$
2. $16 \div 4 \cdot 2$
3. $12 - 8 \div 4 + 6$
4. $3 + 5 \cdot 4$
5. $4 \cdot (6 + 4) \div 2$
6. $84 - 28 \div (4 \cdot 7)$

Exercises •

Evaluate each expression.

1. $6 + 5 \bullet 2$
2. $24 \div 6 - 2$
3. $4^2 + 7 - 2$
4. $-4 + 8 \div 2$
5. $27 \bullet -3 + 5$
6. $-4 + 9 - 6$
7. $162 - 3^3 \bullet 3$
8. $6 \bullet 3^2 + 6 \bullet 0.5$
9. $1.2 \bullet 4^2 + 8.5 \bullet 2^4$
10. $(6 - 5) \bullet 2.5$
11. $(5 + 2) \bullet (6 - 7)$
12. $(5 - 20) \div 3$
13. $2 \bullet [7 - (9 - 5)]$
14. $[16 \bullet (2 - 1)] \div 2^5$
15. $[(8^2 - 4) - 6] \div 6$

Write whether each statement is *true* or *false*.

16. $6 \bullet 3 + 4 = 42$
17. $24 - 2 \bullet 8 = 176$
18. $6^2 - 12 \div 2 + 1 = 13$
19. $(5 + 1) \bullet 6 = 36$
20. $16 \div (8 + 4) = 6$
21. $14 - 5 - 2 \bullet 2 = 6$

Insert parentheses to make each equation true.

22. $18 + 4 \bullet 3 = 66$
23. $18 \div 3 + 6 = 2$
24. $2^5 \div 2^2 + 28 \div 4 = 15$

Problem SOLVING •

Use the table at the right to answer questions 25–26.

25. Mrs. Swartz has a budget of $50 to buy sweets for her next tea party. Can she buy 4 danishes, 1 pie, and 3 cakes?

26. If Mrs. Swartz's budget is increased to $100, what can she buy? List 4 combinations.

Sophie's Sweets	
Danish	$2.00
Pie	$8.00
Cake	$12.00

Constructed RESPONSE •

27. Pat and Monica now want to take a class trip to the aquarium. The admission is $10 for adults and $7 for children. How much will it cost for 4 adults and 32 children to visit the aquarium?

   a. Write an expression for the cost of the adults. Write an expression for the cost of the children.

   b. Write an expression for the total cost of adults and children.

   c. Use the order of operations to determine the total cost.

MiXeD REVIEW •

Write each in standard form.

28. 5^4
29. 8^3
30. 2^4
31. 7^3

Objective: to understand the properties of addition and multiplication

When Thomas Jefferson wrote the Declaration of Independence, he stated that certain truths could be assumed by all people. In mathematics, certain properties are assumed to be true. The charts below list some of these properties.

Commutative and Associative Properties

Commutative Property of Addition	**Commutative Property of Multiplication**
The order in which addends are added does not change the sum.	The order in which factors are multiplied does not change the product.
$4 + 7 = 7 + 4$	$6 \cdot 4 = 4 \cdot 6$
$11 = 11$	$24 = 24$
Associative Property of Addition	**Associative Property of Multiplication**
The way in which addends are grouped does not change the sum.	The way in which factors are grouped does not change the product.
$(4 + 3) + 5 = 4 + (3 + 5)$	$(4 \cdot 2) \cdot 3 = 4 \cdot (2 \cdot 3)$
$7 + 5 = 4 + 8$	$8 \cdot 3 = 4 \cdot 6$
$12 = 12$	$24 = 24$

Inverse and Identity Properties

Inverse Property of Addition	**Inverse Property of Multiplication**
When a number is added to its opposite, the sum is zero.	When a number is multiplied by its reciprocal, the product is one.
$-3 + 3 = 0$	$2 \cdot \dfrac{1}{2} = 1$
Identity Property of Addition	**Identity Property of Multiplication**
When zero is added to a number, the sum is that number.	When a number is multiplied by one, the product is that number.
$-2 + 0 = -2$	$-7 \cdot 1 = -7$

These properties will help you add and multiply mentally. Look for sums and products that are multiples of 10.

Examples

A. $16 + 7 + 14 + 3 =$ Change the order
$\underline{16 + 14} + \underline{7 + 3} =$ of 7 and 14.
$30 \;+\; 10 \;= 40$

B. $(3 \cdot 4) \cdot 25 =$ Change the way
$3 \cdot (4 \cdot 25) =$ the numbers are
$3 \cdot 100 = 300$ grouped.

Replace each ■ with a number to make a true sentence. Identify the property used.

1. $19 + ■ = 3 + 19$
2. $■ • 8 = 8 • 20$
3. $(50 + 18) + 9 = 50 + (■ + 9)$
4. $(17 • ■) • 4 = 17 • (5 • 4)$
5. $■ + 58 = 58 + 123$
6. $56 + (8 + ■) = 56 + (72 + 8)$

Exercises

Compute mentally. Write only your answer.

1. $18 + 13 + 2 + 7$
2. $4 + 13 + 26 + 17$
3. $12 • 2 • 5$
4. $6 • 1$
5. $6 • 11 • 10$
6. $53 + 82 + 57 + 28$
7. $33 + 39 + 15 + 67 + 11$
8. $14 • 5$ THINK: $7 • 2 = 14$
9. $-12 + 0$
10. $4 • \frac{1}{4}$
11. $93 + 46 + 37 + 54$
12. $-12 + 12$

Name the property shown.

13. $4 + 6 + 3 = 6 + 4 + 3$
14. $11 + 0 = 11$
15. $3 • (4 • 10) = (3 • 4) • 10$
16. $-6 • 3 = 3 • -6$
17. $-8 + 8 = 0$
18. $9 • 1 = 9$

State whether each of the following is *true* or *false*. If false, give an example to illustrate your point.

19. Subtraction is commutative.
20. Subtraction is associative.
21. Division is commutative.
22. Division is associative.

Problem SOLVING

23. Is addition of integers a commutative operation? Write *yes* or *no*. Then write an example to illustrate your answer.

24. Putting on your jacket and then your hat is a commutative action. Putting on your socks and then your shoes is *not* a commutative action. Give an example of a commutative action. Then give an example of an action that is *not* commutative.

Test PREP

25. Which expression represents the inverse property of addition?

    a. $4 + 0 = 4$
    b. $\frac{1}{2} • 2 = 1$
    c. $3 • 1 = 3$
    d. $-4 + 4 = 0$

Objective: to use the distributive property to simplify expressions

During a kitchen remodel, a contractor measures two adjoining walls and finds that one is 12 feet by 9 feet, and the other is 8 feet by 9 feet. He needs to know the total area so that he can order the correct amount of drywall. How can he find the total area?

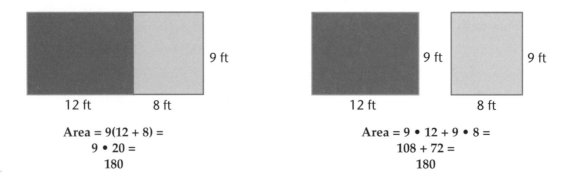

Area = 9(12 + 8) =
9 • 20 =
180

Area = 9 • 12 + 9 • 8 =
108 + 72 =
180

Both expressions are equal. This is an example of the **distributive property**. The distributive property states the product of a number and the sum of two or more numbers is the same as multiplying each addend by the number and then adding the products.

The Distributive Property
$a(b + c) = ab + ac$
$-5(4 + 6) = -5 • 4 + -5 • 6$

Examples

The distributive property can help you write equivalent expressions.

A. $3(2 - 5) = 3 • 2 - 3 • 5$
$3(-3) = 6 - 15$
$-9 = -9$

B. $4 • 8 + 4 • 3 = 4(8 + 3)$
$32 + 12 = 4(11)$
$44 = 44$

The distributive property can help you compute mentally.

C. $4 • 32 =$
$4(30 + 2) =$
$(4 • 30) + (4 • 2) =$
$120 + 8 = 128$

D. $6 • 99 =$
$6(100 - 1) =$
$(6 • 100) - (6 • 1) =$
$600 - 6 = 594$

Replace each ■ with a number to make a true sentence.

1. $5(3 + 4) = (5 \bullet 3) + (5 \bullet ■)$

2. $7(4 - 2) = (7 \bullet ■) - (7 \bullet 2)$

3. $8(40 + 2) = (■ \bullet 40) + (8 \bullet 2)$

4. $5 \bullet 23 = 5(20 + ■)$

5. $9 \bullet 96 = 9(100 - ■)$

6. $9 \bullet 54 = ■(50 + 4)$

Exercises ·

Write an equivalent expression using the distributive property. Then simplify.

1. $2(8 + 1)$

2. $(4 \bullet 30) + (4 \bullet 7)$

3. $-6(5 + 4)$

4. $(-8 \bullet 30) + (-8 \bullet 2)$

5. $5(6 - 1)$

6. $(6 \bullet 3) - (2 \bullet 3)$

Compute mentally.

7. $6 \bullet 99$

8. $-4 \bullet 81$

9. $9 \bullet 22$

10. $-5 \bullet 65$

11. $3 \bullet 61$

12. $6 \bullet 96$

13. $-2 \bullet 59$

14. $8 \bullet 81$

15. $3 \bullet 59$

16. $-7 \bullet 34$

17. $4 \bullet 8.2$

18. $5 \bullet 2.8$

Problem **SOLVING** ·

19. Peyton needs to buy some chicken and some ground beef for a barbeque. The chicken is $2.00 per pound, and the ground beef is $3.00 per pound. He needs to buy 8 pounds of each. Write two equivalent expressions using the distributive property to show how much Peyton will pay for the chicken and ground beef.

20. The kitchen contractor wants to know how much molding he should buy for the kitchen floor. To determine this, he must find the perimeter of the kitchen floor. The formula for perimeter is $2l + 2w$. If the dimensions of the kitchen are 12 feet • 8 feet, write two equivalent expressions using the distributive property. Use the equivalent expressions to find the perimeter of the kitchen floor.

21. Write a number sentence to demonstrate the distributive property. Check your number sentence to make sure it is true.

Constructed **RESPONSE** ·

22. Ricardo completed the problem below. He does not think the problem is correct. Find his error, and correct the problem.

$$4(6 + 9) = (4 + 6) \bullet (4 + 9)$$

Objective: to solve equations using mental math

A mathematical sentence that contains an equals sign, =, is called an **equation**. Many of the relationships in physical science can be expressed as simple mathematical equations. For example, the *distance* that a skateboarder travels is equal to the *rate* of speed multiplied by the *time*. Using variables, $d = r \bullet t$ or $d = rt$.

You can translate sentences into equations. Variables are used to stand for unspecified numbers.

Sentence	Equation
4 added to b is equal to 12.	$b + 4 = 12$
A number decreased by 7 is equal to 5.	$n - 7 = 5$
The product of 7 and c is 42.	$7c = 42$
A number divided by 8 is 4.	$d \div 8 = 4$

When you replace a variable in an equation so that a true sentence results, you have **solved** the equation. You will learn many ways to solve equations. Sometimes an equation can be solved mentally by using number facts or arithmetic skills.

Examples

A. Solve. $6 + x = 9$

$6 + 3 = 9$

$x = 3$

THINK
6 plus what number is equal to 9?

The number 3 is a solution because $6 + 3 = 9$ is a true sentence.

B. Solve. $5y = 55$

$5 \times 11 = 55$

$y = 11$

THINK
5 times what number is equal to 55?

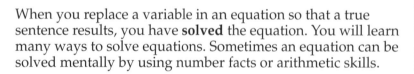

Try THESE

Translate each sentence into an equation.

1. The product of 9 and m is 45.

2. A number increased by 3 is 19.

3. A number divided by 6 is 18.

4. The difference of p and 7 is 30.

Exercises ··

Solve each equation mentally by using number facts or arithmetic skills.

1. $5 + r = 12$

2. $8 + z = 15$

3. $a + 7 = 10$

4. $15 - q = 7$

5. $17 = m - 3$

6. $2 = 14 - b$

7. $2n = 14$

8. $9s = 63$

9. $66 = 11w$

10. $\frac{k}{6} = 4$

11. $\frac{x}{5} = 9$

12. $\frac{18}{u} = 9$

Translate each sentence into an equation. Then solve.

13. Some number plus six is equal to eleven. What is the number?

14. Fifteen decreased by a number is seven. What is the number?

15. A number divided by three gives a result of thirteen. Find the number.

16. When a number is decreased by five, the result is seven. Find the number.

17. The product of a number and six is equal to forty-two. Find the number.

18. Nine plus a number is sixteen. Find the number.

Use the formula for distance at the beginning of the lesson to find the unknown value.

19. distance = 20 miles, rate = 5 miles per hour, time = _____

20. distance = 54 miles, rate = _____, time = 6 hours

Problem SOLVING ···

21. The temperature at 1:00 P.M. is d. The temperature falls 15° by sundown to 55°. What was the temperature at 1:00 P.M.? Write an equation to help you solve the problem.

22. Lily walked 10 miles during her vacation at the beach. She walked the same distance each day and was at the beach for 5 days. How far did she walk each day?

Mind BUILDER

Puzzle

Use four of the five numbers shown to write a number expression with the greatest whole-number value.

1. [?] ÷ [?] − [?] ÷ [?]

2. [?] + [?] × [?] − [?]

Objective: to choose the method of computation

Jesse needs to save $300 for the class trip to Houston. He has already saved $265. He plans to earn $20 mowing lawns and $25 baby-sitting. Will he have enough money for the trip?

> One of the important steps in problem solving is to decide what method you will use to solve the problem.

In this case, Jesse can estimate to find out about how much money he will have.

$$
\begin{array}{r}
\$265 \\
20 \\
+\quad 25 \\
\end{array}
\longrightarrow
\begin{array}{r}
\$270 \\
20 \\
+\quad 30 \\
\hline
\$320 \\
\end{array}
$$

He will have about $320.

When he deposits the money into his savings account, he needs to know the exact amount.

$$265 + 20 + 25 = 310$$

He has saved $310.

As shown above, an *estimate* is appropriate in some situations, but an *exact answer* is needed in others. The following flow chart can help you decide which method of computation to use.

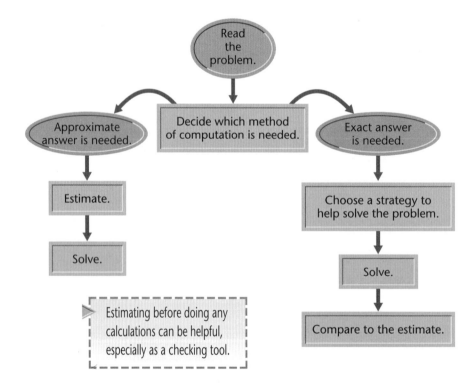

Try THESE ···

Read these situations. Write *exact* if the number must be figured exactly, or write *estimate* if the number can be approximate.

1. the time a plane flight leaves the airport

2. the amount of flour in a cake recipe

3. the prices of grocery items as you place them into your cart

4. the amount of money you deposit into your savings account

5. the attendance at a baseball game

6. a baseball team's win-loss record

Solve ···

Solve each problem. Write the method of computation you used.

1. Will $7.00 buy a loaf of bread at $0.98, 1 lb of ground beef at $2.29, and luncheon meat at $3.29?

2. Will $20.00 buy a pair of shoes at $18.95 and socks at $2.25?

3. Westerville High School has 500 adult tickets and 750 student tickets for a football game. In the advanced sales, 235 adult tickets and 647 student tickets were sold. How many of each are left to sell at the gate?

4. Juan wants to buy a drum set for $359 and drum cases for $49. He has saved $259. How much more does he need to save?

Use the mileage chart to solve problems 5–7.

	Chicago	Dallas	Los Angeles	New York
Chicago		917	2,054	802
Dallas	917		1,387	1,552
Los Angeles	2,054	1,387		2,786
New York	802	1,552	2,786	

5. How much farther is it from Dallas to New York than from Dallas to Chicago?

6. Which distance is shorter—a trip from Dallas to Los Angeles to New York or a trip from Dallas to New York to Los Angeles?

7. A trip from Chicago to New York takes 18 hours. Is the average speed in miles per hour greater than or less than 50 miles per hour?

1.11 Problem-Solving Application: Choose the Method of Computation **27**

Language and Concepts

Choose the correct word to complete each sentence.

1. In the expression 10^2, 10 is called the _____.

2. When comparing integers, the greater integer is found to the _____ of the lesser integer on the number line.

3. If two addends are negative, their sum is _____.

4. A(n) _____ is used to stand for some number.

5. A(n) _____ tells how many times a number, called the base, is used as a factor.

6. _____ is neither positive nor negative.

7. When you change the order in which the numbers are added, you are using the _____ property of addition.

8. When you change the way in which the factors are grouped, you are using the _____ property of multiplication.

9. Mathematical sentences, like $x + 3 = 10$ and $2y = 15$, are examples of _____.

10. To subtract an integer, add its _____.

associative
base
commutative
equations
exponent
multiply
negative
opposite
right
variable
zero
left
positive

Skills and Problem Solving

Name the absolute value of each integer. Section 1.1

11. -3   12. -5   13. 4   14. 12

Replace each ● with >, <, or = to make a true statement. Section 1.1

15. 8 ● 5   16. -4 ● -2   17. -5 ● 5   18. 3 ● -6

Compute. Sections 1.2–1.3

19. -2 + -6   20. -7 + 5   21. -8 + 0   22. 5 − 6

23. -3 ● -8   24. 9 ÷ -3   25. 0 ● -3   26. -11 − -9

Complete. Section 1.4

27. $5 \cdot 5 = 5^{\blacksquare}$ 28. $12 \cdot 12 \cdot 12 = 12^{\blacksquare}$ 29. $10 = 10^{\blacksquare}$

30. $8^{\blacksquare} = 64$ 31. $\blacksquare^2 = 144$ 32. $\blacksquare^3 = 64$

Evaluate each expression if $n = 8$, $s = 12$, and $p = 3$. Section 1.5

33. $s - n$ 34. np 35. $s^2 - n^2$

36. $4n - 2p$ 37. $6(s - 5)$ 38. $4(n - p)$

Evaluate each expression. Section 1.7

39. $-7 \cdot 9 + 12$

40. $249 - (56 + 27)$

41. $52 - 144 \div 12$

42. $(9 + 4) \cdot (8 - 7)$

43. $34 + 8 \div 2 + 4 \cdot 9$

44. $(84 \div 4) \div -3$

Name the property shown. Section 1.8

45. $(6 \cdot 5) \cdot 2 = 6 \cdot (5 \cdot 2)$

46. $-10 + 10 = 0$

47. $-5 \cdot 1 = -5$

48. $3 + 5 = 5 + 3$

Write an equivalent expression using the distributive property. Section 1.9

49. $3(2 - 9)$

50. $(3 \cdot 6) + (3 \cdot 8)$

Translate each sentence into an equation. Section 1.10

51. 36 times a number is 180.

52. The difference of y and 8 is 14.

53. The sum of x and 7 is 8.

54. A number divided by 5 is 18.

Solve each equation mentally by using number facts or arithmetic skills. Section 1.10

55. $x + 3 = 7$

56. $y - 5 = 21$

57. $4x = 32$

58. $\dfrac{x}{2} = 8$

59. $24 = 4c$

60. $18 = b - 9$

Solve. Sections 1.2–1.11

61. When Aidan woke up, the temperature was 65°. It rose 10° during the day, then a cold front came through after dinner, and the temperature dropped 15°. What was the temperature when Aidan went to bed?

62. Five friends share the cost of a lunch equally. Each person pays $5.00. What is the total cost of the lunch?

63. Using the formula, distance = rate • time, find how long it takes Abigail to run 24 miles at a rate of 6 miles per hour.

64. Sarah Bly's account at the bank is overdrawn by $25. How much does she need to deposit to have a balance of $100?

Chapter 1 Test

Name the absolute value of each integer.

1. 3
2. -9
3. -17
4. 94

Replace each ● with >, <, or = to make a true statement.

5. -3 ● -7
6. 3 ● 7
7. -4 ● 0
8. -2 ● 1

Compute.

9. -4 + -4
10. 6 + -9
11. -7 • 7
12. 0 – -3
13. -3 – 7
14. -16 ÷ 2
15. -1 • -9
16. -98 ÷ -7

Write in standard form.

17. 2 cubed
18. 5^3
19. 15^2
20. 16^1

Evaluate each expression if $a = 5$, $v = 7$, and $h = 4$.

21. av
22. $2h - 2h$
23. $v^2 + 2h$
24. $3(5a + 4)$

Evaluate the expression.

25. $3^2 - (4 + 5)$
26. $(5^2 - 5) ÷ 5$
27. $3 • 2^3 + 1$

Solve each equation mentally by using number facts or arithmetic skills.

28. $a + 8 = 14$
29. $h - 2 = 10$
30. $-4c = 32$

31. $9 - t = 4$
32. $6 = \dfrac{x}{2}$
33. $40 = 5h$

Translate each sentence into an equation. Then solve.

34. Five times a number is thirty-five. Find the number.

35. A number decreased by six is four. Find the number.

Solve.

36. It costs $283 to plant an acre of young trees in a national forest. What is the cost of planting 640 acres?

37. The temperature on a winter day at 6:00 A.M. was -12°. At noon the temperature was 17°. What was the temperature change from 6:00 A.M. to noon?

38. Tom's scores in a game were 90, -50, -70, and 125. What was the total score?

Perfect Squares

What numbers will complete the pattern?

$1^2 = 1, 2^2 = 4, 3^2 = 9,$ _____, _____

Each of the numbers 1, 2, 3, 4, and 5 have been squared. The numbers 1, 4, 9, 16, and 25 are called **perfect squares**. Name the next five perfect squares.

Activity

Is it possible to arrange 144 small squares into one large square? If so, write the exponent that shows 144 is a perfect square.

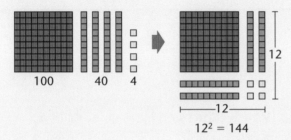

$12^2 = 144$

Arrange the figures for each number into a square. Then write each number as an exponent.

1.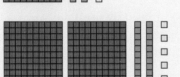

2.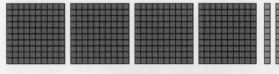

3.

4.

Determine whether each number is a perfect square. Write *yes* or *no*. If it is a perfect square, write the number as an exponent.

5. 400   6. 150   7. 169   8. 324

9. 200   10. 484   11. 196   12. 10,000

Cumulative Test

1. 2^4
   a. 8
   b. 16
   c. 64
   d. none of the above

2. The expression $a - 6$ represents which phrase?
   a. a number increased by 6
   b. 6 less than a number
   c. 6 more than a number
   d. 6 times a number

3. The cost for bowling is $1.50 per game. Which expression shows the cost for bowling n games?
   a. $\$1.50 \div n$
   b. $\$1.50 - n$
   c. $\$1.50 + n$
   d. $\$1.50 \bullet n$

4. $-9 + 16 = $ _____
   a. -25
   b. -7
   c. 7
   d. 25

5. $-4 \bullet -8 = $ _____
   a. -32
   b. -2
   c. 2
   d. 32

6. $-46 \div 2 = $ _____
   a. -92
   b. -23
   c. 23
   d. 92

7. There are about 24 quarts of oil in a case. About how many cases do 5,000 quarts of oil fill?
   a. 208
   b. 209
   c. 100,000
   d. 120,000

8. Which expression has a value of 15 if $x = 3$?
   a. $x - 1$
   b. x^2
   c. $2x + 5$
   d. $5x$

9. Which expression can be written as $4 \times (5 + 6)$?
   a. $(4 + 5) + 6$
   b. $(4 \times 5) + (4 \times 6)$
   c. $(4 \times 5) \times (4 \times 6)$
   d. none of the above

10. The attendance at the fair for 3 days is 24,732, 18,245, and 27,547. What is the estimated total for the 3 days?
    a. 40,000
    b. 70,000
    c. 95,000
    d. none of the above

Decimals

Felicity Quartermaine
Tuscon, AZ

2.1 Comparing, Ordering, and Rounding Decimals

Objective: to compare, order, and round decimals

In the 1988 Winter Olympics, Bonnie Blair won a gold medal in the 500-meter speed skating event. Note that 500 meters is the same as 0.5 or 0.50 kilometers.

The shading in the figures at the right shows that 0.5 and 0.50 have the same value and name the same number. Decimals that name the same number are **equivalent**.

Attaching zeros to the right of a decimal produces equivalent decimals.

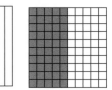

$\frac{5}{10}$ or 0.5 $\frac{50}{100}$ or 0.50

$$0.5 = 0.50 = 0.500 = 0.5000 \ldots$$

 The three dots mean that the pattern never ends.

0.5 = 0.50

To compare decimals, start at the left and compare the digits in each place-value position. In some cases, you may need to attach zeros.

Examples

A. Compare 32.15 and 32.32.

same digits

32.15   **32.32**

In the tenths place, 1 < 3.

32.15 < 32.32

B. Compare 1.35 and 1.3. Attach a zero so that you can compare the digits in the hundredths place.

same digits

1.35   **1.30**

In the hundredths place, 5 > 0.

1.35 > 1.30

Decimal	2.1648	59.10499	0.0965
Nearest Whole Number	2	59	0
Nearest Tenth	2.2	59.1	0.1

To round a decimal, look at the digit to the right of the place being rounded. Then follow the same rules used when rounding whole numbers.

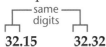 ···

Replace each ● with <, >, or = to make a true statement.

1. 0.6 ● 0.7

2. 0.49 ● 0.44

3. 0.904 ● 0.909

Round to the underlined place-value position.

4. 56.4̲6

5. 98.6̲

6. 8.0̲07

Replace each ● with <, >, or = to make a true statement.

1. 2.03 ● 3.02
2. 3.13 ● 3.130
3. 0.162 ● 0.15
4. 0.601 ● 0.66
5. 2.5 ● 2.07
6. 0.07 ● 0.77

State whether each statement is *true* or *false*.

7. 0.8 > 0.6
8. 0.06 = 0.66
9. 0.09 < 0.9
10. 0.009 > 0.900
11. 9 < 9.001
12. 8.06 < 8.001

Order the numbers in each list from least to greatest.

13. 1.2, 1.23, 2.31, 1.32
14. 0.46, 0.41, 0.64, 0.641
15. 56.18, 56.09, 56.98, 56.81
16. 0.727, 0.277, 0.272, 0.27, 0.722

Choose the correct answer for rounding to the underlined place-value position.

17. $4\underline{6}.50$ a. $46 b. $47 c. $48 d. none
18. $\underline{1}.23$ a. 1.2 b. 1 c. none d. 1.22
19. $4.2\underline{0}5$ a. 4.30 b. 5 c. 4.21 d. none
20. $0.04\underline{8}5$ a. none b. 0.049 c. 0.048 d. 0.05

Round to the given place-value position.

21. 16.09, whole number
22. 23.081, tenths
23. 0.0049, thousandths
24. 0.6051, hundredths

25. The attendance at a football game was 37,000, to the nearest thousand. What is the greatest number of people that could have been in attendance?

26. A certain calculator shows eight digits to the right of the decimal point. What is the least number this calculator will display?

27. Sudsy dish-washing liquid costs $0.247 per ounce, while Cleano cost $0.204 per ounce. Round each to the nearest cent. Which one is cheaper?

28. The winning times in the 50-meter freestyle swimming event for each age group were 25.66 seconds, 25.506 seconds, 25.55 seconds, and 25.65 seconds. Order these times from least to greatest.

2.2 Adding and Subtracting Decimals

Objective: to add and subtract decimals

In the slalom, skiers make two runs. What is the total time for runs of 51.6 seconds and 50.94 seconds?

THINK
Estimate:
50 + 50 = 100

To find the total time, add 51.6 and 50.94. Follow these steps to add or subtract decimals.

Step 1	Step 2
Line up the decimal points. Attach a zero if needed. $\quad$ 51|60 $+$ 50|94	Add or subtract as with whole numbers. $\quad\quad$ 1 $\quad$ 51.60 $+$ 50.94 $\quad$ 102.54

Examples

A. 8.1 − 4.75

$$\begin{array}{r} {\scriptstyle 7\ 10\ 10} \\ 8.\cancel{10} \\ -\ 4.75 \\ \hline 3.35 \end{array}$$ 8.1 = 8.10

B. $10 + $1.74 + 6¢

$$\begin{array}{r} {\scriptstyle 1} \\ \$10.00 \\ 1.74 \\ +\quad 0.06 \\ \hline \$11.80 \end{array}$$ $10 = 10.00
6¢ = $0.06

When you do not need to know exactly how much or how many, you can **estimate** the sum. One type of estimation is **front-end estimation**.

Estimate the sum of 12.6 + 8.38 + 6.95 using front-end estimation.

Step 1	Step 2	Step 3
Add the front-end digits. $\quad$ 12.6 $\quad\quad$ 8.38 $+\ $ 6.95 $\quad$ 26	Estimate the sum of the remaining digits. $\quad$ 12.6 $\quad\quad$ 8.38 → 1 $+\ $ 6.95 → $+$ 1 $\quad\quad\quad$ 2	Add the results. $\quad$ 26 $+\quad$ 2 $\quad$ 28

Add or subtract.

1.   0.7
  + 0.1
	2. $0.14
	  + 0.63
		3. 0.5
		  − 0.4
			4. 0.68
			  + 0.5
				5. 42.3
				  + 0.97

Exercises ....

Add or subtract.

1.   3.04
  + 0.6
	2. 64.6
	  − 5.5
		3. 8
		  + 4.7

4.   20.14
  − 8.093
	5. 2.42
	  − 0.5
		6. 419.6
		  + 0.42

7. 0.7 + 3.9   **8.** 7.9 + 0.03   **9.** 1.8 − 0.9

10. 6.51 − 0.8   **11.** $8.17 + $17   **12.** $8.06 − $2.34

13. $12 + 67¢ + $1.52   **14.** 8.6 + 0.34 + 2.9   **15.** 0.23 + 2.01 + 16

★16. 0.915 − 0.00431   **17.** What is the sum of the addends 20.3, 4, and 0.84?

Use the digits 8, 5, 1, and 7 to make the least possible sum or difference.
Use each digit only once in each problem.

18. ■■.6
+ ■.■   **19.** 8 ■.■
+ ■.■   **20.** ■■.■
− ■.2   **21.** ■■
− ■■.9

Problem SOLVING ....

Use front-end estimation to answer questions 22–25.

22. Andrea has $10 to spend. Is it possible for her to buy a T-shirt and a poster?

23. Can Luis buy a paperweight and two pens for $5?

24. How many pens can you buy for $6?

25. Is the difference between a hat and a poster more or less than $3?

26. Garcia buys some stamps for $0.25 each and a money order for $10.17. He spends a total of $10.92. How many stamps does he buy?

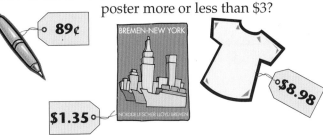

89¢

$1.35

$5.98

$2.38

$8.98

Objective: to solve problems by eliminating possibilities

The Sanchez family recently purchased some sporting equipment. They bought 3 items and spent $48.20. Which items did they buy?

1. READ

You know how many items they bought and the total cost.

2. PLAN

Look for items that cost more than $48.20. Eliminate these items. Estimate the sums of other combinations of three items. Do you need to consider all other combinations?

3. SOLVE

cost of bicycle > $48   Eliminate the bicycle from any combination.

glove:	$3	$48	total	Eliminate having
net:	+ 7	− 10		both the glove and
	$10	$38	no item near this	net in any combination.

Estimate other possible combinations.

dart board: $23		dart board: $23	
glove:	3	net:	7
skates:	+ 19 about	skates:	+ 19 about
	$45 $3 low		$49 right

22.50 + 6.75 + 18.95 = 48.20 ✔

The Sanchez family bought a dart board, fishing net, and roller skates.

4. CHECK

The answer meets the requirement of three items that cost a total of $48.20.

Use the display on p. 38 to find items that cost the amount given.

1. 2 items: $41.45
2. 3 items: $155.69
★3. 4 items: $174.19

Solve ···

1. It is an even number. It is greater than 4×8. It is less than $100 \div 2$. The sum of its digits is 6. What is the number?

2. It is not an even number. It is less than 113. It is a 3-digit number. The sum of its digits is odd. What is the number?

3. Casey threw five darts at the dart board. Each dart hit the board. Which of the following numbers could have been his score: 16, 31, 4, 37, 28?

★4. Yoko has a bag of marbles. It contains between 50 and 100 marbles. If she separated the marbles into 8 piles, there are 5 left. If she separates the marbles into 9 piles, there are 4 left. How many marbles are in Yoko's bag?

★5. Rae, Carol, and Alma are friends. Their hobbies are sculpturing, fixing cars, and gardening. Their occupations are doctor, teacher, and lawyer. Use the following clues to find their hobbies and occupations.

   a. The gardener and the teacher both graduated from the same college.

   b. Both the lawyer and Rae have poodles, as does the sculptor.

   c. The doctor bandaged the sculptor's broken thumb.

   d. Carol and the lawyer have been friends for 5 years.

   e. Alma beat both Carol and the gardener in tennis.

MiXeD **REVIEW** ···

Estimate.

6. $2.7 + 3.4$
7. $2.89 - 1.05
8. $88.9 - 19.4$
9. $10.15 - 9.83$
10. $12 + 0.7 + 4.23 + 9.075$
11. $7 - 96¢$

2.4 Multiplying Decimals

Objective: to multiply decimals

Juan buys 4 souvenir pennants at the baseball park for $8.95 each. To find the total cost, multiply $8.95 by 4.

Estimation is helpful in placing the decimal point in the product.

The cost should be about $9 × 4, or $36.

$$
\begin{array}{r}
\$8.95 \\
\times \quad 4 \\
\hline
\$35.80
\end{array}
$$

$8.95 ← 2 decimal places

$35.80 ← 2 decimal places   The answer is reasonable, since $35.80 is close to the estimate of $36.

Examples

Multiply decimals as you would whole numbers. The estimate helps you place the decimal point.

A.
$$
\begin{array}{r}
1.94 \\
\times \quad 8.2 \\
\hline
388 \\
15\ 52 \\
\hline
15.908
\end{array}
$$

1.94 ← 2 decimal places
× 8.2 ← 1 decimal place

B.
$$
\begin{array}{r}
2.09 \\
\times \ 0.04 \\
\hline
0.0836
\end{array}
$$

2.09 ← 2 decimal places
× 0.04 ← 2 decimal places

A zero is placed here to make 4 decimal places.

> **Rule**
> The number of decimal places in the product is the same as the sum of the number of decimal places in the factors.

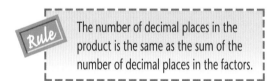

Try THESE

Copy. Place the decimal point in the product.

1.
$$
\begin{array}{r}
0.5 \\
\times \ 3 \\
\hline
15
\end{array}
$$

2.
$$
\begin{array}{r}
4.1 \\
\times \ 2 \\
\hline
82
\end{array}
$$

3.
$$
\begin{array}{r}
\$5.81 \\
\times \quad 7 \\
\hline
\$4067
\end{array}
$$

4.
$$
\begin{array}{r}
12 \\
\times \ 2.6 \\
\hline
312
\end{array}
$$

5.
$$
\begin{array}{r}
\$8.45 \\
\times \quad 24 \\
\hline
\$20280
\end{array}
$$

Multiply.

1. $\begin{array}{r} 0.7 \\ \times\, 0.7 \\ \hline \end{array}$ 2. $\begin{array}{r} 2.1 \\ \times\, 0.6 \\ \hline \end{array}$ 3. $\begin{array}{r} 6.4 \\ \times\, 0.8 \\ \hline \end{array}$ 4. $\begin{array}{r} 3.5 \\ \times\, 0.3 \\ \hline \end{array}$ 5. $\begin{array}{r} 9.7 \\ \times\, 0.5 \\ \hline \end{array}$

6. $\begin{array}{r} 0.75 \\ \times\, 0.08 \\ \hline \end{array}$ 7. $\begin{array}{r} 1.41 \\ \times\, 0.34 \\ \hline \end{array}$ 8. $\begin{array}{r} \$2.86 \\ \times\quad 0.5 \\ \hline \end{array}$ 9. $\begin{array}{r} 0.987 \\ \times\quad 0.6 \\ \hline \end{array}$ 10. $\begin{array}{r} 0.24 \\ \times\, 0.006 \\ \hline \end{array}$

11. 0.89×0.65 12. 1.63×0.98 13. 0.608×1.0203

14. What is the product of 16.5 and 0.98?

Evaluate each expression when $a = 2.1$, $b = 11.31$, and $c = 0.4$

15. ac 16. $3b$ 17. bc 18. abc

Use the chart to the right to solve problems 19–21.

19. Andrea eats two oranges in one day. How many milligrams of riboflavin does she receive from the oranges?

20. Hernando eats a grapefruit and two peaches during the day. How much thiamine does he receive from the fruit?

★21. Name a combination of three fruits that would give a total of 0.15 milligrams of vitamin B_2 and at least 80 milligrams of vitamin C.

Vitamin Content of Fruit (in milligrams)			
Fruit	Vitamin B_1 (thiamine)	Vitamin B_2 (riboflavin)	Vitamin C
Apple	0.017	0.03	6
Banana	0.045	0.07	12
Peach	0.02	0.05	7
Orange	0.13	0.05	66
Grapefruit	0.10	0.04	88

22. Last year, consumers spent $0.8 billion for golf equipment. They spent four times as much for athletic shoes. How much was spent for athletic shoes?

23. When Tai's baseball team visited Japan, $1 in American money could be exchanged for 126.30 Japanese yen. Tai exchanged $50. How much in yen did he receive?

24. How is addition with decimals different from multiplication with decimals?

2.5 Dividing Decimals

Objective: to divide decimals

Melinda is competing in the floor-exercise event at a gymnastics meet. The judges have awarded her scores of 7.8, 8.0, 7.7, 7.6, 8.3, and 8.0, for a total of 47.4. To find the average score, divide 47.4 by 6.

Estimate:
$48 \div 6 = 8$

Step 1	Step 2	Step 3
Place the decimal point in the quotient as shown. $$6\overline{)47.4}$$ There are not enough tens to divide without renaming.	Divide the ones. $$\begin{array}{r} 7 \\ 6\overline{)47.4} \\ -42 \\ \hline 5\,4 \end{array}$$	Divide the tenths. $$\begin{array}{r} 7.9 \\ 6\overline{)47.4} \\ -42 \\ \hline 5\,4 \\ 5\,4 \\ \hline 0 \end{array}$$

Melinda's average score is 7.9.   Check by multiplying.

More Examples

Sometimes there is never a remainder of 0. In such cases, the quotient is usually rounded.

A.
$$\begin{array}{r} 0.105 \\ 12\overline{)1.260} \\ -1\,2 \\ \hline 60 \\ -60 \\ \hline 0 \end{array}$$

> Attach zeros to the dividend until the remainder is zero.

B. Find $14 \div 3$ to the nearest tenth.

$$\begin{array}{r} 4.66 \\ 3\overline{)14.00} \\ 12 \\ \hline 2\,0 \\ 1\,8 \\ \hline 20 \end{array}$$
4.66 rounds to 4.7.

> To round a quotient to a certain place value, divide to one extra place. Then round.

We can also divide a decimal by a decimal.

Divide 37.5 by 1.5.

Step 1	Step 2
Multiply 1.5 and 37.5 by 10. Why?	Divide as with whole numbers.

Step 1:

$$1.5\overline{)37.5} \longrightarrow 1.\underset{\smile}{5}\overline{)37.\underset{\smile}{5}}$$

$$1.5 \times 10 = 15$$

$$37.5 \times 10 = 375$$

Step 2:

$$\begin{array}{r} 25. \\ 1.5\overline{)37.5} \\ -30 \\ \hline 7\ 5 \\ -7\ 5 \\ \hline 0 \end{array}$$

Estimate:

$$\begin{array}{r} 20 \\ 2\overline{)40} \end{array}$$

The answer is reasonable, since it is close to the estimate.

Another Example

C. $0.\underset{\smile}{14}\overline{)3.\underset{\smile}{5}}$

$$\begin{array}{r} 25. \\ 014.\overline{)350.} \\ -28 \\ \hline 70 \\ -70 \\ \hline 0 \end{array}$$

▷ To divide by a decimal, multiply the divisor and dividend by a power of 10 so that the divisor is a whole number. Then divide as with whole numbers.

Try THESE

Copy. Place the decimal point and necessary zeros in the quotient.

1. $\overset{42}{2\overline{)8.4}}$

2. $\overset{161}{6\overline{)96.6}}$

3. $\overset{24}{33\overline{)79.2}}$

4. $\overset{20}{5\overline{)10.2}}$

5. $\overset{2}{0.7\overline{)0.14}}$

Exercises

Divide.

1. $6\overline{)1.08}$

2. $9\overline{)12.6}$

3. $0.8\overline{)2.4}$

4. $0.04\overline{)0.092}$

5. $5\overline{)\$1.95}$

6. $32\overline{)\$2.88}$

7. $0.008\overline{)0.072}$

8. $2\overline{)0.01}$

9. $7\overline{)163.8}$

10. $0.053\overline{)0.00954}$

★11. $2.584 \div 8$

★12. $1 \div 2$

★13. $\$3.01 \div 43$

14. $132.03 \div 8.1$

15. $896.8 \div 0.16$

16. $6.27 \div 66$

Divide. Round each quotient as indicated.

17. $6\overline{)23.9}$, nearest whole number

18. $0.8\overline{)6.51}$, nearest tenth

19. $0.8\overline{)\$5.43}$, nearest cent

20. $90.1\overline{)\$8,675}$, nearest dollar

21. $1.95 \div 0.02$, nearest tenth

22. $6 \div 0.733$, nearest hundredth

23. $\$0.84 \div 9$, nearest cent

24. $711.5 \div 3.5$, nearest whole number

Problem SOLVING

25. In 9 softball games, Lisa has 14 hits. To the nearest tenth, how many hits is this per game?

26. A fund-raising relay team ran 249.5 kilometers on a 0.4-kilometer track. To the nearest lap, how many laps did the relay team run?

★ 27. Find two numbers that have a quotient of 0.07 and a product of 6.3?

Constructed RESPONSE

28. Josie bought 5 pounds of ground beef for $7.99, and Jack bought 4.5 pounds of ground beef for $7.29. Who had the better buy? Explain.

Mid-Chapter REVIEW

Round to the underlined place-value position.

1. 2.6̲8

2. 8̲.995

3. 5.61̲05

Add or subtract.

4. $14.32 - 5.65$

5. $6 + 2.1 + 3.58 + 8.210$

6. $\$5 - 32¢$

Multiply or divide.

7. 6.3×2.1

8. $\$1.44 \div 24$

9. $\$115 \div 4.6$

Cumulative Review

Compute.

1. $\begin{array}{r} 91 \\ -\ 55 \\ \hline \end{array}$

2. $\begin{array}{r} \$265 \\ +\ 93 \\ \hline \end{array}$

3. $\begin{array}{r} 77 \\ \times\ 4 \\ \hline \end{array}$

4. $\$714 \div 7$

Replace each ● with <, >, or = to make a true statement.

5. 206 ● 260

6. 4,918 ● 4,198

7. 12,413 ● 12,412

8. 0.7 ● 0.9

9. 0.60 ● 0.06

10. 0.75 ● 7.5

11. 0.400 ● 0.40

12. 9.85 ● 9.9

13. 46.014 ● 46.009

Round to the underlined place-value position.

14. 2̲46

15. $8̲5

16. 8̲29

17. 2,8̲96

18. 1,0̲84

19. 3̲9,504

20. 0.6̲4

21. 0.8̲7

Write in standard form.

22. 10^3

23. 2^3

24. 5^2

25. 4^3

Estimate.

26. $\begin{array}{r} 645 \\ +\ 862 \\ \hline \end{array}$

27. $\begin{array}{r} 70.85 \\ -\ 3.96 \\ \hline \end{array}$

28. $\begin{array}{r} \$88 \\ \times\ 9 \\ \hline \end{array}$

29. $\begin{array}{r} 24 \\ \times\ 76 \\ \hline \end{array}$

Solve.

30. The sale price on a pair of sweat pants is $7.89 plus $0.55 tax. The original price was $10.63. Find the sale price plus tax.

31. The average person's heart beats 259,200 times in 60 hours. *About* how many times does the heart beat each hour?

32. Can William buy a piece of pizza at $1.95 and a soda at $0.95 if he only has $3.00?

33. Bill Almon buys items at the athlete's store that cost $10.00, $8.99, and $0.43. Find the amount of change Mr. Almon should receive from $20.02.

2.6 Scientific Notation

Objective: to represent numbers in scientific notation and standard form

In a recent year, about 130 million people watched the Super Bowl on television. Numbers, like 130,000,000, can be expressed in scientific notation. **Scientific notation** is a way of renaming numbers as a product of two factors. The first factor is equal to or greater than 1 but less than 10. The second factor is a power of 10. You can rename greater numbers and lesser numbers.

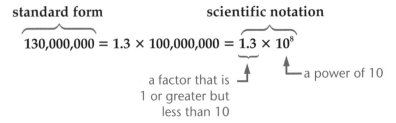

Observe the patterns with exponents:

$10^3 = 1,000$

$10^2 = 100$

$10^1 = 10$ What do you notice about the value of each power of 10

$10^0 = 1$ (the base number) as the exponent decreases?

$10^{-1} = 0.1$

$10^{-2} = 0.01$ Negative exponents are used to rename numbers between 0 and 1 in scientific notation.

$10^{-3} = 0.001$

You can change from scientific notation to standard form as follows.

$$3.08 \times 10^4 = 3.08 \times 10,000$$
$$= 3.0800$$
$$= 30,800$$

> Multiplying by 10,000 or 10^4 results in moving the decimal point four places to the right.

Examples

A. Write in standard form.

     5.0×10^{-7}

     .0000005.0

     Move the decimal 7 places to the left.

     $5.0 \times 10^{-7} = 0.0000005$

B. Write in scientific notation.

     0.008

     Move the decimal 3 places to the right.

     8.0 then add the power of 10.

     8.0×10^{-3}

Write as a power of 10.

1. 0.001
2. 10,000
3. 0.000001
4. 0.01
5. 100,000
6. 1,000,000

Exercises

Write in standard form.

1. 4.9×10^{-4}
2. 6×10^4
3. 1.5×10^{-3}
4. 2.3×10^3
5. 4.6×10^4
6. 2.05×10^{-4}
7. 1.65×10^3
8. 8.06×10^1

Write in scientific notation.

9. 968,000
10. 8,600
11. 0.009
12. 0.0003
13. 867
14. 0.00016
15. 0.00000001
16. 1,650

Problem SOLVING

17. Last year, consumers spent $3.2 billion for athletic shoes. Write this number in scientific notation.

18. The area of Colorado is 103,729 square miles. Write the number in scientific notation.

19. One cubic centimeter equals 0.061 cubic inches. Rename cubic inches using scientific notation.

20. What is the relationship of the exponent and the number of places the decimal point is moved?

Mind BUILDER

More Scientific Notation

Multiply 2×10^1 by 4×10^2.

$(2 \times 10^1) \times (4 \times 10^2)$

$= (2 \times 4) \times (10^1 \times 10^2)$

$= 8 \times (10 \times 10 \times 10)$

$= 8 \times 10^3$ or 8,000

Divide 6×10^4 by 3×10^3.

$(6 \times 10^4) \div (3 \times 10^3) = \frac{6}{3} \times \frac{10^4}{10^3}$

$= 2 \times \frac{10 \times \cancel{10} \times \cancel{10} \times \cancel{10}}{\cancel{10} \times \cancel{10} \times \cancel{10}}$

$= 2 \times 10^1$ or 20

Multiply or divide.

1. $(3 \times 10^2) \times (2 \times 10^4)$
2. $(7.2 \times 10^{12}) \times (1.3 \times 10^1)$
3. $(9 \times 10^5) \div (3 \times 10^2)$
4. $(8 \times 10^9) \div (2 \times 10^7)$

5. Explain how addition can be used when you multiply powers of 10.

6. Explain how subtraction can be used when you divide powers of 10.

Objective: to be able to convert within the metric system

Joan ran a 5-kilometer race this weekend. She wants to know how many meters she ran. We can convert between units in the metric system to figure this out.

The **metric system** is a base-ten system. The metric prefixes are associated with the decimal places as shown below.

Kilo-	Hecto-	Deka-	Meter Gram Liter	Deci-	Centi-	Milli-
			•			
thousands	hundreds	tens	ones	tenths	hundredths	thousandths

To convert between metric units you can multiply or divide. **Multiply** to change from larger units to smaller units. **Divide** to change from smaller units to larger units.

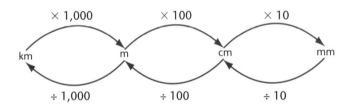

You are changing from a larger unit to a smaller unit, so multiply.
Since 1,000 m = 1 km, multiply by 1,000.

1,000 × 5 = 5,000 m   Joan ran 5,000 meters.

Example

Dave brought 1,400 milliliters of water to the race. How many liters did Dave bring?

1,400 milliliters = ■ liters

You are changing from a smaller unit to a larger unit, so divide.

Since 1 L = 1,000 mL, divide by 1,000.

$$\begin{array}{r} 1.4 \\ 1{,}000\overline{)1{,}400} \end{array}$$ Dave brought 1.4 liters of water.

Try THESE

Fill in the ■ with the correct amount.

1. 3.5 m = ■ cm
2. 85 g = ■ mg
3. 456 mL = ■ L
4. ■ cm = 500 mm
5. 68 mg = ■ g
6. ■ L = 62 kL

Exercises

State whether you multiply or divide to change between units.

1. centimeters to millimeters
2. grams to kilograms
3. liters to milliliters
4. kilograms to milligrams

Fill in the ■ with the correct amount.

5. 0.25 L = ■ mL
6. 6,051 m = ■ km
7. 1.15 cm = ■ m
8. 603 kg = ■ g
9. 8.50 L = ■ mL
10. ■ kg = 6.55 g
11. 2.53 km = ■ m
12. 4.3 cm = ■ mm
13. 5.35 kL = ■ mL

Compare using <, >, or =.

14. 40 g _____ 4 mg
15. 1,500 g _____ 150 kg
16. 4.5 cm _____ 45 mm

Order the measurements from least to greatest.

17. 43 cm; 4.59 m; 4,832 m
18. 0.893 kg; 819 kg; 8,350 mg

19. A can of soup contains about 550 mg of sodium. How many grams of sodium are in 8 cans of soup?

20. Sharon made a citrus punch. She used 2.2 L of orange juice, 150 mL of lemon juice, 100 mL of lime juice, and 4.1 L of seltzer water. How many liters of punch did Sharon make?

21. There are three trees in the Davis' backyard: a maple tree at 279 cm tall, an oak tree at 2.794 m tall, and a pine tree at 2,791 mm tall. Which tree is the tallest?

Constructed **RESPONSE** ·····································

22. Joel ran 4.2 kilometers each day for 4 days, while Dana ran 3,105 meters each day for 3 days. Who ran further? Explain.

Test **PREP** ··

23. Kelly walked 4.8 km. How many meters did she walk?

    a. 48   b. 480   c. 4,800   d. 48,000

24. A paper clip is 2.35 cm. How many meters long is the paper clip?

    a. 0.00235   b. 0.0235   c. 0.235   d. 20.35

Mind **BUILDER**

Mental Math

Multiplying a number by 0.5 has the same result as dividing that number by 2. Multiplying a number by 0.25 has the same result as dividing that number by 4. Study the examples.

$$1,232 \times 0.5 = 616 \qquad 1,468 \times 0.25 = 367$$
$$1,232 \div 2 = 616 \qquad 1,468 \div 4 = 367$$

Compute mentally. Write only the answer.

1. $2,212 \times 0.5$ 2. $1,424 \times 0.25$ 3. $7,258 \times 0.5$

4. $6,672 \times 0.5$ 5. $5,424 \times 0.25$ 6. $2,456 \times 0.25$

7. Multiply several numbers by 0.2. Complete this statement:
   Multiplying a number by 0.2 is the same as dividing a number by ____.

Farmer Brown's Cabbage Patch

Farmer Brown always plants cabbage patches shaped in squares like those shown below. He planted 1 cabbage the first year, 4 cabbages the second year, 9 cabbages the third year, and so on. This year he planted 29 more cabbages than last year. How many cabbages does he have this year? How many did he have last year?

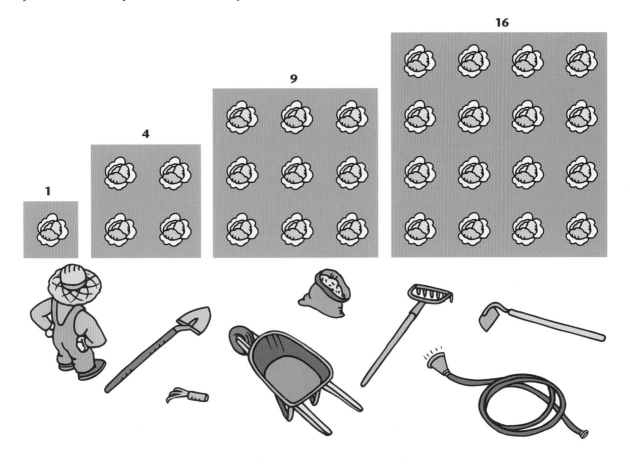

Extension

Identical cubes are stacked in a corner as shown at the right. There are 15 cubes in the bottom layer, and each layer has one more cube than the layer above it. How many layers are there in all?

2.8 Problem-Solving Strategy: Multi-Step Problems

Objective: to solve multi-step problems

The Jackson family bicycles on weekends in Darby Creek Park. How many kilometers shorter is the path directly from A to B than the path from A to B through F?

Darby Creek Bike Path (km)

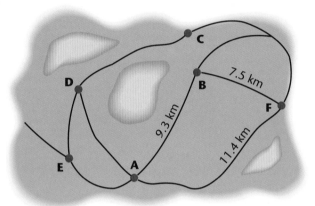

 You need to find the distances on the map. The distance from A to B is 9.3 km, the distance from A to F is 11.4 km, and the distance from F to B is 7.5 km.

 To find the distance from A to B through F, add 11.4 and 7.5. Then subtract 9.3, the distance from A to B.

> **Estimate:**
> $11 + 8 = 19$
> $19 - 9 = 10$
> $n = (11.4 + 7.5) - 9.3$

 $(11.4 + 7.5) - 9.3 = 9.6$

The distance from A to B is 9.6 km shorter than the distance from A to B through F.

 Since 9.6 km is close to the estimate of 10 km, the answer is reasonable.

 •

Choose the operations needed to solve each problem.

1. In the first two events, a gymnast scores ■ and ■ points. What must he score in the third event in order that his total score is ■ points?

2. Running shoes usually sell for ■ dollars. They are on sale for ■ dollars. How much money is saved if ■ pairs of running shoes are bought?

3. The two legs of a trip from Albuquerque to Los Angeles are ■ miles and ■ miles long. A car gets ■ miles per gallon? How many gallons of gas are needed for the trip?

4. Carmen spends ■ dollars, ■ dollars, and ■ dollars on running supplies. Tax is ■ dollars. How much change does she receive from ■ dollars?

1. Sonia has $20.50 to spend. After she buys a T-shirt for $4.95, does she have enough money to buy a sweater for $16.99?

2. The cross-country team buys 18 uniforms for $22.50 each. The tax on the uniforms is $21.78. Find the cost plus tax of the uniforms.

3. Ken earns 2.5¢ for each daily paper and 4¢ for each Sunday paper he delivers. One week he delivers 324 daily papers and 74 on Sunday. How much does he earn?

4. Thomas buys a dinner for $8.95. The tax is $0.36, and he leaves a tip of $1.30. How much change does he receive from $20.00?

Use the chart to solve problems 5–7.

5. Using the chart, how can you determine the number of games Montreal has played?

6. To find a baseball team's winning percentage (Pct.), divide the number of wins by the number of games played. If Montreal wins 2 of the next 4 games, find its Pct.

7. The chart also lists each team's record at home. Use estimation to determine which team has the best Pct. at home.

National League Standings					
East	**W**	**L**	**Pct.**	**Home**	**Road**
Pittsburgh	17	6	0.739	8–1	9–5
New York	16	6	0.727	6–2	10–4
Montreal	10	11	0.476	6–5	4–6
Chicago	10	13	0.435	2–4	8–9
St. Louis	9	14	0.391	4–5	5–9
Philadelphia	7	13	0.350	5–4	2–9

Constructed RESPONSE ·

8. Greta is making bouquets of roses and lilies. Roses cost $2.50 each, and lilies cost $3.25 each.

   a. How much will a bouquet with 4 roses and 2 lilies cost?

   b. How much will a bouquet with 5 roses and 7 lilies cost?

   c. Which bouquet is cheaper, one with 5 roses or one with 3 lilies? Explain.

Mixed REVIEW ·

Compute.

9. -16 + -11

10. -25 + 17

11. -5 − 18

12. 23 − -16

13. 16 • -6

14. -13 • -27

15. 312 ÷ -24

16. -72 ÷ -9

Write *true* or *false*.

1. The ones place is always located directly to the left of the decimal point.

2. When comparing two decimals, the one with more digits is always greater.

3. When rounding a decimal to a given place, you should round a number down if it is followed by a 5.

4. To add or subtract decimals, line up the numbers by place-value position.

5. A shortcut for multiplying a decimal by 100 is to add two zeros to the right of the number.

6. To divide a decimal by 0.35, first move the decimal point two places to the right.

7. The number 1.5×10^3 is written in scientific notation.

Skills and Problem Solving

Replace each ● with <, >, or = to make a true statement. Section 2.1

8. 0.8 ● 0.79   9. 1.605 ● 1.645   10. 2.61 ● 2.610

Order the numbers in each list from least to greatest. Section 2.1

11. 2.051, 2.501, 2.105   12. 0.618, 0.0861, 0.1068

Round to the underlined place-value position. Section 2.1

13. 6.8̲43   14. 0.46̲38   15. $29.6̲42

Add or subtract. Section 2.2

16. $16.15
    +   0.89

17.   0.217
    − 0.028

18.   12.088
    + 8.96

19. $16
    − 1.43

20.   4.06
     1.95
   + 28.074

Use front-end estimation to find the estimation of the sum. Section 2.2

21. 7.9 + 8.2 + 8.15   22. 6.95 + 12.20 + 7.81

Multiply. Section 2.4

23.
$$\begin{array}{r} 0.37 \\ \times\ 0.8 \\ \hline \end{array}$$

24.
$$\begin{array}{r} 11.36 \\ \times\ 2.8 \\ \hline \end{array}$$

25.
$$\begin{array}{r} \$12.56 \\ \times\quad 37 \\ \hline \end{array}$$

26.
$$\begin{array}{r} 0.009 \\ \times\ 0.68 \\ \hline \end{array}$$

27.
$$\begin{array}{r} 3.07 \\ \times\ 0.098 \\ \hline \end{array}$$

28. 6.2×10

29. $3.6 \times 1,000$

30. 2.87×100

Divide. Section 2.5

31. $8\overline{)24.8}$

32. $0.4\overline{)2.4}$

33. $0.72\overline{)4.896}$

34. $0.018\overline{)38.34}$

Write in scientific notation. Section 2.6

35. $31,000$

36. 0.000651

37. 0.0902

38. $672,000$

Write in standard form. Section 2.6

39. 5.3×10^5

40. 2.81×10^{-3}

41. 9.444×10^3

42. 7.01×10^{-6}

Fill in the ■ with the correct amount. Section 2.7

43. $58 \text{ mL} = ■ \text{ L}$

44. $250 \text{ kg} = ■ \text{ g}$

45. $58 \text{ m} = ■ \text{ cm}$

Solve. Sections 2.3 and 2.8

46. The sum of a number's digits is 4. It is an odd number. It is greater than 110 and less than 210. What is the number?

47. Dena Early buys 4 boxes of note cards for $2.75 each. How much change does she receive from $20.00?

48. The times of the four runners in a relay are 10.26, 9.85, 9.9, and 9.79 seconds. How many seconds less than 40 seconds was the total time?

In Your Own Words

49. Explain the pattern of the value of the places at the left and right of the ones place.

Chapter 2 Test

Write *true* or *false*.

1. $0.09 > 0.75$ **2.** $0.36 = 0.351$ **3.** $7.043 > 7.034$

Compute.

4. $\$3.85 - \$1.74$ **5.** $21.3 + 104.4$ **6.** $81.5 - 14.763$

7. $7.5 + 6.2$ **8.** $\$8.16 - \$4.37$ **9.** $12 - 8.604$

10. $\$7.56 + \$8.31 + 28¢$ **11.** $643 + 2.05 + 10.4 + 3.798$ **12.** 7.2×4

13. 0.403×37 **14.** $\$10.20 \times 0.25$ **15.** 4.006×10

16. $42.6 \div 10^2$ **17.** 0.08×10^3 **18.** $0.5\overline{)11.5}$

19. $0.6 \div 0.48$ **20.** $0.296 \div 0.008$

Divide. Round each quotient to the nearest hundredth.

21. $7\overline{)29}$ **22.** $3\overline{)21.4}$ **23.** $0.4\overline{)28.48}$ **24.** $0.43\overline{)7.39}$

Write in standard form.

25. 3×10^4 **26.** 2.5×10^{-3} **27.** 4.76×10^{-2} **28.** 9.03×10^5

Fill in the ■ with the correct amount.

29. $1.2 \text{ L} = ■ \text{ mL}$ **30.** $261 \text{ cm} = ■ \text{ m}$ **31.** $3 \text{ g} = ■ \text{ kg}$

Solve.

32. Tai-Lee plays a card game called Choices. Each card has a point value of either 2, 4, 6, 8, or 10. He draws six cards at random. Which of the following numbers could be his total score: 25, 64, 38, 10, 49?

33. Jana buys a dress for $25.98 and a blouse for $14.99. The sales tax is $2.46. What is her change from a $50 bill?

34. You are grocery shopping. You need a gallon of milk, two loaves of bread, and orange juice. You have $10. Do you have enough money?

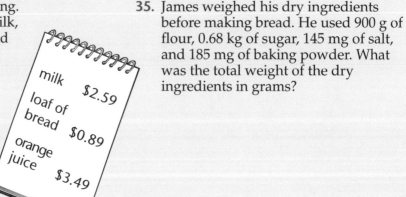

milk $2.59

loaf of bread $0.89

orange juice $3.49

35. James weighed his dry ingredients before making bread. He used 900 g of flour, 0.68 kg of sugar, 145 mg of salt, and 185 mg of baking powder. What was the total weight of the dry ingredients in grams?

Change of Pace

Sequences and Magic Squares

Lists of numbers following a certain pattern are called **sequences**.

8, 10, 12, 14, 16, . . . Each number in this pattern is 2 more than the number before it.

25.5, 15.5, 5.5, . . . Each number in this pattern is 10 less than the number before it.

You can use sequences to make **magic squares**. In a magic square, the sum (called the magic sum) along each row, column, and diagonal is the same.

Use the sequence 5.5, 6.5, 7.5, 8.5, . . . to make a magic square. First find the pattern, and then list the first nine numbers in the sequence. Then place the numbers in the appropriate square as shown below.

The pattern is to add 1. The first nine numbers in the sequence are 5.5, 6.5, 7.5, 8.5, 9.5, 10.5, 11.5, 12.5, and 13.5.

What is the magic sum?

2nd	7th	6th
9th	5th	1st
4th	3rd	8th

6.5	11.5	10.5
13.5	9.5	5.5
8.5	7.5	12.5

Describe each sequence. Then make a magic square for each sequence, and find the magic sum.

1. 9, 8.5, 8, 7.5, . . .

2. 9.25, 9.5, 9.75, 10, . . .

3. 12.1, 13.2, 14.3, 15.4, . . .

4. 0.005, 0.010, 0.015, 0.02, . . .

Copy and complete each magic square. Find the magic sum.

5.
3.3	?	7.7
?	6.6	?
5.5	?	9.9

6.
?	0.35	?
0.45	0.25	?
?	0.15	?

7.
?	13	?
15	?	7
?	?	?

8.
9	?	?
?	13.5	?
12	?	?

9. Make up your own magic square using sequences.

Cumulative Test

1. $43.6 - 18.49 = $ ____
   a. 24.11
   b. 24.57
   c. 25.01
   d. none of the above

2. $6.4\overline{)1{,}312}$
   a. 2.05
   b. 20.5
   c. 205
   d. none of the above

3. Estimate the product of 19 and 3.1.
   a. 6
   b. 16
   c. 22
   d. 60

4. Which expression is equal to $3(2 + 5)$?
   a. $(3 \times 2) \times (3 \times 5)$
   b. $(3 \times 2) + (3 \times 5)$
   c. $(3 + 2) \times (3 + 5)$
   d. none of the above

5. Sue's batting average is 0.376. What is the place-value position of the 6?
   a. hundredths
   b. ones
   c. tenths
   d. thousandths

6. What replacement for ■ makes the sentence $0.8 \times ■ = 800$ true?
   a. 10
   b. 100
   c. 1,000
   d. 10,000

7. What is the value of $-2a + 3$ if $a = 3$?
   a. 6
   b. 9
   c. 3
   d. none of the above

8. Diablo wants to buy eight dozen eggs. Two dozen eggs cost $1.70. Which problem cannot be solved using the information given?
   a. How much change will Diablo get?
   b. How much do one dozen eggs cost?
   c. How much do eight dozen eggs cost?
   d. none of the above

9. Kay has $10.00. She spends $5.45 for a dinner and leaves $0.85 for a tip. How much money is left?
   a. $3.70
   b. $4.55
   c. $5.40
   d. $9.15

10. What is the total cost for a 4-line and a 6-line ad if both are run for 3 days?

Daily Messenger—Classified Ad Rates				
Lines	Sunday	1 Day	3 Days	5 Days
2	$ 3.50	$ 3.00	$ 8.50	$14.00
4	6.50	5.50	16.00	26.50
6	9.00	8.00	23.50	39.00
8	11.50	10.25	30.25	50.25

   a. $16.00
   b. $23.50
   c. $39.50
   d. $40.00

Fractions, Decimals, and Percents

Tina Harrison
Wellington, FL

3.1 Prime Factorization

Objective: to write a number as a product of its prime factors

Musical instruments produce sound by making vibrations. Each sound is one of a kind.

Likewise, disregarding order, every composite number can be expressed as a product of prime factors in exactly one way. This product is called the **prime factorization** of a number. The prime factorizatrion of a number is a way to express a **composite number** as a product of **prime numbers**. A composite number has more than two factors, and a prime number has exactly two factors, itself and 1.

Use factor trees, like the ones shown below, to find the prime factorization of 40.

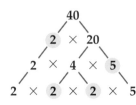

Start with any 2 factors.

Continue to factor.

Circle prime numbers as they appear.

All factors are prime.

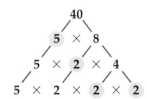

Can you make another factor tree for 40?

The prime factorization of 40 is 2 × 2 × 2 × 5.

Using exponents, $40 = 2^3 \times 5$.

> Write the factors in order from least to greatest according to the base number. Disregard exponents when putting the factors in order.

Example

Find the prime factorization of 36.

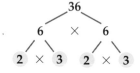 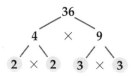

The prime factorization of 36 is $2^2 \times 3^2$.

Try THESE

Use number facts to find the least prime factor of each number.

1. 8	2. 16	3. 23	4. 25	5. 49
6. 77	7. 90	8. 125	9. 135	10. 143

Complete.

1.	**2.**	**3.** 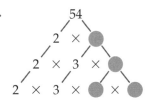	**4.** 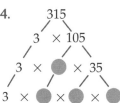

Use factor trees to find the prime factorization of each number. Write your answer using exponents.

5. 16	**6.** 42	**7.** 65	**8.** 96
9. 116	**10.** 125	**11.** 171	**12.** 198
13. 108	**14.** 88	**15.** 64	**16.** 100
17. 216	**18.** 432	★**19.** 1,242	★**20.** 1,296

Tell whether the value of each expression is *prime* or *composite*.

21. $2a + 3b$ when $a = 3$ and $b = 5$ **22.** $6x + 1$ when $x = 3$ **23.** $3x^2 + 3$ when $x = 2$

Problem SOLVING

24. What is the missing factor? $2^3 \times n \times 3^2 = 360$

★**25.** The product of two whole numbers is 1,000,000, but neither factor contains a zero. Find the factors.

26. What is the only even prime number?

Constructed RESPONSE

27. Find, describe, and correct the error in Dan's prime factorization of 48.

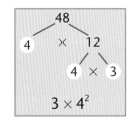

3.2 Greatest Common Factor

Objective: to find the greatest common factor of two or more numbers

Musical instruments, like guitars, electric keyboards, and drums, are used in a rock band. Violins, french horns, and drums are used in an orchestra. Drums are common to both the rock band and the orchestra.

Similarly, groups of numbers have **common factors**. The **factors** of 24 and 30 are listed below.

factors of 24:   1, 2, 3, 4, 6, 8, 12, 24

factors of 30:   1, 2, 3, 5, 6, 10, 15, 30

The common factors, shown in red, are 1, 2, 3, and 6. The greatest of these is called the **greatest common factor (GCF)**. The GCF of 24 and 30 is 6.

The GCF is the greatest whole number that is a factor of two or more given whole numbers.

Another Example

You can also find the GCF by using prime factorization.
Consider 14 and 42.

Step 1	Step 2	Step 3
Write the prime factorization of each number. 14 2 × 7 42 3 × 14 2 × 7	Find the common factors. $14 = 2 \times 7$ $42 = 2 \times 3 \times 7$ The common factors are 2 and 7.	Multiply the common factors to find the GCF. The GCF of 14 and 42 is 2×7, or 14.

Relatively prime numbers are two or more nonzero numbers whose greatest common factor is 1.

factors of 9:   1, 3, 9   The GCF is 1.

factors of 16:   1, 2, 4, 8, 16   9 and 16 are relatively prime.

Try THESE

Find the GCF of each group of numbers.

1. factors of 9: 1, 3, 9
   factors of 12: 1, 2, 3, 4, 6, 12

2. factors of 8: 1, 2, 4, 8
   factors of 10: 1, 2, 5, 10

3. $5 = 5$
   $25 = 5 \times 5$

4. $30 = 2 \times 3 \times 5$
   $45 = 3 \times 3 \times 5$

5. $12 = 2 \times 2 \times 3$
   $18 = 2 \times 3 \times 3$
   $24 = 2 \times 2 \times 2 \times 3$

Find the GCF of each group of numbers.

1. 8, 12
2. 12, 18
3. 10, 15
4. 12, 20
5. 12, 16
6. 15, 24
7. 40, 125
8. 16, 56
9. 14, 28
10. 56, 96
11. 35, 42, 84
12. 36, 50, 130
13. $2 \times 3 \times 5, 2 \times 3^2$
★14. $2^2 \times 3 \times 5^2, 2^3 \times 3 \times 7$

15. Write two numbers for which 5 is the GCF.

16. Write three numbers for which 8 is the GCF.

Find the GCF of each set of algebraic expressions.

17. $14a^2, 21a^3$
18. $12y, 18y^2$
★19. $27x^3y, 18x$

Find the two numbers in each group that are relatively prime.

20. 5, 9, 30
21. 6, 15, 35
22. 14, 15, 35
23. 21, 22, 33
24. 30, 42, 49
25. 35, 45, 72

Problem SOLVING

26. Roberto is 14 years old. The GCF of his age and his younger sister's age is 7. How old is his sister?

★27. Find the two least composite numbers that are relatively prime.

Constructed RESPONSE

28. A florist is making bouquets of flowers. She has 210 carnations, 350 roses, and 140 lilies. If the florist makes the bouquets the same and uses every flower, how many bouquets can she make, and how many of each flower will be in each bouquet? Explain.

29. Is the statement "Two composite numbers are never relatively prime" true or false? Support your answer.

Mind BUILDER

Perfect Numbers

A *perfect number* is equal to the sum of its proper factors. *Proper factors* are all factors of a number except the number itself. In *abundant numbers,* the sum of the proper factors is greater than the number. In *deficient numbers,* the sum of the factors is less than the number itself.

Number	Sum of Proper Factors	Perfect, Abundant, Deficient
4	1 + 2 = 3	deficient
6	1 + 2 + 3 = 6	perfect
12	1 + 2 + 3 + 4 + 6 = 16	abundant

Classify the numbers 2 through 30 as *perfect, abundant,* or *deficient.*

3.3 Least Common Multiple

Objective: to find the least common multiple of two or more numbers

The rocks in Juan's collection can be separated into groups of 4 or groups of 6. What is the least number of rocks that could be in his collection?

When you multiply a number by nonzero whole numbers 1, 2, 3, and so on, you are finding **multiples** of the number. The multiples of 4 and 6 are listed below.

4: 4, 8, **12**, 16, 20, **24**, . . .

6: 6, **12**, 18, **24**, 30, . . .

The first two common multiples of 4 and 6 are 12 and 24. What is the next common multiple?

Multiples of both numbers, shown in blue, are called **common multiples**. The least nonzero common multiple is called the **least common multiple (LCM)** of the numbers.

Since the LCM of 4 and 6 is 12, there are at least 12 rocks in Juan's rock collection.

More Examples

You can also find the LCM in one of the following two ways.

A. Find the LCM of 6 and 15 using prime factorization.

6 = ②×③
15 = ③×⑤

Circle common factors, and then circle each remaining factor.

The LCM is the product of the factors, using each common factor only once.

The LCM is 2 × 3 × 5, or 30.

B. Find the LCM of 8 and 12.

Multiples of 8: 8, 16, 24, . . .

Multiples of 12: 12, 24, . . .

The LCM is 24. List a number of multiples until you find the first common nonzero multiple.

Try **THESE** ·

Find the LCM of each group of numbers.

1. 6 and 9

6: 6, 12, 18, 24, . . .

9: 9, 18, 27, 36, . . .

2. 20 = ②×②×⑤

12 = ②×②×③

3. 4, 8, and 16

4: 4, 8, 12, 16, . . .

8: 8, 16, 24, 32, . . .

16: 16, 32, 48, 64, . . .

4. 5 = 5

10 = ②× 5

15 = ③×⑤

Exercises

Find the LCM of each group of numbers.

1. 2, 4
2. 3, 4
3. 6, 10
4. 14, 21
5. 36, 9
6. 25, 30
7. 35, 12
8. 21, 28
9. 2, 3, 5
10. 2, 4, 10
11. 8, 3, 4
12. 10, 20, 30
13. 18, 32
14. 16, 24
15. 25, 81
16. 52, 132

17. Copy and complete the following chart.

Numbers	GCF	LCM	GCF × LCM
2, 3	1	6	6
3, 4	?	?	?
4, 8	?	?	?
4, 6	?	?	?
8, 12	?	?	?

Problem SOLVING

18. What do you notice about the product of the GCF and the LCM in the chart above?

19. The GCF of 48 and 60 is 12. Use your observations from the chart above to find the LCM.

20. Find a pair of numbers that have 9 as their GCF.

21. Describe the LCM of two relatively prime numbers. Give examples to support your answer.

★22. Kendra attends a computer club meeting the first and third Thursday of each month. She also has drill team practice every other school day. If Kendra has both activities scheduled for Thursday, January 20, what is the next date she will have both activities scheduled?

★23. The LCM of two numbers is $2^2 \times 3 \times 5^2$. The GCF of the same numbers is 2×5. If one of the numbers is $2 \times 3 \times 5$, what is the other number?

Test PREP

24. Find the least common multiple of 15 and 45.
   a. 675
   b. 15
   c. 45
   d. 90

25. Find the greatest common factor of 42 and 70.
   a. 7
   b. 2
   c. 21
   d. 14

Objective: to convert between fractions and decimals

During lunch $\frac{1}{2}$ of the students prefer turkey sandwiches, $\frac{2}{5}$ prefer grilled cheese, and $\frac{1}{4}$ prefer a salad. Place the lunch choices in order from least preferred to most preferred.

It is sometimes easier to look at fractions as decimals. You can convert fractions to decimals.

We can write $\frac{2}{5}$, $\frac{1}{2}$, and $\frac{1}{4}$ as decimals by dividing.

$$
\begin{array}{r}
0.4 \\
5\overline{)2.0} \\
-2\,0 \\
\hline
0
\end{array}
\qquad
\begin{array}{r}
0.5 \\
2\overline{)1.0} \\
-1\,0 \\
\hline
0
\end{array}
\qquad
\begin{array}{r}
0.25 \\
4\overline{)1.00} \\
-\ \ 8 \\
\hline
20 \\
-20 \\
\hline
0
\end{array}
$$

▷ Divide the numerator by the denominator.

You find that $\frac{2}{5}$ is 0.4 as a decimal. A decimal, like 0.4, is called a **terminating decimal** because the division ends or terminates with 0 as the last remainder.

Not all decimals are terminating. Some are **repeating decimals**. A repeating decimal, such as 0.333333, is shown by a bar over any digits that repeat.

$0.333333 \ldots = 0.\overline{3}$

Examples

A. Write $\frac{4}{20}$ as a decimal.

$$
\begin{array}{r}
0.2 \\
20\overline{)4.0} \\
-4\,0 \\
\hline
0
\end{array}
$$

$\frac{4}{20}$ is 0.2 as a decimal.

B. Write $\frac{5}{3}$ as a decimal.

$$
\begin{array}{r}
1.66 \\
3\overline{)5.00} \\
-3 \\
\hline
20 \\
-18 \\
\hline
20 \\
-18 \\
\hline
2
\end{array}
$$

$\frac{5}{3}$ is $1.6\overline{6}$ as a decimal.

We can also convert decimals to fractions.

C. Write 0.6 as a fraction.

$0.6 = \dfrac{6}{10}$ 6 is in the tenths place.

$= \dfrac{3}{5}$ Simplify. The GCF of 6 and 10 is 2.

D. Write 4.75 as a mixed number.

$4.75 = 4\dfrac{75}{100}$ 5 is in the hundredths place.

$= 4\dfrac{3}{4}$ The GCF of 75 and 100 is 25.

Try THESE

Copy and complete.

Fraction	$\frac{1}{4}$	?	?	$\frac{9}{100}$	$\frac{1}{50}$	?	$\frac{4}{5}$	?	$\frac{1}{8}$
Decimal	?	0.5	0.3	?	?	0.4	?	0.65	?

Exercises

Write each fraction as a terminating or repeating decimal.

1. $\dfrac{7}{8}$

2. $\dfrac{15}{16}$

3. $1\dfrac{1}{2}$

4. $\dfrac{7}{12}$

5. $4\dfrac{3}{8}$

6. $\dfrac{11}{30}$

7. $\dfrac{9}{21}$

8. $3\dfrac{7}{8}$

9. $\dfrac{7}{20}$

10. $\dfrac{11}{12}$

11. $\dfrac{19}{50}$

12. $\dfrac{9}{25}$

13. $7\dfrac{4}{5}$

14. $5\dfrac{11}{25}$

15. $3\dfrac{1}{20}$

Write each decimal as a fraction or mixed number in simplest form.

16. 0.7

17. 0.4

18. 7.1

19. 9.75

20. 0.008

Replace each ● with <, >, or = to make a true statement.

21. $\dfrac{1}{2}$ ● 0.2

22. $\dfrac{4}{5}$ ● 0.8

23. 0.76 ● $\dfrac{3}{4}$

24. $\dfrac{1}{3}$ ● 0.3

25. 0.9 ● $\dfrac{9}{10}$

26. 0.83 ● 0.83

27. $\dfrac{4}{9}$ ● 0.4444

28. 0.37 ● $\dfrac{3}{8}$

Estimate using rounding. Then write each fraction as a decimal and compute.

29. Find the product of 8.25 and $6\frac{1}{2}$.

30. Divide 1.75 by $\frac{4}{5}$.

31. Subtract $6\frac{7}{8}$ from 10.875.

32. Add $4\frac{3}{4}$, $5\frac{1}{2}$, and 8.1265.

Problem SOLVING

33. The record height for a giraffe is 6.1 meters. Express 6.1 as a mixed number in simplest form.

34. The largest saltwater crocodile ever measured was $25\frac{1}{2}$ feet long. Write $25\frac{1}{2}$ as a decimal.

The Million-Dollar Giveaway

The students in Carlos's social studies class were to imagine that they each had $1 million to spend for improvements in their community.

Carlos liked number patterns, so he spent the money in this way.

$\frac{1}{2}$ to build a youth center

$\frac{1}{4}$ to build a park

$\frac{1}{8}$ to build a senior-citizen center

$\frac{1}{16}$ to buy equipment for his school

. . . and so on until Carlos had a list of ten items.

Did Carlos spend more or less than $1 million?

Extension

If Carlos spent his money using the following pattern and a list of ten items, would Carlos have spent more or less than $1 million?

$\frac{1}{3}, \frac{1}{6}, \frac{1}{12}, \frac{1}{24}, \ldots$

Cumulative Review

Replace each ● with <, >, or = to make a true statement.

1. 43 ● 4.3
2. 0.39 ● 3.9
3. 1.90 ● 1.9
4. 4.59 ● 50.6
5. 0.781 ● 0.78
6. 8.005 ● 8.05

Estimate.

7. $\begin{array}{r} 721 \\ -\ 198 \end{array}$

8. $\begin{array}{r} \$7.32 \\ +\ 8.64 \end{array}$

9. $\begin{array}{r} \$12.36 \\ \times\ \ \$4.57 \end{array}$

10. $4.1\overline{)15.67}$

11. $0.6\overline{)3.63}$

Compute.

12. $3.25 + 5.069$
13. $63.52 - 41.30$
14. $4.75 - 2.08$
15. $\$9 - 3.37$
16. $108 \bullet 0.6$
17. $4.8 \div 4$
18. $6.5 \div 0.5$
19. $0.0027 \div 0.3$
20. $14.98 \div 3.3$
21. $\$3.25 \bullet 100$
22. $10.23 \bullet 10$

Evaluate each expression if $r = 4$, $s = 3$, $t = 0.5$, and $w = 2$.

23. $r^2 + t$
24. $r \bullet s$
25. $(w + s) \bullet t$
26. $w + r \bullet t$

Evaluate each expression.

27. $8 + 9 - 3 + 5$
28. $7 \bullet 5 + 22 \bullet 32$
29. $(9 + 4) \bullet (8 - 7)$
30. $24 \div 6 + 2$
31. $3^2 \bullet 4 \div 2$
32. $18 - (9 + 3) + 24$
33. $5 \bullet 6 \div 10 + 1$
34. $12 + 6 \div 3 - 5$
35. $7 - 2 \bullet 8 \div 4$

Solve

36. Mr. Collier buys two $2.98 books and a $0.15 newspaper. The tax is $0.39. How much change does he receive from $10.00?

37. Ms. Rodriguez has $125 to spend. Can she buy a dress and a sweater for $35 each and a pair of shoes for $28?

38. An electric clock costs 22¢ a month to operate. How much, in dollars, does it cost to operate for 1 year?

39. One loaf of bread is used to make 12 sandwiches. Tom used $2\frac{1}{2}$ loaves to make sandwiches for a party. How many sandwiches did he make?

Objective: to convert between decimals and percents

The River Valley scout troop collected firewood for 54% of the neighborhood families.

We can represent 54% as a decimal.

Remember **percent** means hundredth.

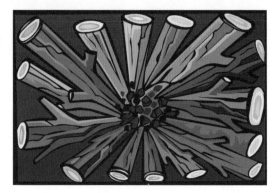

$$54\% = \frac{54}{100} = 0.54$$

÷ 100 move decimal point left

54% ⟶ 0.54

× 100 move decimal point right

When converting a percent to a decimal, divide the percent by 100. This is the same as moving the decimal point two places to the left and dropping the percent sign. When converting a decimal to a percent, multiply the decimal by 100, or move the decimal point two places to the right and add a percent sign.

Examples

A. Write 28% as a decimal.

$$28\% = 28\%$$
$$= 0.28$$

B. Write 0.3 as a percent.

$$0.3 = 0.30$$
$$= 30\%$$

Large and Small Percents

We can also convert percents that are between 0 and 1 or greater than 100.

C. Write 156% as a decimal.

$$156\% = 156\%$$
$$= 1.56$$

D. Write 0.006 as a percent.

$$0.006 = 0.006$$
$$= 0.6\%$$

Tell which direction to move the decimal point.

1. Write 52% as a decimal.
2. Write 195% as a decimal.
3. Write 0.68 as a percent.
4. Write 0.007 as a percent.

Exercises

Write each percent as a decimal.

1. 12%	2. 97%	3. 64%	4. 83%
5. 75%	6. 66%	7. 150%	8. 183%
9. 37.5%	10. 1.2%	11. 216.3%	12. 812%

Write each decimal as a percent.

13. 0.86	14. 0.05	15. 0.09	16. 0.62
17. 1.25	18. 2.53	19. 0.416	20. 0.015
21. 0.004	22. 0.125	23. 6.108	24. 4.1

Problem SOLVING

For exercises 25–28 use the chart to the right. Write each percent as a decimal for the following elements.

25. Oxygen
26. Magnesium
27. Nickel
28. Titanium

★29. Square A is 10 cm by 10 cm. Square B is 7 cm by 7 cm. What percent of square A is the area of square B?

Earth's Chemical Composition	
Element	Percentage
Iron	34.6%
Oxygen	29.5%
Silicon	15.2%
Magnesium	12.7%
Nickel	2.4%
Titanium	0.05%

Constructed RESPONSE

30. Last year you earned $965 for baby-sitting. This year you earned 105% of last year's amount. Did you earn more or less this year? Explain.

3.6 Fractions and Percents

Objective: to convert between fractions and percents

The Middle School Student Council conducted a survey to determine how many people like ketchup on their French fries. Of 100 students, 65 like ketchup on their French fries. The grid at the right is shaded to show 65 out of a 100.

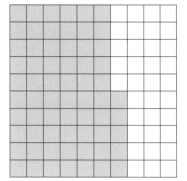

65 out of 100 can be written as a percent.

A **percent** is a ratio that compares a number to 100.

Percent means hundredth.

65 out of 100 $\longrightarrow \dfrac{65}{100} \longrightarrow$ 65%

Fractions and percents are different names for the same number.

Examples

A. Write 5% as a fraction.

$5\% = \dfrac{5}{100}$ Write the percent as a fraction with a denominator of 100.

$= \dfrac{1}{20}$ Simplify the fraction.

B. Write $\frac{1}{4}$ as a percent.

$\dfrac{1}{4} = \dfrac{25}{100} = 25\%$ To write the fraction as a percent, write an equivalent fraction with a denominator of 100.

C. Write $\frac{4}{5}$ as a percent.

$\dfrac{4}{5} = \dfrac{80}{100} = 80\%$

D. Write 35% as a fraction.

$35\% = \dfrac{35}{100} = \dfrac{7}{20}$

You can find the percents of numbers using the relationships between fractions and percents.

E. What is 40% of 25?   You know that 40% is also $\frac{2}{5}$. $40\% = \dfrac{40}{100} = \dfrac{2}{5}$

40% of $25 = \dfrac{2}{5} \cdot 25 = \dfrac{2 \cdot 25}{5} = 10$

Try THESE ....

Write each ratio as a percent.

1. 17 out of 100

2. 84 out of 100

3. 30 out of 100

4. 21 m out of 100 m

5. $6 out of $100

6. 9.5 out of 100

Write the percent as a fraction or mixed number in simplest form.

1. 20%
2. 25%
3. 35%
4. 75%
5. 48%
6. 55%
7. 8%
8. 120%
9. 110%
10. 150%
11. $33\frac{1}{3}$%
12. $16\frac{2}{3}$%

Write the fraction as a percent.

13. $\frac{1}{20}$
14. $\frac{3}{4}$
15. $\frac{11}{20}$
16. $\frac{9}{25}$
17. $\frac{7}{100}$
18. $\frac{9}{20}$
19. $\frac{3}{5}$
20. $\frac{7}{8}$
21. $\frac{1}{8}$
22. $\frac{3}{2}$
23. $\frac{1}{12}$
24. $\frac{2}{3}$

Find the percent of the number.

25. 20% of 50
26. 75% of 16
27. 60% of 20
28. 25% of 28
29. 80% of 400
30. 10% of 70
31. 40% of 80
32. 90% of 30

Problem SOLVING

33. Carter has typed 67 pages of a 100-page report. What percent of the report does he have yet to type?

34. There are 33 students in the music room and 17 students in the gym. Of all the students, what percent are in the music room?

35. Order the given ratios from least to greatest. 25%, $\frac{2}{5}$, 22 to 100

Constructed RESPONSE

36. The atmosphere of the Earth is made up of about 78% nitrogen and about 21% oxygen. Write each percent as a fraction. About what percent of the Earth's atmosphere is made up of other gases? What fraction is this?

Mid-Chapter REVIEW

Find the prime factorization of each number. Write your answer using exponents.

1. 54
2. 124
3. 105
4. 81

Find the greatest common factor and least common multiple of each pair of numbers.

5. 12, 36
6. 6, 10
7. 8, 15
8. 9, 27

Convert each fraction to a decimal and a percent.

9. $\frac{4}{5}$
10. $\frac{8}{12}$
11. $\frac{1}{8}$
12. $\frac{3}{8}$

3.7 Comparing and Ordering Rational Numbers

Objective: to compare and order rational numbers

Eric has taken music lessons for years. He knows that an eighth note is held for less time than a quarter note. In math class, he wonders if one-eighth is less than one-fourth. What do you think?

From the model, $\frac{1}{8} < \frac{1}{4}$.

To compare and order fractions, like the ones above, it is best to rewrite each fraction with a common denominator and compare the numerators. The **least common denominator** is the LCM of the original denominators.

Examples

A. Compare $\frac{4}{5}$ and $\frac{3}{4}$.

Step 1	Step 2	Step 3
Find the LCD by finding the LCM of the denominators. 5 = 5, 10, 15, (20), 25 4 = 4, 8, 12, 16, (20), 24 LCD = 20	Rename each fraction using the LCD of 20. $\frac{4}{5} = \frac{16}{20}$ (×4) $\frac{3}{4} = \frac{15}{20}$ (×5)	Compare the renamed fractions. $16 > 15$ $\frac{16}{20} > \frac{15}{20}$ So $\frac{4}{5} > \frac{3}{4}$.

You can also compare and order fractions and percents by writing them as decimals, then comparing the decimals.

B. Order $\frac{3}{4}, \frac{2}{3}$, and 60% from least to greatest.

Step 1	Step 2	Step 3
Write each fraction as a decimal. $\frac{3}{4} = 0.75$ $\frac{2}{3} = 0.6\bar{6}$	Write each percent as a decimal. 60% = 0.60	Order from least to greatest. $0.60 < 0.6\bar{6} < 0.75$ 60%, $\frac{2}{3}, \frac{3}{4}$

The integers, fractions, and decimals, both terminating and repeating, you are comparing and ordering are called **rational numbers**. A rational number is any number that can be expressed as a fraction where the denominator is not 0.

Find the least common denominator for each pair of fractions.

1. $\frac{1}{2}, \frac{1}{4}$
2. $\frac{1}{4}, \frac{1}{8}$
3. $\frac{2}{3}, \frac{3}{4}$
4. $\frac{5}{6}, \frac{4}{15}$

Exercises ···

Replace each ● with >, <, or = to make a true statement.

1. $\frac{2}{3}$ ● $\frac{5}{8}$
2. $\frac{6}{3}$ ● $\frac{10}{15}$
3. $\frac{3}{8}$ ● $\frac{1}{4}$
4. $\frac{5}{8}$ ● $\frac{11}{16}$

5. $\frac{4}{6}$ ● $\frac{6}{9}$
6. 70% ● $\frac{5}{12}$
7. $\frac{3}{4}$ ● $\frac{-5}{6}$
8. $\frac{14}{20}$ ● $\frac{5}{10}$

9. $-1\frac{3}{4}$ ● $\frac{3}{4}$
10. $\frac{-8}{8}$ ● $\frac{9}{9}$
11. $\frac{5}{12}$ ● $\frac{3}{16}$
12. $\frac{-1}{2}$ ● $\frac{3}{4}$

13. $\frac{-3}{2}$ ● $-1\frac{1}{2}$
14. $\frac{2}{5}$ ● 45%
15. $\frac{3}{11}$ ● 30%
16. $2\frac{3}{4}$ ● $2\frac{4}{6}$

17. $\frac{5}{3}$ ● $\frac{6}{4}$
18. $-1\frac{1}{4}$ ● $-1\frac{1}{2}$
19. 80% ● $\frac{5}{6}$
20. $|1\frac{1}{2}|$ ● $|-1\frac{1}{2}|$

Order the rational numbers in each list from least to greatest.

21. $\frac{3}{8}, \frac{3}{4}, \frac{5}{16}, \frac{1}{2}$
22. $\frac{2}{3}, \frac{-3}{5}, 55\%, \frac{7}{10}$
23. $\frac{-1}{2}, 42\%, -0.51, \frac{11}{20}$

Problem SOLVING ···

24. Which race is longer, a $\frac{7}{16}$-mile race or a $\frac{3}{8}$-mile race?

★25. A set of measuring cups has the following sizes: $\frac{1}{2}, \frac{1}{3}, \frac{1}{4}, 1, \frac{2}{3}$, and $\frac{3}{4}$ of a cup. Order them from largest to smallest.

26. Is $\frac{5}{6}$ yard of material enough for a pattern calling for $\frac{3}{4}$ yard?

27. The density property states that between any two fractions on a number line, there is another fraction. Name a fraction that lies between each set of given fractions below.

a. $\frac{1}{4}, \frac{1}{2}$
b. $\frac{5}{8}, \frac{2}{3}$
c. $\frac{7}{24}, \frac{1}{3}$
d. $\frac{17}{36}, \frac{1}{2}$

Mind BUILDER

Latin

Many of the terms used in mathematics come from Latin words. Explain why these words were chosen.

Latin word	meaning
numeratore	number
denominatore	names
frangere	to break

3.8 Problem-Solving Strategy: Guess and Check

Objective: to solve problems using the guess-and-check strategy

Ayita and her parents spent $12 for tickets to the zoo. A student's ticket is exactly two-thirds as much as an adult ticket. Find the cost of each ticket.

To solve this problem, use the guess-and-check strategy.

- First make a sensible guess for a solution.
- Check the guess to see if it is correct.
- Decide how to improve the next guess.
- Make another guess and check this guess.
- Repeat these steps until the problem is solved.

You need to find the cost of each ticket. You know that a student ticket is two-thirds an adult ticket. You also know the total for three tickets.

Guess the cost of one adult ticket. Then find two-thirds of that cost. See if the total cost of three tickets is $12.

First guess that an adult ticket costs $6. A student ticket would cost $\frac{2}{3}$ of $6, or $4.

$6 + $6 + $4 = $16   Since 16 > 12, try a number less than 6.

Guess again. Guess $3.
A student ticket would cost $\frac{2}{3}$ of $3, or $2.

$3 + $3 + $2 = $8   Since 8 < 12, try a number greater than 3.

Guess again. Guess $4.50. $4.50 is halfway between 3 and 6.
A student ticket would cost $\frac{2}{3}$ of $4.50, or $3.00.

$4.50 + $4.50 + $3.00 = $12.00

So, an adult ticket costs $4.50, and a student ticket costs $3.00.

Explain why the solution is reasonable.

1. Benito's family spent $14 for two adult and two student tickets for the basketball game. If a student ticket costs three-fourths as much as an adult ticket, find the cost of each ticket.

2. Fair tickets cost $3.50 for adults and $1.50 for children. Jason's family spent $12.00 for tickets. They bought more adult tickets than children's tickets. How many of each did they buy?

Solve ....

Use any strategy.

1. The difference between two whole numbers is 14. Their product is 1,800. Find the two numbers.

2. One-half the sum of two consecutive whole numbers is 20.5. Find the numbers.

3. At the school supply store, four pencils and seven pens cost $1.89. Eleven pencils and one pen cost $1.00. What is the cost of one pencil?

★4. Mae is one-third as old as her sister, Joan. In five years, Mae will be one-half as old as Joan. How old is Mae now?

5. A number is squared and the result is 225. What is the number?

6. The sum of four consecutive numbers is 38. Find the numbers.

Constructed RESPONSE ....

★7. Brenda has dimes, nickels, and quarters in her pocket. The 9 coins have a total value of $1.00. She has more nickels than dimes. How many of each coin does Brenda have? Explain.

8. Juan bought 8 pounds of apples to bake pies. He bought twice as many pounds of Granny Smith than of Macintosh. How many pounds of each type of apple did Juan buy? Explain.

MiXeD REVIEW ....

Add or subtract.

9. $0.42 + 1.11$

10. $19 + 0.1$

11. $11.8 - 10.5$

12. $14 - 6.5$

13. $4.4 + 0.015$

14. $20 - 0.7$

Chapter 3 Review

Language and Concepts

Choose the correct term to complete each sentence.

1. The word *percent* means (ten, hundredth).

2. The fraction $\frac{1}{2}$, the decimal 0.5, and 50% are different names for the same (variable, number).

3. Another word for *factor* is (divisor, fraction).

4. The (LCM, GCF) of two numbers is always less than or equal to the numbers.

5. A fraction is in simplest form when the GCF of its numerator and denominator is (0, 1).

6. The fraction $\frac{1}{8}$ can be written as a (terminating, repeating) decimal.

Skills and Problem Solving

Find the prime factorization of each number. Write your answer using exponents. Section 3.1

7. 8
8. 56
9. 121
10. 484

Find the GCF of each group of numbers. Section 3.2

11. 8, 16
12. 12, 18, 21

Find the LCM of each group of numbers. Section 3.3

13. 4, 7
14. 10, 15

Write each fraction as a terminating or repeating decimal. Section 3.4

15. $\frac{2}{5}$
16. $\frac{1}{12}$
17. $\frac{6}{11}$
18. $\frac{15}{12}$

Write each decimal as a fraction or mixed number. Section 3.4

19. 0.8
20. 0.05
21. 7.3
22. 4.18

Replace each ● with <, >, or = to make a true statement. Section 3.4

23. $0.5 \bullet \frac{1}{5}$
24. $\frac{2}{3} \bullet 0.6$
25. $0.4 \bullet \frac{2}{5}$
26. $\frac{6}{10} \bullet 0.6$

Write each percent as a decimal. Section 3.5

27. 11%   28. 4%

29. 56%   30. 125%

Write each decimal as a percent. Section 3.5

31. 0.42   32. 0.08

33. 0.006   34. 3.18

Write the percent as a fraction in simplest form. Section 3.6

35. 40%   36. 18%

37. 125%   38. $87\frac{1}{2}$%

Write the fraction as a percent. Section 3.6

39. $\frac{4}{5}$ 40. $\frac{3}{8}$

41. $\frac{7}{20}$ 42. $\frac{9}{10}$

Replace each ● with >, <, or = to make a true statement. Section 3.7

43. $\frac{3}{4}$ ● 70%   44. $-\frac{2}{3}$ ● $\frac{4}{5}$

45. 35% ● $\frac{7}{20}$ 46. $\frac{9}{10}$ ● 99%

Solve. Section 3.8

47. The difference between two numbers is 8. The product is 105. Find the two numbers.

48. Mrs. Snyder took her class to the history museum to learn about the presidents. The children's admission was $2.50, and the adult admission was $5.00. She bought five times as many children's tickets as she did adult tickets and spent a total of $70.00. How many of each type of ticket did she buy?

Chapter 3 Test

Write the prime factorization of each number using exponents.

1. 33
2. 91
3. 324
4. 450

Find the GCF of each group of numbers.

5. 4, 16
6. 8, 12
7. 9, 15
8. 4, 6, 9

Find the LCM of each group of numbers.

9. 4, 10
10. 8, 36
11. 5, 8
12. 3, 9, 27

Write each fraction or mixed number as a decimal.

13. $\frac{4}{5}$
14. $\frac{11}{16}$
15. $1\frac{1}{3}$
16. $3\frac{2}{3}$
17. $5\frac{3}{20}$

Write each decimal as a fraction or mixed number in simplest form.

18. 0.4
19. 0.09
20. 0.55
21. 6.2
22. 3.75

Write each fraction as a percent.

23. $\frac{3}{5}$
24. $\frac{4}{5}$
25. $\frac{10}{12}$
26. $\frac{4}{10}$
27. $\frac{18}{25}$

Replace each ● with <, >, or = to make a true statement.

28. $\frac{2}{5}$ ● 0.35
29. 0.60 ● $\frac{5}{8}$
30. $\frac{3}{4}$ ● 0.75
31. $\frac{3}{8}$ ● 0.38

Write each percent as a decimal.

32. 18%
33. 6%
34. 130%
35. 95%
36. 52%

Write each decimal as a percent.

37. 0.48
38. 0.7
39. 0.09
40. 1.28
41. 3.55

Solve.

42. Find an odd number between 10 and 25 that is divisible by 3 but is not divisible by 5.

43. Jeremy had some nickels and dimes in his pocket. The 14 coins have a value of 95¢. How many of each coin does he have?

Change of Pace

More Factor Patterns

You already know that prime numbers have exactly two factors. What numbers have exactly three factors? or four factors?

The numbers from 2 through 15 have been placed in the chart according to the number of factors each has.

Exactly 2	Exactly 3	Exactly 4	Exactly 5	Exactly 6
2	4	6		12
3	9	8		
5		10		
7		14		
11		15		
13				

Can you see a pattern in any of the columns? Can you conclude that there is no number that has exactly five factors?

1. Draw the chart on a separate piece of paper.

2. Find how many factors are in each of the numbers 16 through 30.

3. Place the numbers 16 through 30 in the correct column.

4. What is different about the number 16?

5. Repeat this procedure with numbers 31–50.

6. What do you find as the numbers get larger?

Cumulative Test

1. What is the greatest common factor of 12 and 15?
   a. 1
   b. 3
   c. 4
   d. none of the above

2. 3^4
   a. 12
   b. 27
   c. 81
   d. 243

3. What is the least common multiple of 6 and 9?
   a. 3
   b. 54
   c. 36
   d. 18

4. Which expression has a value of 70?
   a. $(17 - 3) \cdot 2 + 3$
   b. $17 - (3 \cdot 2) + 3$
   c. $17 - 3 \cdot (2 + 3)$
   d. $(17 - 3) \cdot (2 + 3)$

5. A number is a multiple of 10. It is divisible by which numbers?
   a. 2 and 5
   b. 3 and 5
   c. 3 and 7
   d. 4 and 7

6. Find the difference of 67.32 and 6.518.
   a. 0.224
   b. 2.24
   c. 60.802
   d. 73.838

7. Diego buys 4 tickets for a game. Lisa buys 3 tickets. Diego pays $28 for his tickets. How much does each ticket cost Diego? Which fact is not needed?
   a. Diego buys 4 tickets.
   b. Diego pays $28 for the tickets.
   c. Lisa buys 3 tickets.
   d. none of the above

8. What is the prime factorization of 30?
   a. $22 \cdot 3 \cdot 5$
   b. $2 \cdot 3 \cdot 5$
   c. $2 \cdot 32 \cdot 5$
   d. $2 \cdot 2 \cdot 3 \cdot 5$

9. Which number is both odd and composite?
   a. 7
   b. 14
   c. 19
   d. 25

10. The chart shows the scores of high schools at a track meet. Which school scored the most points?

Central	65.8
East	64.95
Grove	65
Liberty	65.75
Ridge	65.83

   a. Central
   b. East
   c. Liberty
   d. Ridge

Computing Fractions

Nicholas Parlato
Calvert Day School

4.1 Adding Fractions and Mixed Numbers

Objective: to add fractions and mixed numbers

Cars use about $\frac{4}{9}$ of the energy consumed by the transportation industry. Buses and trains use $\frac{1}{6}$. Add $\frac{4}{9}$ and $\frac{1}{6}$ to find the part of the transportation energy used by cars, buses, and trains.

> Will the sum be greater or less than 1?

Step 1	Step 2	Step 3
Find the LCD. $$\frac{4}{9} \quad 9: 9, 18, 27, 36$$ $$+ \frac{1}{6} \quad 6: 6, 12, 18, 24$$ $$\text{LCD} = 18$$	Rename each fraction. $$\frac{4}{9} = \frac{8}{18}$$ $$+ \frac{1}{6} = \frac{3}{18}$$	Add. $$\frac{4}{9} = \frac{8}{18}$$ $$+ \frac{1}{6} = \frac{3}{18}$$ $$\frac{11}{18}$$

Cars, buses, and trains use $\frac{11}{18}$ of the transportation energy.

More Examples

A. $\frac{7}{10} + \frac{9}{10} = \frac{16}{10}$ Will the sum be greater or less than 1?

$= 1\frac{6}{10}$ or $1\frac{3}{5}$

> Write the sum as a mixed number in simplest form.

B. $\frac{5}{6} = \frac{20}{24}$ $6 = 2 \times 3$

$+ \frac{5}{8} = \frac{15}{24}$ $8 = 2 \times 2 \times 2$

LCD: $2 \times 3 \times 2 \times 2$ or 24

$\frac{35}{24} = 1\frac{11}{24}$

> You can use prime factorization to find the LCD.

C. $1\frac{1}{10} = 1\frac{1}{10}$ Will the sum be greater than or less than $3\frac{1}{2}$?

$+ \quad 2\frac{1}{2} = 2\frac{5}{10}$

$3\frac{6}{10} = 3\frac{3}{5}$

Try THESE

Find the LCD.

1. $\frac{1}{4}$
    $+ \frac{1}{8}$

2. $\frac{2}{3}$
    $+ \frac{1}{2}$

3. $1\frac{2}{8}$
    $+ 2\frac{2}{5}$

4. $2\frac{5}{6}$
    $+ 4\frac{3}{10}$

Add. Write each sum in simplest form.

1. $\dfrac{1}{2}$
$+\dfrac{3}{4}$

2. $\dfrac{3}{10}$
$+\dfrac{5}{10}$

3. $5\dfrac{1}{2}$
$+2\dfrac{1}{3}$

4. $\dfrac{1}{2}$
$+\dfrac{1}{3}$

5. $3\dfrac{1}{5}$
$+6\dfrac{1}{2}$

6. $9\dfrac{1}{3}$
$+8\dfrac{3}{8}$

7. $10\dfrac{1}{4}$
$+\ 4\dfrac{2}{3}$

8. $\dfrac{2}{9}$
$+\dfrac{1}{6}$

9. $\dfrac{1}{6}$
$+\dfrac{3}{8}$

10. $\dfrac{2}{8}$
$+\dfrac{3}{10}$

11. $7\dfrac{3}{5} + 11\dfrac{1}{4}$

12. $4\dfrac{4}{5} + 7\dfrac{7}{10}$

13. $\dfrac{2}{4} + \dfrac{2}{6}$

14. $12\dfrac{7}{12} + 9\dfrac{1}{6}$

15. $3\dfrac{1}{4} + \dfrac{1}{2} + \dfrac{7}{8}$

16. $5\dfrac{3}{4} + 2\dfrac{5}{6} + 2\dfrac{1}{2}$

17. $2\dfrac{2}{3} + 1\dfrac{1}{2} + 3\dfrac{5}{6}$

Evaluate each expression if $r = \dfrac{2}{3}$, $s = 4\dfrac{1}{6}$, $t = \dfrac{5}{6}$, and $v = 7$.

18. $r + t$

19. $s + t$

20. $s + v$

21. $r + t + v$

22. Is addition of fractions associative? Write an example to illustrate your answer.

23. Jade made snack mix. She used $4\dfrac{1}{2}$ pounds of peanuts, $2\dfrac{3}{4}$ pounds of pretzels, and $1\dfrac{2}{3}$ pounds of almonds. How many pounds of snack mix did she make?

24. Ms. Bower needs $1\dfrac{1}{2}$ yd of green fabric and $2\dfrac{2}{3}$ yd of brown fabric to make tree costumes for the spring play. How much fabric does she need in all?

   a. $3\dfrac{3}{5}$ yd b. $4\dfrac{1}{6}$ yd c. $1\dfrac{1}{6}$ yd d. $5\dfrac{1}{3}$ yd

25. The length of a rectangle is $7\dfrac{3}{4}$ in. and the width is $3\dfrac{1}{2}$ in. What is the perimeter?

   a. $20\dfrac{1}{2}$ in. b. $22\dfrac{1}{2}$ in. c. $21\dfrac{3}{8}$ in. d. $10\dfrac{1}{4}$ in.

4.2 Subtracting Fractions and Mixed Numbers

Objective: to subtract fractions and mixed numbers

After Sara's birthday party, $\frac{3}{8}$ of her birthday cake was left. The next day Sara ate $\frac{1}{6}$ of the leftover cake. How much cake is left now?

Subtract $\frac{1}{6}$ from $\frac{3}{8}$ to find the difference.

Step 1	Step 2	Step 3
Find the LCD. $\frac{3}{8}$ 8: 8, 16, 24, 32 $-\frac{1}{6}$ 6: 6, 12, 18, 24 LCD = 24	Rename each fraction. $\frac{3}{8} = \frac{9}{24}$ $-\frac{1}{6} = \frac{4}{24}$	Subtract. $\frac{3}{8} = \frac{9}{24}$ $-\frac{1}{6} = \frac{4}{24}$ $\frac{5}{24}$

Sara has $\frac{5}{24}$ of her cake left.

Examples

A.
$$\frac{3}{5} = \frac{6}{10}$$
$$-\frac{1}{2} = \frac{5}{10}$$
$$\frac{1}{10}$$

B.
$$8\frac{3}{4} = 8\frac{9}{12}$$
$$-5\frac{1}{6} = 5\frac{2}{12}$$
$$3\frac{7}{12}$$

Estimate
$$8\frac{3}{4} \qquad 9$$
$$-5\frac{1}{6} \qquad -5$$
$$\qquad\qquad 4$$

How does this compare to the estimate?

Subtract $3\frac{4}{5}$ from $6\frac{2}{10}$.

Step 1	Step 2	Step 3
Rename each fraction. $6\frac{2}{10} = 5\frac{10}{10} + \frac{2}{10} = 5\frac{12}{10}$ $5\frac{12}{10} = 5\frac{12}{10}$ $-3\frac{4}{5} = -3\frac{8}{10}$	Subtract the fractions. $6\frac{2}{10} = 5\frac{12}{10}$ $-3\frac{4}{5} = -3\frac{8}{10}$ $\frac{4}{10}$	Subtract the whole numbers. $6\frac{2}{10} = 5\frac{12}{10}$ $-3\frac{4}{5} = -3\frac{8}{10}$ $2\frac{4}{10} = 2\frac{2}{5}$

Subtract. Write each difference in simplest form.

1. $\dfrac{5}{8} - \dfrac{2}{8}$ 2. $\dfrac{9}{10} - \dfrac{2}{5}$ 3. $6\dfrac{3}{5} - 2\dfrac{1}{5}$ 4. $5\dfrac{3}{4} - 2\dfrac{1}{2}$

Exercises

Subtract. Write each difference in simplest form.

1. $\dfrac{3}{4}$ $-\dfrac{1}{8}$ 2. $\dfrac{5}{6}$ $-\dfrac{2}{3}$ 3. $\dfrac{15}{16}$ $-\dfrac{3}{4}$ 4. $10\dfrac{11}{12}$ $-7\dfrac{1}{4}$ 5. $15\dfrac{3}{4}$ $-4\dfrac{1}{8}$ 6. $19\dfrac{9}{10}$ $-14\dfrac{2}{5}$

7. $\dfrac{5}{6}$ $-\dfrac{3}{8}$ 8. $\dfrac{7}{8}$ $-\dfrac{5}{12}$ 9. $10\dfrac{3}{8}$ $-6\dfrac{9}{16}$ 10. $12\dfrac{15}{16}$ $-4\dfrac{5}{6}$ 11. $\dfrac{14}{15}$ $-\dfrac{5}{6}$ 12. $\dfrac{7}{12}$ $-\dfrac{2}{9}$

13. $\dfrac{8}{9} - \dfrac{7}{12}$ 14. $10\dfrac{1}{4} - 3\dfrac{3}{10}$ 15. $31\dfrac{3}{4} - 12\dfrac{2}{9}$ 16. $20\dfrac{9}{16} - 18$

Compute. Write each result in simplest form.

17. $\left(\dfrac{5}{8} - \dfrac{1}{4}\right) + \dfrac{3}{8}$ 18. $\dfrac{3}{4} - \left(\dfrac{1}{2} + \dfrac{1}{4}\right)$ ★19. $\dfrac{1}{5} + \left(\dfrac{7}{10} - \dfrac{1}{2}\right)$ ★20. $\left(\dfrac{2}{3} + \dfrac{3}{4}\right) - \dfrac{1}{6}$

Problem SOLVING

21. An oil company's stock sold for $38\dfrac{7}{8}$ on Monday and $38\dfrac{1}{4}$ on Tuesday. How many points did the stock drop?

★22. The sum of two numbers is $\dfrac{7}{8}$. One addend is $\dfrac{5}{6}$. What is the other?

23. Two drops of paint fell on a ruler. One fell on the $6\dfrac{5}{16}$-inches mark, and the other fell on the $9\dfrac{3}{16}$-inches mark. How far apart were the drops?

24. You have a 12-foot board. After cutting a $3\dfrac{1}{2}$-foot piece and a $2\dfrac{3}{4}$-foot piece, how much of the board remains?

25. Separate the set below into two sets so that the sums of the fractions in the two sets are equal.
$\dfrac{1}{3}, \dfrac{1}{4}, \dfrac{1}{2}, \dfrac{1}{6}, \dfrac{1}{12}$

Constructed RESPONSE

26. Is it possible to add or subtract two fractions with like denominators and get an answer with a different denominator? Explain. If it is possible, give an example.

Objective: to solve problems involving measurement

Buildings are insulated to keep them warm in the winter and cool in the summer. The diagram at the right shows a section of the outside wall of a house. Notice that the measurements are given as fractions or mixed numbers. How thick is the entire wall?

$\frac{5''}{8}$ — Drywall

$3\frac{1}{2}''$ — Insulation

$\frac{3''}{4}$ — Sheathing

$\frac{7''}{8}$ — Siding

To find the total thickness, add the measurements.

Estimate: $1 + 4 + 1 + 1 = 7$

Add the measurements.

Find the LCD.   Rename as necessary and add.

$3\frac{1}{2}$ 2: 2, 4, 6, 8 $3\frac{4}{8}$

$\frac{5}{8}$ 8: 8, 16, 24 $\frac{5}{8}$

$\frac{3}{4}$ 4: 4, 8, 12, 16 $\frac{6}{8}$ **THINK** $2\frac{6}{8}$

$+\ \frac{7}{8}$ $+\ \frac{7}{8}$ $8\overline{)22}$

                                                              $\underline{16}$

                                                              6

$3\frac{22}{8} = 3 + 2 + \frac{6}{8} = 5\frac{6}{8} = 5\frac{3}{4}$

The wall is $5\frac{3}{4}$ inches thick.   Does this agree with your estimate?

Try THESE

1. What is the total thickness of three boards that are $\frac{5}{16}$ in., $\frac{5}{8}$ in., and $\frac{7}{8}$ in. thick?

2. A rough board $\frac{7}{8}$ in. thick has $\frac{1}{16}$ in. taken off by planing on one side. Find the thickness.

3. During the first hour of flight, an airplane uses $16\frac{3}{4}$ gallons of fuel. During the second hour, $20\frac{1}{2}$ gallons are used. If the tank was full at the start, how much fuel was left in the 60-gallon tank?

4. A cabinet 6 ft $4\frac{1}{4}$ in. long is built along a wall that measures 12 ft $2\frac{1}{2}$ in. What is the length of the remaining space?

5. Gabriela has 27 yards of material. She uses $10\frac{7}{8}$ yards to make curtains and $14\frac{3}{4}$ yards for a bedspread. How much material is left?

6. How many feet of fence are needed to fence in the front yard? Use the diagram to the right.

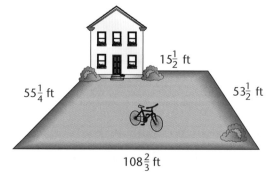

$15\frac{1}{2}$ ft

$55\frac{1}{4}$ ft

$53\frac{1}{2}$ ft

$108\frac{2}{3}$ ft

1. A green pencil is $3\frac{5}{8}$ inches long. A red pencil is $4\frac{1}{8}$ inches long. How much longer is the red pencil?

2. Parking at an airport costs 50¢ for each half hour or fraction of a half hour. How much does it cost to park 100 minutes?

Use the map to solve problems 3–5.

3. How many miles farther is it from Clearfork to the forest reserve than from Clearfork to the oil field?

Storage Tanks · $1\frac{1}{2}$ mi · Oil Field · $1\frac{9}{10}$ mi · Clearfork · $3\frac{2}{5}$ mi · Forest Reserve

4. You are on the road between the oil field and storage tanks, $\frac{2}{3}$ of a mile from the oil field. How far away are the storage tanks?

5. You are between Clearfork and the forest reserve, $1\frac{1}{2}$ miles from the reserve. How many miles are you from the oil field?

Use the chart to solve problems 6–7.

6. What three parts account for three-fourths of the total heat loss?

7. Rank the parts in order from greatest to least heat loss.

Part of House	Fraction of Total Heat Loss
Exterior walls	$\frac{1}{8}$
Ceiling	$\frac{3}{8}$
Doors	$\frac{1}{20}$
Windows	$\frac{3}{25}$
Basement	$\frac{2}{25}$
Air leakage	$\frac{1}{4}$

Constructed RESPONSE

8. Jen walked $\frac{3}{5}$ of a mile on Monday and $\frac{1}{4}$ of a mile on Tuesday. Joe walked $\frac{1}{8}$ of a mile on Monday and $\frac{4}{5}$ of a mile on Tuesday.

   a. How far did Jen walk?   b. How far did Joe walk?   c. Who walked farther? Explain.

Mid-Chapter REVIEW

Add or subtract.

1. $\frac{2}{5} + \frac{1}{2}$

2. $\frac{2}{3} + \frac{2}{15}$

3. $3\frac{1}{4} + 3\frac{5}{8}$

4. $6\frac{2}{9} + 1\frac{1}{6}$

5. $\frac{5}{6} - \frac{1}{6}$

6. $\frac{4}{5} - \frac{3}{4}$

7. $3\frac{1}{3} - \frac{5}{6}$

8. $9\frac{2}{3} - 6\frac{5}{6}$

Problem Solving

The Secret Formula

Professor Wells poured "The Secret Formula" into a glass until it was one-half full. Then, he poured "The Secret Formula" into a second glass until it was one-fourth full. The second glass was twice as large as the first glass. Both glasses were then filled with water.

That afternoon, the absent-minded lab assistant mixed the contents of both glasses in a third container.

"The Secret Formula" is what part of the final mixture?

Extension

Suppose the professor mixes a solution that is $\frac{5}{100}$ "The Secret Formula" with twice as much solution that is $\frac{15}{100}$ "The Secret Formula." What part of the mixture is "The Secret Formula"?

Cumulative Review

Solve each equation mentally.

1. $x + 7 = 28$
2. $t - 11 = 13$
3. $9d = 27$
4. $\frac{n}{3} = 4$

Find the greatest common factor (GCF) of each group of numbers.

5. 4, 16
6. 12, 15
7. 5, 11
8. 9, 12, 24

Write each fraction in simplest form.

9. $\frac{6}{9}$
10. $\frac{8}{10}$
11. $\frac{9}{15}$
12. $\frac{12}{20}$
13. $\frac{25}{35}$

Replace each ● with <, >, or = to make a true statement.

14. $\frac{3}{8}$ ● $\frac{5}{8}$
15. $\frac{5}{16}$ ● $\frac{1}{4}$
16. $\frac{10}{14}$ ● $\frac{5}{7}$
17. $\frac{5}{7}$ ● $\frac{11}{12}$

Compute. Write each result in simplest form.

18. $\frac{1}{8} + \frac{3}{4}$
19. $\frac{5}{6} + \frac{5}{12}$
20. $\frac{4}{9} + \frac{7}{15}$
21. $1\frac{1}{2} + 3\frac{1}{2}$

22. $\frac{15}{16} - \frac{11}{16}$
23. $\frac{5}{7} - \frac{2}{3}$
24. $2 - \frac{3}{4}$
25. $8\frac{3}{4} - 4\frac{5}{8}$

Solve.

26. One loaf of bread is used to make 12 sandwiches. Tom used $2\frac{1}{2}$ loaves to make sandwiches for a party. How many sandwiches did he make?

27. Judy Carson spent $45.60 for gasoline in January, $31.20 in February, and $40.90 in March. To the nearest dollar, find the average amount she spent a month.

28. Ben delivers 39 newspapers each day. He earns $0.07 for each newspaper. Does he earn more or less than $20.00 in 6 days?

29. Marla paid $1.98 for a package of four pens. She also paid $0.11 tax. How much change did she receive from a five-dollar bill?

Objective: to multiply fractions and mixed numbers

A half-gallon container of rainbow sherbet is made up of equal parts of orange, raspberry, and lime sherbet. Marybeth only likes orange sherbet and wants to know how many gallons of orange sherbet are in a half-gallon of rainbow sherbet.

We can multiply fractions to find out how many gallons of orange sherbet are in a half-gallon of rainbow sherbet. We need to find out how much $\frac{1}{3}$ of $\frac{1}{2}$ is.

Multiply. $\frac{1}{3} \cdot \frac{1}{2} = \frac{1}{6}$

A half-gallon container has $\frac{1}{6}$ of a gallon of orange sherbet.

Examples

When the numerator and denominator have a common factor, you can simplify (cancel) before multiplying by dividing the numerator and denominator by the same factor. Also, make sure to change each mixed number to an **improper fraction** before multiplying.

A. $\frac{4}{5} \times \frac{3}{8} = \frac{4 \times 3}{5 \times 8}$

$= \frac{\overset{1}{\cancel{4}} \times 3}{5 \times \cancel{8}_2}$

$= \frac{3}{10}$

> The GCF of 4 and 8 is 4. Divide the numerator and the denominator by 4. Notice that this answer is in simplest form.

B. $\frac{1}{4} \times \frac{12}{20} \times \frac{3}{6} = \frac{1 \times \overset{1}{\cancel{12}} \times 3}{\cancel{4}_1 \times 20 \times \cancel{6}_2}$

$= \frac{3}{40}$

C. $\frac{3}{5} \times 4\frac{5}{6} = \frac{\overset{1}{\cancel{3}}}{5} \times \frac{29}{\cancel{6}_2}$

$= \frac{29}{10} = 2\frac{9}{10}$

Rename the mixed number.
$\frac{20 + 9}{10} = 2 + \frac{9}{10}$

D. $1{,}500 \times 1\frac{2}{3} = \frac{\overset{500}{\cancel{1{,}500}}}{1} \times \frac{5}{\cancel{3}_1}$

$= 2{,}500$

Try THESE

Rename each mixed number as an improper fraction.

1. $1\frac{7}{8}$ 2. $1\frac{7}{12}$ 3. $2\frac{1}{2}$ 4. $2\frac{4}{5}$ 5. $3\frac{2}{3}$

Exercises

Multiply. Write each product in simplest form.

1. $\frac{1}{3} \times 7$

2. $\frac{5}{6} \times 10$

3. $\frac{3}{7} \times \frac{2}{3}$

4. $\frac{5}{8} \times \frac{2}{3}$

5. $\frac{7}{9} \times \frac{3}{5}$

6. $\frac{2}{5} \times 1\frac{1}{4}$

7. $1\frac{3}{5} \times \frac{3}{4}$

8. $\frac{7}{8} \times 1\frac{3}{7}$

9. $2 \times 1\frac{1}{3}$

10. $4\frac{3}{8} \times 4$

11. $\frac{1}{2} \times \frac{2}{3} \times \frac{3}{4}$

12. $\frac{2}{3} \times \frac{3}{5} \times \frac{6}{7}$

13. $3\frac{3}{4} \times 2\frac{2}{3}$

14. $2\frac{5}{6} \times 1\frac{7}{8}$

15. $2\frac{2}{3} \times 2{,}100$

16. $3\frac{3}{4} \times 1\frac{1}{5}$

17. $\frac{3}{4} \times \frac{5}{8} \times \frac{4}{5}$

18. $\frac{5}{6} \times \frac{2}{3} \times \frac{3}{5}$

19. $1\frac{1}{2} \times \frac{4}{5} \times 2\frac{1}{16}$

20. $3\frac{1}{15} \times 1\frac{1}{4} \times 1\frac{1}{3}$

Evaluate each expression if $a = \frac{1}{2}$, $b = \frac{2}{3}$, $c = \frac{1}{4}$, $d = 3\frac{1}{2}$, and $e = 8$.

21. $a \times b$

22. b^2

23. $a \times b \times d$

24. $b + a \times e$

Problem SOLVING

25. A theater has 500 seats. Three-fourths of the seats are filled. How many seats are filled?

26. An animal preserve is $\frac{3}{4}$ of a park. A wooded area is $\frac{1}{2}$ of the animal preserve. What part of the park is wooded?

27. Sonia's beagle puppy weighs $6\frac{2}{3}$ pounds. A full-grown beagle weighs $3\frac{3}{10}$ times as much. Estimate the weight of a full-grown beagle.

★28. What is the product of the first 99 terms of the sequence $\frac{1}{2}, \frac{2}{3}, \frac{3}{4}, \frac{4}{5}, \ldots$?

29. Farmer Joe's horse pasture is $15\frac{2}{3}$ meters long and $12\frac{1}{4}$ meters wide. What is the area of Farmer Joe's horse pasture?

Constructed RESPONSE

30. The product of two numbers is 12. One of the factors is $\frac{2}{3}$. Find the other factor. Explain how you found the other factor.

Objective: to divide fractions and mixed numbers

Brad's kitten eats $\frac{1}{2}$ of a can of cat food each day. How many days will five cans last? To solve this problem, you can count the number of halves in 5. This is the same as dividing 5 by $\frac{1}{2}$.

There are 10 halves, so $5 \div \frac{1}{2} = 10$. Five cans will last 10 days.

Brad's sister, Patty, solved the problem this way. Since each can will last 2 days, multiply 5 by 2.

Compare the two methods.

Brad's Method	*Patty's Method*
$5 \div \frac{1}{2} = 10$	$5 \times 2 = 10$
$5 \div \frac{1}{2} = 5 \times \frac{2}{1}$	5×2

THINK
How many halves are in 5?

> The reciprocal of a fraction is found by "inverting" the fraction. The numerator and denominator are interchanged.

The numbers $\frac{1}{2}$ and 2 have a special relationship. They are called **reciprocals** because their product is 1. To divide by a fraction, multiply by its reciprocal.

Examples

A. $\dfrac{3}{4} \div \dfrac{9}{10} = \dfrac{3}{4} \times \dfrac{10}{9}$

$= \dfrac{\overset{1}{\cancel{3}} \times \overset{5}{\cancel{10}}}{\underset{2}{\cancel{4}} \times \underset{3}{\cancel{9}}}$

$= \dfrac{5}{6}$

B. $5\dfrac{1}{4} \div 4\dfrac{1}{2} = \dfrac{21}{4} \div \dfrac{9}{2}$ Rename each mixed number.

$= \dfrac{21}{4} \times \dfrac{2}{9} = \dfrac{\overset{7}{\cancel{21}} \times \overset{1}{\cancel{2}}}{\underset{2}{\cancel{4}} \times \underset{3}{\cancel{9}}}$

$= \dfrac{7}{6} = 1\dfrac{1}{6}$

Try THESE ·

Complete.

1. $\dfrac{1}{3} \div \dfrac{4}{7} = \dfrac{1}{3} \times \dfrac{\blacksquare}{\blacksquare} = \dfrac{\blacksquare}{\blacksquare}$

2. $\dfrac{2}{5} \div \dfrac{7}{10} = \dfrac{2}{5} \times \dfrac{\blacksquare}{\blacksquare} = \dfrac{\blacksquare}{\blacksquare}$

3. $2\dfrac{1}{4} \div 3\dfrac{3}{8} = \dfrac{9}{4} \div \dfrac{27}{8} = \dfrac{\blacksquare}{\blacksquare} \times \dfrac{\blacksquare}{\blacksquare} = \dfrac{\blacksquare}{\blacksquare}$

4. $1\dfrac{3}{5} \div 3\dfrac{1}{5} = \dfrac{8}{5} \div \dfrac{16}{5} = \dfrac{\blacksquare}{\blacksquare} \times \dfrac{\blacksquare}{\blacksquare} = \dfrac{\blacksquare}{\blacksquare}$

Divide. Write each quotient in simplest form.

1. $\frac{1}{4} \div \frac{3}{8}$

2. $\frac{1}{3} \div \frac{5}{6}$

3. $\frac{1}{8} \div \frac{3}{4}$

4. $\frac{3}{5} \div \frac{3}{4}$

5. $\frac{4}{9} \div \frac{4}{7}$

6. $\frac{4}{5} \div \frac{8}{9}$

7. $\frac{4}{7} \div \frac{9}{14}$

8. $\frac{3}{5} \div \frac{9}{10}$

9. $\frac{1}{2} \div \frac{1}{2}$

10. $\frac{3}{8} \div \frac{3}{8}$

11. $1\frac{3}{4} \div 3$

12. $1\frac{5}{8} \div 2$

13. $8 \div 2\frac{2}{5}$

14. $8 \div \frac{1}{3}$

15. $1\frac{3}{5} \div \frac{5}{8}$

16. $10 \div \frac{2}{5}$

17. What is the quotient of $\frac{2}{5}$ divided by $\frac{7}{10}$?

18. Find the quotient if $4\frac{2}{3}$ is divided by $1\frac{3}{5}$.

Problem SOLVING ···

19. Chloe needs $2\frac{1}{2}$ cups of sugar for a cookie recipe. She uses a measuring scoop that holds $\frac{1}{4}$ cup. How many scoops of sugar does she need?

20. Half of a casserole is divided equally among four persons. How much of the original casserole does each person get?

★ 21. Find the pattern of the following numbers: $1, \frac{1}{2}, \frac{1}{4}, \frac{1}{8}, \frac{1}{16}, \cdots$.

Constructed RESPONSE ···

22. A pie crust calls for $1\frac{1}{2}$ cups of butter. Each stick of butter is $\frac{1}{2}$ cup. If Derek needs to make 5 pie crusts, is 14 sticks of butter enough? Explain.

MiXeD REVIEW ···

Compute.

23. $\frac{4}{9} + \frac{3}{9}$

24. $\frac{7}{15} + \frac{12}{15}$

25. $\frac{1}{2} - \frac{3}{7}$

26. $\frac{1}{6} \times \frac{3}{4}$

27. $2\frac{5}{6} + 8\frac{2}{3}$

28. $12\frac{7}{8} - 5\frac{1}{2}$

29. $3\frac{3}{4} \times 1\frac{2}{3}$

30. $\frac{1}{4} + \frac{1}{2} + \frac{3}{8}$

Language and Concepts

Choose the letter of the correct term or abbreviation to complete each sentence.

1. To add fractions with like denominators, add the _____.

2. To add fractions with unlike denominators, rename the fractions using the _____ of the denominators.

3. One way to simplify fractions is to find the _____ of the numerator and denominator.

4. The statement $1\frac{1}{2} + (\frac{3}{4} + \frac{7}{8}) = (1\frac{1}{2} + \frac{3}{4}) + \frac{7}{8}$ is an example showing addition of fractions is _____.

5. One way to _____ with fractions and mixed numbers is to use rounding.

a. associative
b. commutative
c. compute
d. denominators
e. estimate
f. GCF
g. LCM
h. numerators
i. numerators and denominators

Skills and Problem Solving

Add. Write each sum in simplest form. Section 4.1

6. $\frac{2}{7} + \frac{3}{7}$

7. $\frac{1}{9} + \frac{5}{9}$

8. $\frac{2}{6} + \frac{1}{3}$

9. $\frac{3}{4} + \frac{8}{9}$

10. $5\frac{1}{5} + 3\frac{3}{5}$

11. $1\frac{8}{9} + 8\frac{5}{9}$

12. $8\frac{1}{3} + 2\frac{1}{6}$

13. $4\frac{7}{8} + 7\frac{2}{3}$

Subtract. Write each difference in simplest form. Section 4.2

14. $\frac{7}{11} - \frac{1}{11}$

15. $\frac{11}{16} - \frac{3}{16}$

16. $\frac{3}{4} - \frac{11}{20}$

17. $\frac{5}{6} - \frac{5}{8}$

18. $3\frac{7}{15} - 1\frac{2}{15}$

19. $10\frac{2}{3} - 6\frac{5}{9}$

20. $11\frac{11}{12} - 5\frac{2}{3}$

21. $28\frac{4}{5} - 15\frac{1}{2}$

Multiply. Write each product in simplest form. Section 4.4

22. $\frac{1}{2} \times \frac{1}{3}$

23. $\frac{5}{6} \times \frac{2}{3}$

24. $\frac{2}{5} \times 12$

25. $6 \times \frac{1}{8}$

26. $\frac{3}{7} \times \frac{7}{12}$

27. $\frac{7}{15} \times \frac{10}{21}$

28. $5 \times 2\frac{3}{5}$

29. $\frac{4}{5} \times 1\frac{2}{3}$

30. $2\frac{7}{9} \times 2\frac{1}{10}$

31. $2\frac{3}{8} \times 3\frac{3}{7}$

Name the reciprocal of each number. Section 4.5

32. $\frac{1}{5}$

33. $\frac{3}{7}$

34. 4

35. $\frac{7}{4}$

36. 12

Divide. Write each quotient in simplest form. Section 4.5

37. $4 \div \frac{1}{3}$

38. $\frac{5}{6} \div 10$

39. $\frac{3}{4} \div \frac{7}{8}$

40. $\frac{2}{5} \div \frac{3}{7}$

41. $1\frac{3}{5} \div 4$

42. $6 \div 2\frac{1}{2}$

43. $3\frac{2}{3} \div \frac{11}{12}$

44. $4\frac{1}{3} \div 2\frac{8}{9}$

45. $5\frac{1}{3} \div 2\frac{5}{6}$

46. $7\frac{2}{5} \div 4\frac{1}{2}$

Solve. Sections 4.3–4.5

47. Benito has two pieces of ribbon. One piece is $6\frac{1}{4}$ feet long, and the other is $11\frac{1}{4}$ feet long. Find the total length.

48. Angela runs $1\frac{1}{2}$ miles on Monday, $2\frac{1}{3}$ miles on Tuesday, and $1\frac{5}{6}$ miles on Wednesday. How many miles does she run in all?

49. The cost to operate a Boeing 737-500 for an hour is $1,743. How much does it cost to operate a Boeing 737-500 for $\frac{2}{3}$ of an hour?

50. A golden eagle can fly 120 miles an hour. How far can a golden eagle fly in $\frac{2}{3}$ of an hour?

51. Logan and his friends ate $\frac{3}{8}$ of a cake, while Sherrie and her friends ate $\frac{1}{4}$ of the cake. Each piece was $\frac{1}{16}$ of the cake. How many pieces were eaten?

Add or subtract. Write each sum or difference in simplest form.

1. $\frac{1}{6} + \frac{1}{6}$

2. $\frac{5}{8} + \frac{7}{8}$

3. $5\frac{3}{8} + 4\frac{1}{8}$

4. $10\frac{7}{9} + 5\frac{5}{9}$

5. $\frac{5}{8} - \frac{3}{8}$

6. $\frac{7}{10} - \frac{3}{10}$

7. $7 - 3\frac{2}{3}$

8. $9\frac{3}{10} - 7\frac{9}{10}$

9. $\frac{1}{5} + \frac{1}{3}$

10. $\frac{1}{5} + \frac{3}{10}$

11. $\frac{5}{6} + \frac{4}{9}$

12. $4\frac{1}{2} + 3\frac{1}{3}$

13. $9\frac{2}{5} + 5\frac{1}{10}$

14. $11\frac{5}{8} + 15\frac{5}{12}$

15. $\frac{1}{3} - \frac{1}{4}$

16. $\frac{5}{6} - \frac{7}{12}$

17. $\frac{5}{8} - \frac{3}{10}$

18. $12\frac{3}{4} - 7\frac{3}{8}$

19. $7\frac{2}{3} - 3\frac{3}{5}$

20. $18\frac{1}{6} - 13\frac{4}{9}$

Multiply or divide. Write each answer in simplest form.

21. $\frac{1}{4} \times \frac{1}{5}$

22. $\frac{2}{3} \times \frac{1}{9}$

23. $\frac{3}{4} \times 12$

24. $7 \times \frac{2}{5}$

25. $\frac{6}{7} \times \frac{14}{15}$

26. $1\frac{2}{3} \times 9$

27. $\frac{3}{7} \times 2\frac{1}{3}$

28. $1\frac{3}{4} \times 3\frac{1}{3}$

29. $5 \div \frac{1}{5}$

30. $\frac{1}{6} \div 3$

31. $\frac{1}{3} \div \frac{5}{12}$

32. $\frac{6}{7} \div \frac{2}{7}$

33. $6 \div 8\frac{2}{5}$

34. $8\frac{5}{8} \div 4\frac{3}{5}$

35. $12\frac{4}{5} \div 3\frac{2}{4}$

36. $6\frac{1}{2} \div \frac{11}{15}$

Solve.

37. Kyung has a 12-foot board. He cuts off a $4\frac{1}{2}$-foot piece and a $1\frac{3}{4}$-foot piece. How much of the board remains?

38. A greyhound can run 64 kilometers an hour. How far can the greyhound run in $\frac{3}{4}$ hour?

39. Bernadette bought two pieces of ribbon. One piece is $6\frac{1}{4}$ feet long, and the other is $11\frac{1}{2}$ feet long.

    a. Find the total length of the ribbon.

    b. If the ribbon cost $1.50 a foot, how much did Bernadette pay for the ribbon?

40. A dragonfly flies 3 miles in $3\frac{3}{5}$ minutes. How far can the dragonfly fly in 1 minute?

Change of Pace

Addition with Rulers

You can use two rulers to show addition with mixed numbers. Suppose you wish to add $1\frac{1}{8}$ and $2\frac{1}{4}$. Place two rulers as shown below.

The edge of the yellow ruler lines up with $1\frac{1}{8}$ on the blue ruler. Read directly down from $2\frac{1}{4}$ on the yellow ruler. The sum of $1\frac{1}{8}$ and $2\frac{1}{4}$ is $3\frac{3}{8}$ on the blue ruler.

Use the rulers below to complete exercises 1–5.

1. What number is shown at **A** on the blue ruler?

2. What number is shown at **A** on the yellow ruler?

3. What is the sum of the answers from exercises 1 and 2?

4. What number is shown at **B** on the yellow ruler?

5. What is the sum of the answers from exercises 1 and 4?

Use two rulers to find each sum.

6. $\frac{5}{8} + 3\frac{1}{4}$ 7. $1\frac{3}{4} + 3\frac{1}{8}$ 8. $2\frac{7}{8} + 3\frac{7}{8}$ 9. $3\frac{5}{16} + 4\frac{7}{8}$

10. Explain how you could use two rulers to show subtraction.

Cumulative Test

1. What is the greatest common factor of 8 and 12?
   a. 1
   b. 2
   c. 4
   d. none of the above

2. $\frac{7}{16} + \frac{3}{4} + \frac{3}{8} = $ _____
   a. $\frac{13}{28}$
   b. $\frac{9}{16}$
   c. $1\frac{9}{16}$
   d. none of the above

3. $2\frac{1}{5} - \frac{1}{3} = $ _____
   a. $1\frac{1}{2}$
   b. $1\frac{13}{15}$
   c. $2\frac{1}{2}$
   d. none of the above

4. $62.841 - 53.619 = $ _____
   a. 10.238
   b. 9.222
   c. 10.319
   d. 9.523

5. A license plate number is divisible by 3 and 5. Which could *not* be the number?
   a. 320
   b. 345
   c. 375
   d. 390

6. $4.21 + 3.9 + 6.33 = $ _____
   a. 10.93
   b. 14.44
   c. 14.33
   d. 10.21

7. What number is represented at **A** on the number line?

   a. $6\frac{1}{2}$ b. $7\frac{1}{2}$
   c. 7   d. 8

8. Which expression is an example of the identity property of addition?
   a. $4 + 6 = 6 + 4$
   b. $7 + \text{-}7 = 0$
   c. $10 + 1 = 1 + 10$
   d. $8 + 0 = 8$

9. How many hours is Adventure Park open each week?
   a. 43
   b. 46
   c. 58
   d. 62

Adventure Park Hours	
Monday	closed
Tuesday–Friday	1:00 P.M.–10:00 P.M.
Saturday–Sunday	10:00 A.M.–11:00 P.M.

10. Out of 478 students in the seventh grade, 293 are girls. Forty-seven students live on a farm. Which question can be answered using this information?
    a. How many boys live on a farm?
    b. How many girls do not live on a farm?
    c. How many students are not girls?
    d. How many students are not in the seventh grade?

Linear Equations and Inequalities

Matthew Cahn
Calvert Day School

5.1 Writing Expressions and Equations

Objective: to write variable expressions and equations

Juanita makes a cake for a bake sale. The icing contains 2 times as much sugar as the cake.

THINK

If the cake contains 1 cup of sugar, then the icing uses 2 • 1 cups of sugar.

If the icing contains 4 cups of sugar, then the cake uses 4 ÷ 2 cups of sugar.

THINK

If the cake contains c cups of sugar, then the cake uses 2 • c cups of sugar.

If the icing contains w cups of sugar, then the cake uses w ÷ 2 cups of sugar.

You can translate phrases into algebraic expressions. Use variables to represent unnamed numbers. In the box below are some key translating words.

Addition	Subtraction	Multiplication	Division
Plus	Minus	Times	Divided by
Increased by	Decreased by	Multiplied by	Quotient of
More than	Less than	Product of	
Sum of	Difference of		
Added to	Subtracted from		

Examples

A. Translate each phrase into an algebraic expression.

some number increased by six	$h + 6$
five multiplied by some number	$5z$
the difference of b and nine	$b - 9$

An **equation** is a mathematical sentence with an equals sign. You can translate many sentences into equations.

B. Translate each sentence into a mathematical equation.

Five more than x is seventeen.	$x + 5 = 17$
A number decreased by four is twenty-five.	$n - 4 = 25$
Two less than one-fourth of a number equals three.	$\frac{1}{4}h - 2 = 3$

Match the phrase with its algebraic expression.

1. eight more than n
2. eight times n
3. a number decreased by eight
4. a number divided by eight

a. $n - 8$
b. $n \div 8$
c. $n + 8$
d. $n \bullet 8$

Exercises

Translate each phrase into an algebraic expression.

1. seventeen more than a
2. ten less than p
3. five times k
4. the quotient of t and twenty-nine
5. the difference of a number and sixteen
6. the product of two hundred fifteen and a number

Translate each sentence into an equation.

7. The sum of m and fifteen is forty-five.
8. Five decreased by r is two.
9. The quotient of d and seven is six.
10. The product of five and y is thirty.
11. Three more than four times y is equal to twenty-seven.
12. Six less than twice g is equal to fourteen.
13. Five times the difference of a number and eighteen is forty-two.
14. The sum of six times a number and three is forty-eight.

Translate into words.

15. $b + 6$
16. $8 - e$
17. $r \div 7$
18. $18a$
19. $14g = 7$
20. $d - 1 = 42$
21. $100 \div t = 5$
22. $26 + \frac{1}{2}v = 9$

Problem SOLVING

23. Overnight the temperature dropped by 15°. It is now 60°. Write an equation to find the original temperature.

24. The Cubs scored c points. The Bucks scored two more points than the Cubs. Write an expression for the number of points scored by the Bucks.

25. There were 100 points on a test. Sam missed t questions. Each question was worth 5 points. Sam earned an 85 on the test. Write an equation for the number of questions Sam missed on the test.

26. Is "eight less than a number" the same as "the difference of eight and a number"? Explain.

5.2 Simplifying Expressions

Objective: to simplify expressions by collecting like terms

Every Sunday when the laundry is done, Bob matches up his socks. He finds the two socks that are the same and puts them in the drawer together.

To simplify algebraic expressions, you match the **terms** and combine them. Terms are separated by either addition or subtraction signs. The expression $7 + 3x + 5x$ has 3 terms. Terms that have the same variable are called **like terms**. Examples of like terms are $3x$ and $5x$, y and $\frac{1}{2}y$, and $2.4ab$ and $-8ab$.

Examples

Notice how the distributive property is used to combine like terms in the examples below.

A. $3x + 5x = (3 + 5)x$
$\quad\quad\quad = 8x$

Remember the distributive property is reflexive.

That is, $a(b + c) = ab + ac$ or $ab + ac = (b + c)a$.

B. $y + \frac{1}{10}y = 1y + \frac{1}{10}y$
$\quad\quad\quad\quad = (1 + \frac{1}{10})y$
$\quad\quad\quad\quad = 1\frac{1}{10}y$

> y is the same as $1y$.

A term can be made up of a **coefficient** and a variable, or it can be **constant**, only a number. A coefficient is the number in front of a variable in a term.

Coefficient $8xy$ Variables 12 Constant

C. $2.4ab + 8ab = (2.4 + 8)ab$
$\quad\quad\quad\quad\quad = 10.4ab$

D. $-5x + 3x - 6 = (-5 + 3)x - 6$
$\quad\quad\quad\quad\quad\quad = -2x - 6$

E. $6y + 7x$

$6y$ and $7x$ are not like terms, so they cannot be combined.

 **THESE** ·

Determine if the pair of terms in each exercise are like terms. Write *yes* or *no*.

1. $\frac{1}{2}x, \frac{1}{3}x$

2. $5y, 5x$

3. $-2y, 6y$

4. $1.9a, 4b$

5. $10x, 40x$

6. $1.3z, \frac{-3}{4}z$

7. $\frac{2}{5}w, w$

8. $5rs, s$

How many terms are in each expression?

9. $5 - n + 2m$

10. $17 - \dfrac{y}{4} + 1.9x$

11. $25 - 3w + 2w + 4$

12. $3a + 6 - \dfrac{2}{9}a + b$

13. $\dfrac{7x}{2} - 2$

14. $3.4abc$

Exercises ・・

Find the like terms in each expression.

1. $6x + 7x + 2$

2. $9a + 9a + 9b$

3. $5t + 5s + 5xs$

4. $2c + 8c - 4 + 8y$

5. $y + 1.2y + 1.2z$

6. $6r + r - 5r$

Simplify.

7. $\dfrac{3}{4}p + 10p$

8. $x + 7x$

9. $r + r + 8rst$

10. $6d - \dfrac{1}{2}d + \dfrac{1}{2}$

11. $y + 1.3y + 1.3x$

12. $15 - 6x + 5x + 3$

13. $2 + 17x - 5x + 9$

14. $12y - 12y$

15. $6x - 6y$

16. $\dfrac{2}{3} + 4x - 5x + 7$

17. $-6y + 3x - 2y$

18. $4m - 6n - 8m + 7n$

19. $p + 1 - 3 + 2p + 5$

20. $4t - 6s + 12s - 10t$

21. $-7a + 3 - 5b + 6 - 2b$

Problem SOLVING ・・・

22. Write and simplify an expression for the perimeter of the rectangle on the right.

★23. Write an expression for two more than twice a number increased by five times the same number, and simplify.

$x + 8$

x

Constructed RESPONSE ・・

24. When the expressions $5x$ and $6x^2$ are added together, is the sum $11x^3$? Explain

Test PREP ・・・

25. Which expression is equivalent to $5x - 9x + 2 + 7x + 1$?

   a. $16x + 3$ b. $3x + 3$ c. $6x$ d. $7x + 3$

26. Which equation is equal to "three times the sum of a number and five is twelve"?

   a. $3x + 5 = 12$ b. $3 + 5x = 12$ c. $15x = 12$ d. $3(x + 5) = 12$

Objective: to solve equations using addition and subtraction

In science class, Judy put the same amount of salt on both sides of a scale. If she adds more to one side, will the scale be balanced? What happens if she adds the same amount to both sides? What happens if she takes away the same amount from both sides?

Balancing a scale is like balancing an equation; both sides must be equal. When you add or subtract the same number from both sides of an equation, the result is a balanced equation. It is called an **equivalent equation**.

$$x + 6 = 9$$
$$x + 6 - 6 = 9 - 6$$
$$x = 3$$

To check the solution, replace x with 3 in the first equation.

$$3 + 6 = 9$$
$$9 = 9 \qquad \text{The solution is 3.}$$

Subtraction Property of Equality
Subtracting the same number from each side of an equation results in an equivalent equation.
Addition Property of Equality
Adding the same number to each side of an equation results in an equivalent equation.

Another Example

Solve. $t - 5 = 12$

$$t - 5 = 12$$
$$t - 5 + 5 = 12 + 5 \qquad \text{Add 5 to each side.}$$
$$t = 17$$

Check: $t - 5 = 12$

$$17 - 5 = 12 \qquad \text{Replace } t \text{ with 17.}$$
$$12 = 12$$
The solution is 17.

Try THESE ....

Name the number you would subtract from each side to solve each equation.

1. $x + 9 = 15$
2. $n + 12 = -18$
3. $5 + g = 11$
4. $14 = 10 + p$
5. $0.28 = 2 + w$
6. $7 + g = 10$

Name the number you would add to each side to solve each equation.

7. $k - 6 = 12$
8. $d - 4 = -14$
9. $r - 40 = 29$
10. $3 = s - 12$
11. $2.5 = r - 6.8$
12. $4.8 = j - 2.4$

....

State whether the given number is a solution of the equation.

1. $n + 6 = -10$, $n = 4$

2. $5 + k = 12$, $k = 6$

3. $26 = y + 11$, $y = 14$

4. $4 = 12 - x$, $x = 4$

5. $h + 2.1 = 5.6$, $h = 3.5$

6. $-18 = r + 6$, $r = -24$

Solve each equation. Check your solution.

7. $e + 7 = 15$

8. $r + 18 = 26$

9. $a - 6 = -19$

10. $y + 2 = -1$

11. $24 = 10 + h$

12. $n + -1 = 5$

13. $5 + g = 12$

14. $-15 = c + 8$

15. $y - 5 = -9$

16. $c + 0.7 = 1.6$

17. $r - 3 = -2$

18. $-6 = p - 16$

19. $4.2 = x - 0.9$

20. $j - 6 = 23$

21. $m - 6 = -4$

22. $b - 3 = -4$

23. $k - 1.8 = -10.5$

24. $3.14 = x - 1.73$

Translate each sentence into an equation. Then solve the equation.

25. The sum of nine and a number is twenty-one.

26. Seven is ten less than m.

27. Five more than a number is twenty-three.

28. Eight subtracted from a number is ten.

....

29. Laura practiced the piano for 2 hours on Monday. She practiced for a total of 10 hours that week. How many hours did she practice the rest of the week? Write an equation, and solve.

★30. Use the figure to the right to write an equation, and solve it for the missing side, knowing that the perimeter is 30 yd.

12 yd   12 yd

31. Damon bought a sandwich and a soda for lunch. The sandwich costs $3.50. The total bill was $5.25. How much was the soda? Write an equation, and solve.

32. Barbara is 8 years older than her sister, Beverly. Write an equation, and solve it to find Beverly's age, when Barbara is 16.

Mind BUILDER

Operation Expressions

Each whole number 1 through 15 can be expressed using the numerals 1, 2, 3, and 4 exactly once with any of the operation signs.

For example, $1 = (1 + 4) \div (2 + 3)$.

Write an expression for each of the other numbers.

Objective: to solve equations using multiplication and division

Celia has a recipe for apple salad that makes 8 servings.

When Celia makes 4 servings, she divides the number of servings and the amount of each ingredient by 2.

When Celia makes 24 servings, she multiplies the number of servings and the amount of each ingredient by 3.

In a similar manner, you can use division and multiplication to solve equations.

$6n = 48$

$\dfrac{6n}{6} = \dfrac{48}{6}$ Divide each side by 6.

$n = 8$

Check your solution by replacing n with 8.

$6 \cdot 8 = 48$

Division Property of Equality
Dividing each side of an equation by the same nonzero number results in an equivalent equation.
Multiplication Property of Equality
Multiplying each side of an equation by the same number results in an equivalent equation.

More Examples

A. Solve. $\dfrac{x}{7} = 9$

$\dfrac{x}{7} \cdot 7 = 9 \cdot 7$

$x = 63$ Multiply each side by 7.

Check: $\dfrac{63}{7} = 9$

B. Solve. $-5x = 75$

$\dfrac{-5x}{-5} = \dfrac{75}{-5}$

$x = -15$ Divide each side by -5.

Check: $-5 \cdot -15 = 75$

Try THESE

Name the operation and the number you would use to solve each equation.

1. $4x = 12$
2. $-6 = \dfrac{b}{5}$
3. $9 = \dfrac{k}{8}$
4. $-4t = 52$
5. $6n = 48$
6. $15 = \dfrac{g}{2}$
7. $-15a = 180$
8. $6 = \dfrac{b}{3}$

··

Solve each equation. Check your solution.

1. $9n = 45$

2. $-36 = 6d$

3. $72y = 0$

4. $-9c = 81$

5. $\dfrac{h}{5} = 55$

6. $21 = \dfrac{g}{6}$

7. $-8x = -64$

8. $\dfrac{a}{7} = -6$

9. $\dfrac{w}{1.3} = 10$

10. $9.68 = 0.4c$

11. $1.2d = 54$

12. $\dfrac{r}{3} = 61$

13. $5a = -35$

14. $-3k = 18$

15. $\dfrac{b}{5} = -8$

16. $-7x = -56$

Translate each sentence into an equation. Then solve the equation.

17. Six multiplied by t is fifty-four.

18. The quotient of y and three is eighteen.

19. The product of b and eleven is sixty-six.

20. t divided by seven is two hundred twelve.

Problem SOLVING ···

21. A basket of apples was divided among 3 friends.

    a. Write an expression for the number of apples each person received.

    b. Suppose each person received 9 apples. Write and solve an equation to find out how many apples there were in all.

22. Dan makes $35,000 a year. If he gets paid 25 times a year, how much is each paycheck?

23. A shipment of shoes contained t pairs at a cost of $25 each. The total cost of the shoes was $225. Write and solve an equation to find the total number of pairs of shoes in the shipment.

★24. The product of two numbers is 24. Their quotient is 6. What are the two numbers?

MiXeD REVIEW ···

Evaluate each expression if $a = 6$, $b = 8$, $c = 4$, and $d = 0.5$.

25. $db + a$

26. $10d - c$

27. $100 - 2a - 17c$

28. $2ab - 4cd$

Simplify.

29. $4 + (7 \cdot 38)$

30. $42 \div (101 - 94)$

31. $(73 \cdot 6) - 53$

32. $3 \cdot 83 + 6$

Let's Have a Pizza Party!

Six friends plan a pizza party. They soon find that they cannot share a pizza because each person likes different toppings on their pizza. Their solution is to order six different individual pizzas: cheese, pepperoni, pepperoni and mushrooms, anchovies, The Works, and vegetarian. Using the clues below, can you tell who ordered what?

1. Mariana likes only one item besides cheese, and it is not pepperoni.

2. Julie sits next to the person who ordered the vegetarian pizza.

3. Tony hates all types of fish.

4. The person who ordered mushrooms sits across from Corey.

5. Masao ordered The Works.

6. Renaldo does not like vegetables.

7. Corey and Julie sit next to each other.

8. Julie and Tony both like pepperoni.

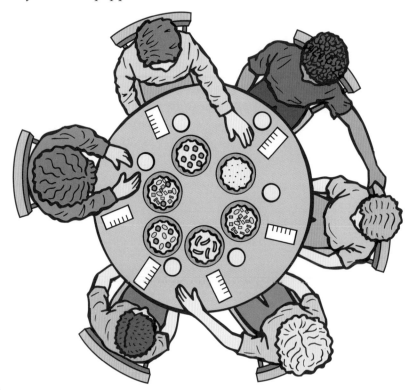

Extension

Make Up a Problem
Write a problem similar to the one above. Be sure to write enough clues, so there is only one answer.

Cumulative Review

Replace each ● with <, >, or = to make a true statement.

1. 0.65 ● 0.56
2. 1.61 ● 1.60
3. 0.781 ● 0.78
4. 6.009 ● 6.09
5. $\frac{1}{2}$ ● 0.5
6. 0.70 ● $\frac{3}{4}$
7. 80% ● $\frac{3}{5}$
8. 0.075 ● 75

Compute.

9. $14 − 6.85
10. 256.85 − 45.879
11. 15.4 • 6.8
12. 40.6 • 5.3
13. 8.94 + 23.547
14. 45 ÷ 12
15. 0.064 ÷ 0.8
16. 0.6 ÷ 0.012
17. $\frac{1}{2} + \frac{2}{5}$
18. $\frac{5}{7} - \frac{1}{3}$
19. $\frac{3}{4} \bullet \frac{4}{5}$
20. $1\frac{1}{2} \div \frac{3}{4}$

Find the value of each expression.

21. 4 + 52 − 3
22. (8 − 4) + (6 + 4)
23. 6.3 + 2.52 − 4.1
24. 2(4 − 2)
25. 6 • 3 + 8 − 6 ÷ 2
26. 5 + 6 − (5 − 3)

Write each fraction in simplest form.

27. $\frac{4}{16}$
28. $\frac{2}{12}$
29. $\frac{4}{10}$
30. $\frac{9}{24}$
31. $\frac{16}{24}$

Replace each ■ with a number so that the fractions are equivalent.

32. $\frac{2}{3} = \frac{■}{12}$
33. $\frac{5}{12} = \frac{■}{24}$
34. $\frac{5}{9} = \frac{■}{18}$
35. $\frac{3}{8} = \frac{■}{40}$

Solve.

36. Ellen Varney buys 306 skeins of red yarn, 245 skeins of blue yarn, and 198 skeins of green yarn. How many skeins of yarn does she buy altogether?

37. A cabin is built on a 5-acre lot. The cabin is rented 196 days. What is the total rent if the cabin rents for $24.00 a day?

38. Each tent is put up with 12 poles. How many tents can be put up with 200 poles?

39. A train travels 15,157 miles in 23 days. What is the average distance the train travels each day?

40. A camping trailer and interest cost $2,034. There are 18 equal monthly payments. What is each payment?

41. Mr. Lopez pays $19.00, $15.00, $22.00, and $12.50 for four pieces of pottery. Find the average cost to the nearest cent.

Objective: to solve two-step equations

A cake is made in stages. The ingredients are mixed, the cake is baked, and the icing is applied.

If an equation contains more than one operation, the equation is solved in stages. In general, to solve equations, reverse the order of operations.

- First undo the addition or subtraction.
- Then undo the multiplication or division.

Solve the equation $7k + 5 = 33$.

$$7k + 5 = 33$$
$$7k + 5 - 5 = 33 - 5 \quad \text{First undo the addition by}$$
$$7k = 28 \quad \text{subtracting 5 from each side.}$$
$$\frac{7k}{7} = \frac{28}{7}$$
$$k = 4 \quad \begin{array}{l}\text{Then undo the multiplication}\\\text{by dividing each side by 7.}\end{array}$$

Check:

$$7k + 5 = 33$$
$$7 \times 4 + 5 \overset{?}{=} 33 \quad \text{Replace } k \text{ with 4.}$$
$$28 + 5 \overset{?}{=} 33$$
$$33 = 33 \quad ✔$$

The solution is 4.

Another Example

Solve. $16 = \frac{x}{4} - 7$

$$16 + 7 = \frac{x}{4} - 7 + 7 \quad \begin{array}{l}\text{First undo the subtraction by}\\\text{adding 7 to each side.}\end{array}$$

$$23 = \frac{x}{4}$$

$$23 \times 4 = \frac{x}{4} \times 4 \quad \begin{array}{l}\text{Then undo the division by}\\\text{multiplying each side by 4.}\end{array}$$

$$92 = x$$

You can check the solution by replacing x with 92 in the first equation.

Try THESE •

State what to do *first* and what to do *second* to solve each equation. Then solve the equation.

1. $2x - 8 = 2$
2. $11 = \frac{a}{2} + 3$
3. $\frac{b}{0.3} - 0.5 = 1.5$

Solve each equation. Check your solution.

1. $4y + 3 = 19$ 2. $3x - 8 = 13$ 3. $8k - 21 = 75$

4. $2 + 3m = 17$ 5. $57 = 4z - 9$ 6. $\dfrac{b}{8} - 17 = 13$

7. $19 = \dfrac{h}{3} + 8$ 8. $9 + \dfrac{j}{4} = 12$ 9. $31 = 3 + \dfrac{c}{6}$

10. $0.3x + 0.8 = 1.4$ 11. $1.6m - 0.2 = 3$ 12. $2.1 = 0.5x + 0.6$

13. $\dfrac{t}{0.7} + 9 = 10$ 14. $\dfrac{x}{0.9} - 0.7 = 1.3$ 15. $6.2 = \dfrac{m}{9} - 6.2$

Translate each sentence into an equation. Then solve the equation.

16. Nine less than the quotient of x and two is twelve.

17. Five plus the quotient of n and eight is seven.

18. The sum of eight and the product of two and y is twenty-four.

19. Four less than the product of three and x is twenty-three.

Problem SOLVING

20. Six more than twice Mark's age is thirty-four. How old is Mark?

21. Rita had $15.00. After buying four pens, she had $4.00 left. How much did each pen cost?

22. Write a two-step equation whose solution is five. Explain why this equation has a solution of five.

★23. John is four years older than his sister, Mary. Twice John's age is equal to three times Mary's age. How old is John?

Constructed RESPONSE

24. Look at the equations to the right, and decide who found the correct solution and why.

Cheryl

$5x + 10 = 25$
$+ 10 \quad + 10$

$\dfrac{5x}{5} = \dfrac{35}{5}$

$x = 7$

Brad

$5x + 10 = 25$
$- 10 \quad - 10$

$\dfrac{5x}{5} = \dfrac{15}{5}$

$x = 3$

5.6 Problem-Solving Strategy: Write an Equation

Objective: to solve word problems using equations

Noah is making goody bags for a birthday party. He has 75 pieces of candy. He wants to give each child 3 pieces of candy. Write and solve an equation that can be used to determine how many goody bags Noah can make.

 You need to find the number of goody bags. You know the number of pieces of candy for each child, and you know the total number of pieces of candy Noah has.

 Let g represent the number of goody bags. There are 3 pieces of candy in each bag. Therefore, 3 times the number of bags is equal to 75. The correct equation is $3g = 75$.

 Solve the equation.

$$3g = 75$$

$$\frac{3g}{3} = \frac{75}{3}$$

$$g = 25$$

The solution is 25. Noah can make 25 goody bags.

 If Noah makes 25 bags, each will contain 3 pieces of candy, so he will have used 75 pieces of candy. The solution is correct.

Try THESE

Choose the equation that can best be used to find the answer. Then solve.

1. Faith bought a burger and fries from a local fast-food restaurant. She paid $3.50. She received $5.50 in change. How much did she have before she bought the food?

   a. $m + \$3.50 = \$5.50$ b. $m + \$5.50 = \$3.50$

   c. $m - \$3.50 = \$5.50$ d. $m - \$5.50 = \$3.50$

2. The Valley Car Dealer has 144 cars on its lot. If every row has 8 cars, how many rows of cars are there?

   a. $c + 8 = 144$ b. $\frac{c}{8} = 144$

   c. $c - 8 = 144$ d. $8c = 144$

Write an equation, and solve.

1. Brandon bought 15 books last week at the bookstore. Of those books, 8 were science fiction books. How many other books did he buy?

2. Dustin is having 15 people over to his house for dinner. Each table in his dining room can seat 3 people. How many tables does he have set up?

3. Maggie baked 108 cookies. If Maggie has 36 students, how many cookies will each student receive?

4. Gail is four more than three times as old as Catherine. Gail is 67. How old is Catherine?

5. Dan's Dining Store charges $40 to deliver furniture and $35 an hour to put it together. The Smiths paid $180 to have their dining room table delivered and put together. How many hours did it take Dan to put it together?

6. Gary ran two more than twice as many miles as Lori. Lori ran 5 miles. How many miles did Gary run?

★7. Jason has $8.00 to spend at the grocery store. He must buy a loaf of bread and some milk. The loaf of bread costs $2.50. How many gallons of milk can he buy if each gallon costs $2.75?

Constructed RESPONSE

8. Five friends go out to lunch and split the bill evenly. Each person pays $10.75.

   a. How much is the bill?

   b. If they add in a tip of $10.00, how much does each person pay? Explain.

Mid-Chapter REVIEW

Translate each sentence into a mathematical equation.

1. Ten more than three times a number is twenty-five.

2. The quotient of a number and four is eight.

Simplify.

3. $4x + 5 + 8x$

4. $-2y + 7xy + 9y$

5. $3n + 6m + 7n - 2m$

Solve.

6. $x - 8.1 = 9$

7. $-4y = 36$

8. $\frac{h}{3} + 4 = 10$

9. $-6r - 8 = 16$

5.7 Variables and Inequalities

Objective: to solve problems using variables and inequalities

In a tug-of-war that ends in a tie, the forces on each team are balanced. This represents an equation. What happens if another person joins the red team? Do you think the tug-of-war still represents an equation? Why or why not?

Now the forces are unbalanced. This is a model of an **inequality**. Inequalities are used to compare quantities. The following chart shows several inequality symbols and their meanings.

Inequality	Meaning
$x > 8$	x is greater than 8.
$y < 7$	y is less than 7.
$m \geq 2$	m is greater than or equal to 2.
$n \leq 5$	n is less than or equal to 5.

Exploration Exercise

For each scale, write the equation or inequality that is shown. Each small cube represents 1. The large rectangular solid = x.

1.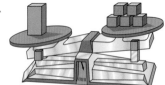

2.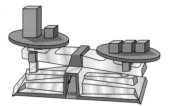

3.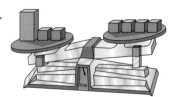

4.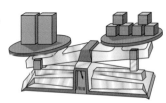

5.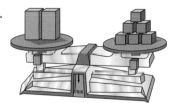

6.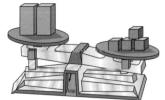

Try THESE

For each equation or inequality, draw a scale that represents it.

1. $x > 4$ 2. $2x < 8$ 3. $x + 2 = 3$ 4. $x + 2 < 5$

Exercises ··

For each inequality, you are given an operation. Perform the operation on each side of the given inequality. Then write the new inequality, and state whether it is *true* or *false*.

1. $2 < 8$, add 4
2. $10 > 4$, add 5
3. $8 \le 8$, add 10
4. $25 < 32$, subtract 11
5. $18 > 17$, subtract 5
6. $2.3 < 2.4$, add 1.5
7. $8 > 2$, multiply by 5
8. $11 < 15$, multiply by 3
9. $12 > 8$, multiply by $\frac{3}{4}$
10. $15 < 27$, divide by 3
11. $25 > 13$, divide by 5
12. $2 < 4$, divide by $\frac{1}{2}$

Problem SOLVING ··

13. Describe the pattern you see in the problems above, 1–12. How is the pattern similar to the addition, subtraction, multiplication, and division properties of equality?

14. Write a statement called addition property of inequality. Do you think similar statements can be written for subtraction, multiplication, and division?

15. Write an inequality for each situation.

    a. The altitude was greater than 2 miles.

    b. The jet can make the trip in less than 4 hours.

    c. The temperature was greater than 8°C.

    d. The balloon can carry no more than 3 passengers.

    e. The temperature was at least 20°F.

MiXeD REVIEW ··

Simplify the decimals.

16. $4.12 + 3.89$
17. $12.8 + 2.17$
18. $137.1 - 27.8$
19. $23.001 - 14.87$
20. $4.8 \cdot 3.9$
21. $21.76 \cdot 4.51$
22. $7.16 \div 2$
23. $8.4 \div 2.1$

5.8 Solving and Graphing Inequalities

Objective: to solve and graph inequalities

James Downey is an air-traffic controller. His job is to track all airplanes within a certain radius of the control tower.

Sometimes in mathematics, you need to keep track of many numbers that are all solutions to one problem.

A mathematical sentence that contains a symbol, such as $<$, $>$, $\leq$, $\geq$, or $\neq$, is called an inequality. The set of all replacements for the variable that makes the inequality true is called the **solution set** of the sentence. You can use a number line to show the solutions to an inequality. Consider the inequality $x > -2$. Study the graph of this solution set below.

An open circle means this point is *not* included in the solution set.

The heavy blue arrow shows that all real numbers to the right of -2 are included.

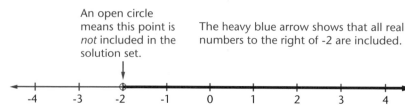

More Examples

A. You can solve inequalities the same way you solve equations.

$$n - 7 > 5$$
$$n - 7 + 7 > 5 + 7$$
$$n > 12$$

To check the solution, replace n with any number greater than 12. For example, use 13.

Check:
$$n - 7 > 5$$
$$13 - 7 \overset{?}{>} 5$$
$$6 > 5 ✔$$

The solution set is {any number greater than 12}. This can also be written as $\{n \mid n > 12\}$.

B. Use a number line to show the solutions to $a \leq \frac{1}{2}$.

A closed circle means this point is included in the solution set.

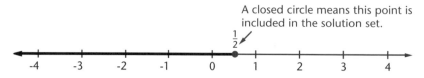

C. Solve the inequality $2p \leq 14$.

$$2p \leq 14$$
$$\frac{2p}{2} \leq \frac{14}{2}$$
$$p \leq 7$$

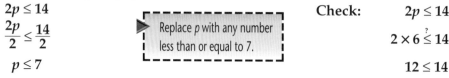

Replace p with any number less than or equal to 7.

Check:
$$2p \leq 14$$
$$2 \times 6 \overset{?}{\leq} 14$$
$$12 \leq 14$$

The solution set is {any number less than or equal to 7}. This can also be written as $\{p \mid p \leq 7\}$.

....

Write the inequality for each of the following.

1.
```
←—+——+——+——+——⊕——+——+——+——+——+——+——→
  -2  -1   0   1   2   3   4   5   6   7   8
```

2.
```
←—+——+——+——+——+——+——+——●——+——+——→
 -3  -2  -1   0   1   2   3   4   5   6   7
```

3.
```
←—+——+——●——+——+——+——+——+——+——+——→
 -6  -5  -4  -3  -2  -1   0   1   2   3   4
          ↑
        -4.25
```

4.
```
←—+——+——+——+——+——+——⊕——+——+——+——→
 -9  -8  -7  -6  -5  -4  -3  -2  -1   0   1
```

....

Use a number line to show the solutions to each of the following inequalities.

1. $y > 2$

2. $x < -3$

3. $m \leq -1$

4. $y < 6$

5. $x \geq -5$

6. $t \geq 0$

7. $x \neq 4$

8. $n \leq -1.5$

Solve each inequality. Check your solution.

9. $m - 7 < 6$

10. $n - 8 > 5$

11. $x + 4 > 9$

12. $p + 5 < 10$

13. $6t < 96$

14. $5m > 45$

15. $\dfrac{b}{3} > 2$

16. $\dfrac{k}{6} > 14$

....

17. Carlos needs to buy at least 7 pairs of socks. They come in packages of 3 pairs. What is the least number of packages he should buy?

★18. The science class is taking a trip to the Science Center. There are 20 students and an unknown number of adult chaperones going. The bus holds at most 35 people. How many adults can chaperone?

19. Write a real-world problem that can be modeled by $x + 2 \leq 4$.

★20. Jessica needs to bake at least 4 more than twice the amount of cookies that she made last week, which was 24. At least how many cookies does Jessica need to bake?

5.9 Problem-Solving Strategy: Using Formulas

Objective: to solve a word problem using a formula

Motion is all around us. People walk, run, ride bicycles and skateboards, and travel from place to place in automobiles and airplanes. At an amusement park, they speed up and down or spin round and round on many rides. One of the earliest goals of scientists was to explain motion.

In order to describe motion, you have to know these qualities:

The *distance* is how far an object has moved.

The *rate*, or speed, is how fast an object moves.

The *time* is how long it takes the object to move.

A formula shows how quantities are related. In this case, the formula is distance = rate $\times$ time. Using variables, $d = rt$.

Example

How far away is lightning if you hear the sound of the thunder 4.5 seconds after you see the flash of lightning? Use 344 meters per second as the speed of sound.

$$d = rt$$
$$= 344 \times 4.5 \quad \text{Replace } r \text{ with 344}$$
$$\text{and } t \text{ with 4.5.}$$
$$344 \times 4.5 = 1{,}548$$

The lightning is 1,548 meters away.

Another Example

Tricia drives from Baltimore to Cincinnati. She drives 495 mi in 9 h. What is her average rate of speed?

Replace
d with 495
and *t* with 9.

$$d = rt$$
$$495 = r \times 9$$
$$r = 55 \text{ mph}$$

$$
\begin{array}{r}
55 \\
9)\overline{495} \\
45 \\
\hline
45 \\
45 \\
\hline
0
\end{array}
$$

The average rate of speed is 55 mph.

Solve for the missing value. Use the formula $d = rt$.

1. $r = 40$ mph, $t = 5$ h

2. $r = 48$ mph, $t = 3.5$ h

3. $d = 200$ ft, $r = 2$ ft/s

4. $t = 3$ s, $d = 993$ m

Translate each sentence into a formula.

5. The *area* of a rectangle is equal to the *length* times the *width*.

6. *Interest* is equal to the *principal* times the *rate* times the *time*.

7. The *distance* is equal to the product of the *rate* and the *time*.

8. The *radius* of a circle is the *diameter* divided by *two*.

9. The *circumference* of a circle is equal to *pi* (π) times the *diameter*.

10. The *volume* of a cube is equal to the length of its *edge cubed*.

Solve ••

Write and solve an equation using the given formula.

1. The Kroger's rectangular garden measures 12 yards by 15 yards. What is the area of their garden? Use $A = lw$.

2. Each side of a square picture is 28 inches long. Find the area. Use $A = s^2$.

3. To the nearest whole number, find the normal blood pressure (P) for a person your age (a). Use $P = 110 + 0.5a$.

4. Luis Cruz drove from Los Angeles to San Francisco. He drove 408 miles in 8 hours. What was his average speed? Use $d = rt$.

5. Chris invested $1,000 for 5 years and earned $500 in interest. At what rate did he invest the money? Use $I = prt$.

6. Joseph is making a rectangular picture frame. The length of the frame is 6 inches, and the perimeter is 30 inches. What is the width? Use $2l + 2w = P$.

Constructed RESPONSE ••

7. Grace runs 10 miles in 2.5 hours. What is her average rate of speed? Use $d = rt$.

8. Hunter runs 15 miles in 3 hours. What is his average rate of speed? Use $d = rt$.

9. Using questions 7 and 8, who runs at a faster rate? Explain.

Chapter 5 Review

Language and Concepts

Choose the correct term to complete each sentence.

1. When you replace a variable in an equation so that a true sentence results, you have (evaluated, solved) the equation.

2. The inequality ($x \geq 2$, $x \leq 2$) means "x is less than or equal to 2."

3. $7a + 2$, $3x$, and $9 - 2c$ are examples of (expressions, equations).

4. A mathematical sentence that contains a symbol, such as $<$, $>$, $\geq$, $\leq$, or $\neq$, is called an (equation, inequality).

5. $8ab$ and $4.2ab$ are examples of (terms, constants).

Skills and Problem Solving

Translate each phrase into an algebraic expression. Section 5.1

6. y increased by eleven

7. five more than e

8. the quotient of e and y

9. the product of eleven and y

Translate each sentence into an equation. Section 5.1

10. Thirty-six times a number is one hundred eighty.

11. The difference of y and eight is fourteen.

12. The sum of x and 7.4 is 8.2.

13. A number divided by five is eighteen.

14. The sum of three and twice a number is eighty-one.

15. Three times a number minus eight is sixteen.

122 Chapter 5 Review

Simplify. Section 5.2

16. $10x + x$

17. $9r + 9s - 2.8s$

18. $4ab + 5b - 2ab + 3b$

19. $2a + 2b - 5a$

20. $xy + 7xy + 8x$

21. $5m + 3mn - 8m$

Solve each equation. Check your solution. Sections 5.3–5.5

22. $36 + p = 49$

23. $n - 16 = 24$

24. $6h = 84$

25. $\dfrac{y}{7} = 3$

26. $7.15 + r = 10$

27. $x - 3.5 = 8.2$

28. $y - 2 = -18$

29. $-3x = 24$

30. $x - 3 = -4$

31. $b - \dfrac{1}{2} = -6$

32. $\dfrac{p}{5} = -2$

33. $-2.4 + r = 4$

34. $2t - 8 = 14$

35. $-3x + 5 = 17$

36. $\dfrac{x}{3} - 8 = 2$

Use a number line to show the solution to each of the following inequalities. Section 5.8

37. $x > 5$

38. $m \leq 3$

39. $d < -2$

Solve each inequality. Section 5.8

40. $x + 3 > 4$

41. $2y \leq 12$

42. $m - 6 < 2$

Use the formula $d = rt$ to solve for the missing variable. Section 5.9

43. $r = 45$ mph, $t = 3$ h

44. $d = 165$ mi, $r = 55$ mph

45. $d = 20$ mi, $t = 2.5$ h

46. $r = 350$ mph, $t = 1.5$ h

Write an equation, and solve. Section 5.6

47. The product of a number and 5 is 3.6. What is the number?

48. Alberto buys 2 dozen eggs. After making omelets, he has 9 eggs left. How many eggs did he use in the omelets?

49. Debbie owns 76 records and tapes. She owns 23 records. How many tapes does Debbie own?

50. Five friends share the cost of a breakfast. Each person pays $4.25. What is the total cost of the breakfast?

51. The phone company charges $10.00 a month for phone service. They also charge $0.15 per minute for each minute used.

    a. Last month, Tim's phone bill was $16.00. How many minutes did he use?

    b. Next month, Tim does not want his phone bill to be more than $20.00. How many minutes can he use his phone? Explain.

In Your Own Words

52. Write a sentence that explains the difference between an equation and an inequality.

Translate each sentence into an equation. Then solve.

1. A number decreased by 9.7 is 15.2.

2. Two times a number is eight and four tenths.

Simplify each expression.

3. $5c + 6d - 2c$

4. $x + 6 + 5x - 7$

5. $-2g + 5g + 9g - 3h$

Solve each equation. Check your solution.

6. $m + 91 = 157$

7. $y - 4 = -9$

8. $19b = 190$

9. $\frac{n}{3} = -12$

10. $0.5y = 0.05$

11. $y + 1.8 = 3.14$

12. $-7 + c = 73$

13. $25.5 = x + 8$

14. $12 = \frac{y}{4}$

15. $2y - 4 = 2.8$

16. $3k - 1 = -10$

17. $\frac{t}{2} - 5 = 7$

Solve each inequality. Use a number line to show the solution to each inequality.

18. $x + 6 > 10$

19. $x - 3 \le 5$

20. $7 + x < 12$

Solve. Use the formula $d = rt$.

21. Find the distance between Carl and a fireworks display if it takes 10 seconds for the sound to reach him. The speed of sound through air is 344 meters per second.

22. In a 24-hour endurance race, a car makes 640 laps of a racetrack that is 6 kilometers per lap. How far did the car travel in 24 hours? What was the average speed?

Write an equation, and solve.

23. Several friends share the cost of renting DVDs. If each person pays $3.50 and the total bill is $28.00, how many people share the cost?

24. Jovita adds 12.5 gallons of gas to fill her gas tank. The tank holds 15 gallons.

   a. How much gas was in the car before she added anything?

   b. If Jovita has only $20.00 and gas costs $2.50 a gallon, how many gallons of gas can Jovita put in the car? Will this fill the gas tank? Explain.

Change of Pace

Relations

You can draw a family tree to show how you are related to other members of your family. Here is an example of a family tree.

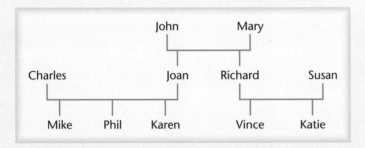

Use these rules to describe the relations in the family tree.

$m(x)$ means "the mother or mother-in-law of x," so m(Katie) is the same as "Susan."

$f(x)$ means "the father or father-in-law of x," so f(Charles) is the same as "John."

$d(x)$ means "the daughter or daughter-in-law of x."

$s(x)$ means "the son or son-in-law of x."

$b(x)$ means "the brother or brother-in-law of x."

$st(x)$ means "the sister or sister-in-law of x."

Use the family tree and the rules above to determine the following people. Some may have more than one answer.

1. m(Joan) = _____

2. f(Mike) = _____

3. s(Richard) = _____

4. b(Karen) = _____

5. d(Mary) = _____

6. b(_____) = Richard

7. st(_____) = Karen

8. s(_____) = Charles

9. $st(f$(Vince)) = _____

10. $f(st$(Vince)) = _____

11. $m(m$(Karen)) = _____

12. $st(s$(_____)) = Katie

13. Is $m(f$(Vince)) the same as $f(m$(Vince))?

14. List three different ways you can describe Karen using the rules above. One way is $d(d$(John)).

1. $43.6 - 18.49 = \underline{\quad}$
   a. 24.11
   b. 24.57
   c. 25.01
   d. none of the above

2. Find the sum of 19.89 and 40.015.
   a. 52.004
   b. 59.905
   c. 60.04
   d. 520.04

3. Which statement is true?
   a. $0.016 < 0.017$
   b. $0.16 < 0.026$
   c. $28.24 > 28.3$
   d. none of the above

4. Which is 63.852 rounded to the nearest tenth?
   a. 60
   b. 63.85
   c. 63.9
   d. 64

5. $-8 \cdot 4 = \underline{\quad}$
   a. 32
   b. -32
   c. 2
   d. -2

6. The expression $x + 9$ represents which phrase?
   a. the product of a number and 9
   b. a number decreased by 9
   c. 9 minus a number
   d. a number increased by 9

7. What is the prime factorization of 42?
   a. $2 \cdot 3^2 \cdot 7$
   b. $2^2 \cdot 3 \cdot 7$
   c. $2 \cdot 3 \cdot 3 \cdot 7$
   d. $2 \cdot 3 \cdot 7$

8. The cost of a car wash is $4.50 per car. Which expression shows the cost for washing n cars?
   a. $\$4.50 \div n$
   b. $\$4.50 - n$
   c. $\$4.50 + n$
   d. $\$4.50 \times n$

9. During June, about how many houses were sold?
   a. 350
   b. 400
   c. 450
   d. 500

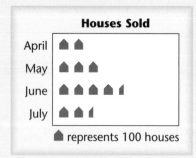

Houses Sold

April
May
June
July

🏠 represents 100 houses

10. Mrs. Linares made a total of 90 place mats. She made 30 the first week and an equal number of place mats during each of the next 5 weeks. How can you find the number of place mats made during each of those 5 weeks?
    a. Divide 30 by 5.
    b. Divide 60 by 5.
    c. Divide 90 by 5.
    d. none of the above

Ratios, Rates, Proportions, and Percents

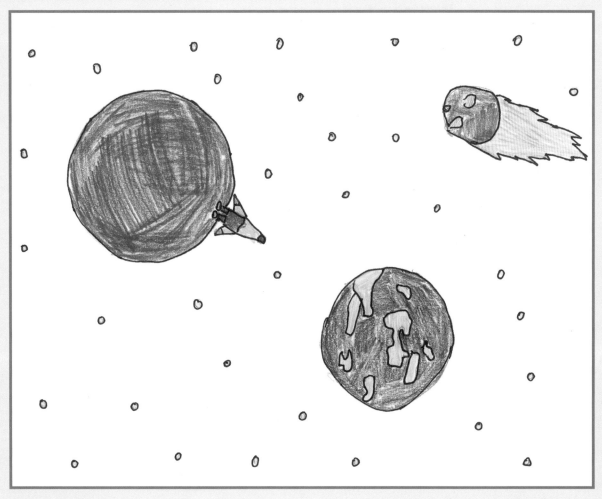

Spencer Peterson
Calvert Day School

Objective: to write and simplify ratios

In 2 hours, Luisa rides her bike 12 kilometers. In the same time, Megan rides her bike 16 kilometers.

You can compare the distance Luisa rides to the distance Megan rides by using a ratio. A **ratio** is the comparison of two numbers by division. The numbers 12 and 16 can be compared as follows:

| 12 to 16 | 12:16 | $\frac{12}{16}$ |

Writing a Ratio

Words	Numbers	Variables
Luisa to Megan	12 to 16	a to b, $b \neq 0$
Luisa/Megan	$\frac{12}{16}$	$\frac{a}{b}$, $b \neq 0$
Luisa:Megan	12:16	$a:b$, $b \neq 0$

Ratios can be written in simplest form.

$\frac{12}{16}$ written in simplest form is $\frac{12 \div 4}{16 \div 4} = \frac{3}{4}$.

Examples

Write the ratio of the first number to the second number in three ways.

A. 3, 5

$3:5$, $\frac{3}{5}$, 3 to 5

B. 14, 8

$14:8$, $\frac{14}{8}$, 14 to 8

C. 21, 9

$21:9$, $\frac{21}{9}$, 21 to 9

Write each ratio as a fraction in simplest form.

D. 6 to 9

$\frac{6}{9} = \frac{2}{3}$

E. 20 to 35

$\frac{20}{35} = \frac{4}{7}$

Try THESE

There are four kinds of road signs in a certain town. The number of each kind is shown at the right. Use this information to write each ratio in three ways.

1. stops to railroads

2. schools to stops

3. yields to schools

4. railroads to yields

5. schools to total signs

6. railroads to total signs

 10

 3

 2

 9

Exercises

Write each ratio as a fraction in simplest form. Do not change improper fractions to mixed numbers.

1. 9 to 7   2. 2 to 4   3. 6:3   4. 4 to 12

5. 16 to 6   6. 9 to 15   7. 18:4   8. 14 to 24

The table shows the number of tulips and roses that two florists sold last month. Use the table to write the specified ratio.

9. Flora's tulips to Flora's roses

10. Pat's tulips to Flora's tulips

11. Pat's roses to all Pat's flowers

12. Flora's roses to Pat's tulips

	Tulips	Roses
Flora's Flowers	56	81
Pat's Petals	31	76

Problem SOLVING

13. Tonio's garden has 25 tulips and 10 daffodils. What is the ratio of the number of tulips to the total number of flowers?

14. It takes Pam 45 minutes to drive to work and 60 minutes to drive home from work. Write the ratio of driving home from work to driving to work in three different ways.

Constructed RESPONSE

15. Mrs. Patterson packed 12 turkey sandwiches, 15 roast beef sandwiches, and 9 ham sandwiches for the school picnic. Her daughter, Kimmy, wanted to write a ratio of the turkey sandwiches to all of the sandwiches. Her work is to the right. Find her error, and correct her work. Explain.

$$\frac{turkey}{sandwiches} = \frac{12}{24}$$

Objective: to write rates and unit rates

Jane drives her car 70 miles in 2 hours. The ratio $\frac{70 \text{ mi}}{2 \text{ h}}$ compares the number of miles to the number of hours Jane drives her car. A ratio of two measurements having different units of measure is called a **rate**.

To find the average distance Jane drives each hour, simplify the rate so that the denominator is 1. A rate with a denominator of 1 is called a **unit rate**.

$$\frac{70 \text{ mi} \div 2}{2 \text{ h} \div 2} = \frac{35 \text{ mi}}{1 \text{ h}} \text{ or } \frac{35 \text{ mi}}{\text{h}}$$

> Divide by the number in the denominator.

The rate $\frac{35 \text{ mi}}{\text{h}}$ is read "35 miles per hour."

Examples

Write each ratio as a unit rate.

A. 24 tickets in 6 minutes

$$\frac{24 \text{ tickets} \div 6}{6 \text{ minutes} \div 6} = \frac{4 \text{ tickets}}{1 \text{ minute}}$$

The unit rate is 4 tickets per minute.

B. 187 miles on 5.5 gallons

$$\frac{187 \text{ miles} \div 5.5}{5.5 \text{ gallons} \div 5.5} = \frac{34 \text{ miles}}{1 \text{ gallon}}$$

The unit rate is 34 miles per gallon.

Unit rates are helpful when comparing items.

C. Which is a better buy, a 28-ounce jar of spaghetti sauce for $2.79 or a 40-ounce jar of spaghetti sauce for $3.25?

28-ounce jar $\quad \frac{\$2.79}{28 \text{ oz}} = 9.8¢$ per ounce

40-ounce jar $\quad \frac{\$3.25}{40 \text{ oz}} = 8.0¢$ per ounce

> To find the better buy, find each unit rate by dividing the cost by the number of ounces. Then compare.

The 40-ounce jar is a better buy.

Try THESE

Write each ratio as a rate.

1. 300 miles in 15 days
2. $400 for 25 tickets
3. 14 liters in 6 days
4. $55 for 11 pounds

Exercises

Write each ratio as a unit rate.

1. 400 miles on 25 gallons
2. 300 cars in 6 hours
3. $105 for 15 tickets
4. $7.70 for 11 kilograms
5. 280 kilometers in 4 hours
6. 8 meters in 10 seconds
7. 286 miles in $5\frac{1}{2}$ hours
8. 27 miles in 0.5 hour
9. 28 revolutions in 2 seconds
10. 12 pounds gained in 16 weeks
11. $425 saved in 10 months
12. 96¢ per dozen

Problem SOLVING

13. A package of paper towels costs $10.00. There are 15 rolls of paper towels in the package. How much does each roll of paper towels cost?

14. Linda can run 24 miles in 4 hours and 15 minutes. Find her average speed in miles per hour.

15. The Martin family travels 336 miles in 7 hours. The Benitez family travels 555 miles in 15 hours. Which family has the greater hourly rate?

★16. Two trains leave the station at the same time traveling in opposite directions. Train A is traveling 6 miles every 10 minutes. Train B is traveling 6 miles every 20 minutes. How far apart are they after 1 hour? How far apart are they after 90 minutes? How far apart are they after 2 hours?

Constructed RESPONSE

17. Ben needs to buy orange juice. He can buy 64 fl oz at the grocery store for $2.00, or he can buy 256 fl oz at the wholesale club for $7.50.

    a. Find the unit price for the grocery store orange juice.

    b. Find the unit price for the wholesale club orange juice.

    c. Where should Ben buy the orange juice if he wants the best deal? Explain.

Test PREP

18. Which of the following has the lowest unit price?

    a. 20 lb for $16.20   b. 26 lb for $23.40   c. 24 lb for $18.72   d. 22 lb for $18.70

19. Which typing time is the fastest?

    a. 320 words in 8 minutes
    b. 350 words in 10 minutes
    c. 600 words in 12 minutes
    d. 225 words in 5 minutes

Objective: to solve proportions

Kimiko is baking cookies for the Computer Club Bake Sale. Her recipe calls for 3 cups of flour for 48 cookies. At this rate, she needs 6 cups of flour for 96 cookies.

The two ratios $\frac{3}{48}$ and $\frac{6}{96}$ name the same number $\frac{1}{16}$, so the ratios are equivalent. A sentence that states that two ratios are equivalent is called a **proportion**.

> *Rule* Two ratios form a proportion if, and only if, their cross products are equal.

Multiply 48 by 6.
Multiply 96 by 3.

288 = 288

You can always use cross products to solve proportions. Sometimes, you can solve them mentally.

Examples

A. $\frac{2}{5} = \frac{x}{50}$

THINK What number can you multiply 5 by to get 50?

$x = 20$

B. $\frac{3}{4} = \frac{y}{30}$

$30 \times 3 = 4 \times y$ Write the cross products.

$90 = 4y$ $4y = 4 \times y$

$\frac{90}{4} = \frac{4y}{4}$ Divide each side by 4.

$22.5 = y$

(*Try* THESE) ·

Use cross products to see if the ratios form a proportion. Replace each ● with = or ≠ (is not equal to) to make a true statement.

1. $\frac{3}{7} \bullet \frac{4}{9}$

2. $\frac{3}{21} \bullet \frac{1}{7}$

3. $\frac{8}{12} \bullet \frac{2}{3}$

4. $\frac{1}{3} \bullet \frac{4}{11}$

Use cross products to see if the ratios form a proportion. Replace each ●
with = or ≠ (is not equal to) to make a true statement.

1. $\frac{3}{5}$ ● $\frac{5}{9}$

2. $\frac{2}{5}$ ● $\frac{4}{10}$

3. $\frac{2}{3}$ ● $\frac{6}{12}$

4. $\frac{4}{8}$ ● $\frac{4}{16}$

5. $\frac{16}{8}$ ● $\frac{8}{3}$

6. $\frac{20}{16}$ ● $\frac{5}{4}$

7. $\frac{4}{10}$ ● $\frac{8}{25}$

8. $\frac{5}{2}$ ● $\frac{40}{16}$

9. $\frac{0.06}{2}$ ● $\frac{0.12}{3}$

★10. $\frac{1.8}{0.9}$ ● $\frac{0.6}{0.3}$

★11. $\frac{1.5}{3}$ ● $\frac{7.5}{15}$

★12. $\frac{4}{6}$ ● $\frac{0.4}{0.9}$

Solve each proportion mentally. Check your answers using cross products.

13. $\frac{15}{1} = \frac{a}{4}$

★14. $\frac{1}{2} = \frac{17}{b}$

★15. $\frac{2}{3} = \frac{8}{h}$

★16. $\frac{27}{t} = \frac{9}{3}$

17. $\frac{1}{7} = \frac{14}{c}$

18. $\frac{4}{z} = \frac{24}{60}$

19. $\frac{2}{8} = \frac{x}{48}$

20. $\frac{y}{4} = \frac{14}{8}$

Solve each proportion.

21. $\frac{2}{5} = \frac{x}{250}$

22. $\frac{15}{3} = \frac{y}{8}$

23. $\frac{18}{20} = \frac{k}{110}$

24. $\frac{3}{9} = \frac{f}{9}$

25. $\frac{3}{10} = \frac{7.5}{n}$

26. $\frac{8}{187.5} = \frac{2}{75}$

27. $\frac{4}{6} = \frac{s}{0.9}$

28. $\frac{9}{40} = \frac{p}{100}$

29. $\frac{15}{40} = \frac{v}{100}$

30. $\frac{75}{54} = \frac{2.5}{c}$

31. $\frac{6.5}{r} = \frac{13}{39}$

32. $\frac{12}{c} = \frac{2}{0.19}$

33. $\frac{8.6}{25.8} = \frac{1}{c}$

34. $\frac{0.25}{0.5} = \frac{z}{4}$

35. $\frac{r}{1.5} = \frac{15}{2.25}$

★36. $\frac{0.3}{0.7} = \frac{3.3}{g}$

Problem SOLVING

37. Gasoline sells for $1.45 a gallon. What is the cost for 14.2 gallons?

38. A recipe calls for $2\frac{1}{2}$ cups of flour for 30 cookies. How much flour is needed for 72 cookies?

39. A piece of rope 30 meters long has a mass of 22 kilograms. What is the mass of 10 meters of the same type of rope?

40. A 10-acre field produced 750 bushels of corn. At that rate, how much corn can be produced from a 14-acre field?

★41. Yoki travels an average of 55 miles per hour (mph) during the first hour of a trip, 50 mph the second hour, 45 mph the third, and so on. How far does she travel in $4\frac{1}{2}$ h?

6.4 Problem-Solving Strategy: Use a Proportion

Objective: to solve problems using proportions

A paddleboat can travel 950 meters in 3 minutes. At that rate, how far does it travel in 15 minutes?

1. READ You know the distance the boat can travel in 3 minutes. You need to find the distance it travels in 15 minutes.

2. PLAN Let *d* represent the distance the boat travels in 15 minutes. Write a proportion, and solve for *d*.

$$\text{meters} \longrightarrow \quad \frac{950}{3} = \frac{d}{15} \quad \longleftarrow \text{meters}$$
$$\text{minutes} \longrightarrow \qquad\qquad\qquad \longleftarrow \text{minutes}$$

3. SOLVE Use paper and pencil.

$$15 \times 950 = 3 \times d$$
$$14{,}250 = 3d$$
$$4{,}750 = d$$

In 15 minutes, the boat can travel 4,750 meters (about 5 kilometers).

4. CHECK In 3 minutes, the boat can travel about 1,000 meters, or 1 kilometer. In 15 minutes, it can travel 5 times as far, or about 5 kilometers. So, the result is reasonable.

Another Example

Many supermarkets provide the unit price, which is the cost per unit. The unit price is similar to the unit rate. Compare the unit prices of the tuna shown below. Which is the better buy? Round to the nearest tenth.

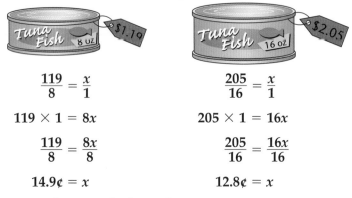

$$\frac{119}{8} = \frac{x}{1} \qquad\qquad\qquad \frac{205}{16} = \frac{x}{1}$$

$$119 \times 1 = 8x \qquad\qquad 205 \times 1 = 16x$$

$$\frac{119}{8} = \frac{8x}{8} \qquad\qquad\qquad \frac{205}{16} = \frac{16x}{16}$$

$$14.9\text{¢} = x \qquad\qquad\qquad 12.8\text{¢} = x$$

The 16 oz can of tuna is the better buy.

· ·

Use unit price to determine the better buy. Round where necessary.

1. juice $1.19 for 16 oz $0.97 for 12 oz

2. hamburger $3.18 for 2 lb $7.40 for 5 lb

3. paper plates $0.88 for 100 $1.49 for 150

4. soup $0.79 for 19 oz $0.45 for 11 oz

5. aluminum foil $0.99 for 75 sq ft $2.49 for 200 sq ft

Write a proportion for each. Then solve.

6. Eighteen pencils cost $1.44. At this rate, what is the cost of seven pencils?

7. Two numbers have a ratio of 1 to 9. If the greater number is 45, what is the lesser number?

Solve ·

1. Alan can type 80 words in 2 minutes. At this rate, how many words can he type in 35 minutes?

2. Two numbers have a ratio of 2 to 3. If the greater number is 21, what is the lesser number?

3. Leo can buy a 5-ounce tube of toothpaste for $0.89, 7 ounces for $1.29, or 9 ounces for $1.59. Which size is the best buy?

4. A recipe for 36 cookies requires $1\frac{1}{2}$ cups of oatmeal. How much oatmeal is needed to make 144 cookies?

5. If 3 pounds of bananas cost $1.00, what is the cost of 7.5 pounds?

6. Gina earns $18.90 in 4.5 hours. What is her hourly rate?

7. Find the cost of your favorite soft drink sold in bottles and cans. Which is the better buy?

★8. A car gets 27.2 miles per gallon of gasoline. Gasoline costs $1.58 per gallon. Find the cost of gasoline required for a 327-mile trip.

★9. Sam usually buys 30 trash bags for $3.89. This week they are on sale for $3.50. Sam also has a coupon to save another $0.30. What is the difference in unit price?

MiXeD REVIEW ·

Solve.

10. $x + 3 = 9$

11. $-4y = 24$

12. $x + 7 = -4$

13. $14 = 2m + 6$

14. $\frac{x}{7} = 9$

15. $3 - 2b = 5$

16. $6m = 84$

17. $\frac{x}{5} + 3 = 7$

Objective: to use proportions with scale drawings

Crescent City
Alturas
Eureka
Redding
Chico
○Sacramento
San Francisco
Oakland
San Jose
Bishop
Bakersfield
Barstow
San Bernadino
Los Angeles   Riverside
San Diego

Scale drawings are used to picture things that are too large or too small to be shown in actual size. On the map of California, 1 cm represents 100 km.

To find the actual distance (d) from Los Angeles to Eureka, measure the map distance, 9.0 cm.

Solve the following proportion to find the actual distance.

map distance (cm)

$$\frac{1}{100} = \frac{9.0}{d}$$

actual distance (km)

$$1 \times d = 100 \times 9.0$$

$$d = 900$$

> The ratio $\frac{1}{100}$ is formed from the fact that 1 cm represents 100 km.

The actual distance from Los Angeles to Eureka is about 900 km.

Try THESE ·

Find the actual distance between the cities. The map distance is given.

1. Bishop, San Francisco, 3.6 cm
2. San Jose, Eureka, 4.2 cm
3. Chico, Redding, 1.2 cm
4. Sacramento, Barstow, 5.5 cm
5. Oakland, San Francisco, 0.3 cm
6. Los Angeles, San Diego, 1.8 cm

The actual distance between two cities is given. Find the map distance. The map scale is 1 cm: 100 km.

7. 135 km
8. 9 km
9. 810 km
10. 333 km

··

On the scale drawing at the right, 1 cm represents 2.5 m. Measure each of the following to the nearest 0.1 cm. Then compute the actual measurement.

1. length of large pool
2. width of large pool
3. length of small pool
4. width of small pool
5. length of refreshment stand
6. width of refreshment stand
7. length of entrance and shower area
8. width of entrance and shower area
★9. perimeter of entire area

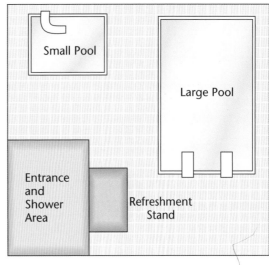

City Swimming Pool

Small Pool

Large Pool

Entrance and Shower Area

Refreshment Stand

Problem SOLVING ···

10. A living room is 6 m wide and 8.5 m long. Make a scale drawing, and estimate the distance between opposite corners.

11. On a city map, 1 cm represents 2.5 km. On the map, the distance from home to work is 3.4 cm. Find the actual distance.

Mind BUILDER

Similarity and Geometry

Two conditions need to be proven to show that two polygons are similar.

- The corresponding angles are congruent.
- The measures of corresponding sides are proportional.

4 in.   8 in.

4 in.

The figures above are *not* similar. Which condition is not met?

Determine whether each statement is *true* or *false*.

1. All squares are similar.
2. All rectangles are similar.
3. All equilateral triangles are similar.
4. All isosceles triangles are similar.

Objective: to solve problems using indirect measurement

Jeremy found that the stop sign at the corner is 7 feet tall and casts a
5-foot shadow. He also measured the shadow cast by his house. He found
it to be 21.5 feet. What is the height of his house?

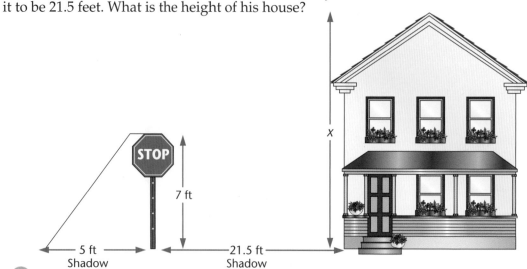

READ You know the height of the stop sign. You also know the
length of the shadows of the sign and the house. You
want to find the height of the house.

PLAN The Sun's rays cause the shadows to be in the same
proportion. Therefore, similar triangles are formed. You
can use the corresponding sides of similar triangles to
find the missing length.

SOLVE Set up and solve a proportion.

shadow

$$\frac{5}{7} = \frac{21.5}{x}$$

height

$$5x = 7 \times 21.5$$
$$\frac{5x}{5} = \frac{150.5}{5}$$
$$x = 30.1$$

The height of Jeremy's house is 30.1 feet.

CHECK The shadow of the house is a little more than 4 times the length of
the shadow of the stop sign. The height calculated for the house,
30.1 feet, is a little more than 4 times the height of the stop sign.
Therefore, the answer is reasonable.

Try THESE

1. Luanna estimates the height of a tree by measuring its shadow and the shadow of a 3-m pole at the same time of day. What is the height of the tree?

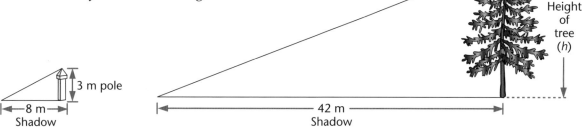

3 m pole

8 m
Shadow

42 m
Shadow

Height of tree (h)

Solve

1. Sylvio placed a mirror on the ground 10 meters from a flagpole. He stood 1.4 meters from the mirror, so he could see the top of the flagpole in the mirror. Sylvio is 1.7 meters tall. What is the height of the flagpole?

2. Doug is 5 feet tall. His father is 6 feet tall. When his father's shadow is 9 feet long, how long will Doug's shadow be?

3. Most TV screens have similar shapes. The measure of the diagonal is used to give the screen size. Suppose the dimensions of a 13-inch screen are $8\frac{1}{2}$ inches by 10 inches. Find the dimensions of a 21-inch screen. Round to the nearest tenth of an inch.

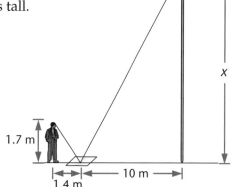

1.7 m

x

10 m

1.4 m

Mid-Chapter REVIEW

Write each ratio as a fraction in simplest form.

1. 5 to 10

2. 4:16

Solve each proportion. Check your answers.

5. $\frac{8}{3} = \frac{b}{12}$

6. $\frac{17.5}{f} = \frac{5}{6}$

Write each rate as a unit rate.

3. $14.50 for 10 gallons

4. $2.52 for 2 maps

Solve.

7. On a map of New Mexico, 1 cm represents 45 km. The distance from Albuquerque to Santa Fe is 2 cm. Find the actual distance.

8. A car traveled 148 miles in 4 hours. At that rate, how far would it travel in $6\frac{1}{2}$ hours?

6.6 Problem-Solving Application: Using Indirect Measurement **139**

Patsy's Pizza-Pie Problem

Patsy, the social director for the After-School Club, was organizing a pizza-pie party for a large group of club members. She wondered aloud, "What is the largest number of pieces of pizza you can get from one pie with 4 cuts? What about 5 cuts?" She practiced on a pizza she had in front of her. The results are shown below. Can you answer Patsy's questions? What is the greatest number of pieces of pizza you can make with 10 cuts?

Extension

What is the greatest number of pieces of pizza you can make with n cuts?

Cumulative Review

Estimate.

1. $\begin{array}{r} 2{,}465 \\ +\ \ 796 \\ \hline \end{array}$

2. $\begin{array}{r} 0.636 \\ -\ 0.089 \\ \hline \end{array}$

3. $\begin{array}{r} 0.71 \\ \times\ 0.56 \\ \hline \end{array}$

4. $27\overline{)244}$

5. $0.67\overline{)0.5762}$

6. $7 \times \frac{2}{3}$

7. $4\frac{4}{5} \times 2\frac{3}{4}$

8. $4 - 1\frac{1}{3}$

9. $2\frac{1}{2} + \frac{3}{4}$

Compute.

10. $29 \div 100$

11. $0.7 \div 10$

12. 0.04×10

13. 100×0.01

Solve each equation.

14. $b + 4.5 = 45$

15. $136 = m - 36$

16. $\frac{x}{0.3} = 30$

17. $6a = 109.2$

Write each number in scientific notation.

18. $340{,}000$

19. 0.00069

20. $72{,}000$

21. 0.000681

Find the greatest common factor for each pair of numbers.

22. $16, 24$

23. $8, 32$

24. $12, 27$

25. $15, 30$

Solve each proportion.

26. $\frac{x}{8} = \frac{5}{4}$

27. $\frac{10}{a} = \frac{7.5}{36}$

28. $\frac{1}{6} = \frac{0.9}{m}$

29. $\frac{7}{10} = \frac{c}{15}$

Solve.

30. The width of a rectangle is 9 m. The ratio of the width to the length is 3 to 7. Find the length of the rectangle.

31. Sasha baked cupcakes. She used $2\frac{1}{3}$ cups of flour, $1\frac{1}{4}$ cups of sugar, and $\frac{2}{3}$ cups of cocoa. How many cups of dry ingredients did Sasha use?

32. On Tuesday, Jacob swam twice as many laps as he did on Monday plus 12 more. If he swam 52 laps on Tuesday, how many did he swim on Monday? Write an equation, and solve.

33. The width of a photograph is 6 inches. Its length is 10 inches. After the photograph is enlarged, the width is 9 inches. What is the new length of the photograph?

Objective: to solve percent problems using estimation

Have you ever heard a statement like this on TV?

Over 75% of dentists surveyed recommend Brand X for fighting cavities.

What important piece of information is missing from this statement?

Examples

A. Suppose 165 dentists were surveyed. About how many recommend Brand X? You can use estimation to find this number.

75% of 165 is ■. **THINK** $75\% = \frac{3}{4}$

$\frac{3}{4}$ **of 165 is ■.** Find a multiple of 4 that is close to 165.

$\frac{3}{4}$ **of 160 is 120.**

Therefore, 75% of 165 is about 120.

In this survey, about 120 dentists recommend Brand X.

B. A different survey reports that over 1,900 dentists recommend Brand Y. If 6,000 dentists were surveyed, what percent recommend Brand Y?

Brand Y ⟶ **1,900** ▶ **2,000** **THINK** 2,000 is close to 1,900.
total dentists ⟶ **6,000** **6,000**

$\frac{2,000}{6,000} = \frac{1}{3}$ or $33\frac{1}{3}\%$ Write $\frac{1}{3}$ as a percent.

In this survey, about $33\frac{1}{3}\%$ of the dentists recommend Brand Y.

 THESE ••

Write each expression so that it will be easy to estimate.

1. 50% of 84

2. 25% of 60

3. $33\frac{1}{3}\%$ of 18

4. 20% of 26

5. $66\frac{2}{3}\%$ of 35

6. 40% of 28.5

7. $12\frac{1}{2}\%$ of 74

8. 24% of 40

9. 51% of 29

Exercises

Determine which is the best estimate.

1. 51% of 400   a. 2   b. 20   c. 200

2. 78% of 32   a. 2.4   b. 24   c. 240

3. 32% of 540   a. 18   b. 180   c. 1,800

4. 12% of 880   a. 1,050   b. 105   c. 10.5

★5. $\frac{1}{4}$% of 800   a. 200   b. 20   c. 2

★6. 125% of 1,200   a. 15   b. 150   c. 1,500

Estimate.

7. 28% of 81   8. 79% of 15   9. 12% of 25

10. 9.5% of 20   11. 31.2% of 125   12. 61% of 156

Estimate each percent.

13. 6 out of 25   14. 9 out of 17   15. 19 out of 60

16. 62 out of 90   ★17. 7 out of 41   ★18. 58 out of 179

Problem SOLVING

19. Luisa made 13 free throws in 18 attempts. About what percent is this?

20. Gary's goal is to save $72. He has saved 48% of that amount. About how much has he saved?

21. Who has the better batting average, Jack with 8 hits in 20 at bats or Jill with 9 hits in 17 at bats?

22. Write a problem that uses the numbers in exercise 10.

MiXeD REVIEW

Solve each proportion.

23. $\frac{t}{7} = \frac{1}{2}$ 24. $\frac{9}{n} = \frac{36}{50}$ 25. $\frac{12}{18} = \frac{y}{24}$ 26. $\frac{0.2}{s} = \frac{1}{12}$

27. $\frac{15}{v} = \frac{6}{8}$ 28. $\frac{5}{8} = \frac{b}{100}$ 29. $\frac{v}{4.8} = \frac{5}{16}$ 30. $\frac{2.25}{1} = \frac{u}{6}$

6.8 Finding the Percent of a Number

Objective: to find the percent of a number

At The Rosewood School, 45% of the 320 students bring a lunch to school everyday. How many students bring a lunch everyday?

Estimate:
$$45\% \longrightarrow \tfrac{1}{2}$$
$$\tfrac{1}{2} \text{ of } 320 = 160$$

We can solve the percent problem above using a proportion or multiplication.

Using a Proportion to Find a Percent
45% means that 45 out of 100 students bring a lunch to school everyday.

$$\frac{\text{Number who bring lunch}}{\text{Total number of students}} \quad \frac{x}{320} = \frac{45}{100}$$

Percent of students who bring lunch.

$$x \cdot 100 = 320 \cdot 45$$

$$\frac{100x}{100} = \frac{14{,}400}{100}$$

$$x = 144$$

Using Multiplication to Find a Percent
You know that 45% of 320 students bring a lunch everyday.

$$45\% \text{ of } 320 = 45\% \cdot 320$$

You need to convert the percent to a decimal.

$$= 0.45 \cdot 320$$

$$= 144$$

At The Rosewood School, 144 students bring a lunch to school everyday.

Examples

A. What number is 40% of 180?

$$a = 40\% \cdot 180$$

$$a = 0.40 \cdot 180 \quad \text{Convert 40\% to 0.40.}$$

$$a = 72$$

72 is 40% of 180.

B. Find 65% of 200.

$$\frac{x}{200} = \frac{65}{100}$$

$$x \cdot 100 = 200 \cdot 65$$

$$100x = 13{,}000$$

$$x = 130$$

130 is 65% of 200.

Try THESE ·

Write the proportion you would use to solve each problem.

1. Find 60% of 10.

2. What number is 90% of 70?

3. What number is 4% of 400?

4. Find 2% of 350.

Solve each problem. Use any method.

1. Find 20% of $14.95.
2. 75% of 48 is what number?
3. What number is 2.5% of 80?
4. Find 40% of $106.99.
5. Find 25% of 160.
6. 50% of 92 is what number?
7. 30% of 60 is what number?
8. Find $12\frac{1}{2}$% of 72.
9. What number is 32% of 450?
10. What number is 6% of 500?
11. Find 73% of $39.00.
12. What number is 200% of 68?
13. Find 50% of 24.
14. What number is 40% of 20?
15. 150% of 8 is what number?
16. What number is $62\frac{1}{2}$% of 400?
17. Find $12\frac{1}{2}$% of 160.
18. 190% of 300 is what number?

Problem SOLVING

19. Erika earns $96 each week. She saves 30% of the amount she earns.

    a. How much money does she save in 4 weeks?

    b. Erika wants to buy a new bike that costs $230. Will she have enough money saved in 8 weeks?

Constructed RESPONSE

20. Andrea used her calculator to find 25% of 28. The display showed 700. Is this answer reasonable? If not, what mistake might Andrea have made?

21. Pete earns $4.41 per hour. Sam earns 105% of this amount per hour. How much more does Sam earn per hour than Pete?

22. Marco bought a bicycle that cost $128. He made a down payment of $37\frac{1}{2}$%. How much does he still owe?

Test PREP

23. A basketball player makes 60% of her free throw shots. If she attempts 15 free throw shots in a game, how many should she make?

    a. 6   b. 15   c. 90   d. 9

24. What is $44\frac{1}{2}$% of 50?

    a. 25.22   b. 22.25   c. 25.20   d. 22.50

25. Write 9.0 as a percent.

    a. 9.0%   b. 90%   c. 900%   d. 9,000%

6.8 Finding the Percent of a Number   145

Objective: to solve percent problems using proportions

Jackie's paycheck last week was $180. She spent $75 for new clothes. What percent of her paycheck did she use to buy new clothes?

> An estimate is a little less than half, or 50%, of her paycheck because $75 is a little less than 50% of $180.

A **percent proportion** can be used to solve this problem. A percent proportion is a comparison of a part of a quantity to the whole quantity called the **base**.

Part: amount spent on clothes
Base: total paycheck $\dfrac{75}{180} = \dfrac{p}{100}$ The percent is written as a fraction out of 100.

Percent Proportion

> The percent proportion is $\dfrac{\text{part}}{\text{base}} = \dfrac{\text{percent}}{100}$.
>
> This can be represented by $\dfrac{a}{b} = \dfrac{p}{100}$, where a = part, b = base, and p = percent.

Examples

A. What percent is $75 of $180?

$\dfrac{75}{180} = \dfrac{p}{100}$ Replace a with 75 and b with 180.

$75 \cdot 100 = 180p$ Multiply.

$\dfrac{7{,}500}{180} = \dfrac{180p}{180}$ Divide.

$41.66 = p$

We can round this to 42.

Jackie spent 42% of her paycheck on new clothes. This answer is reasonable, since it is close to the estimate.

B. 150 is 30% of what number?

$\dfrac{150}{x} = \dfrac{30}{100}$ Replace a with 150 and p with 30.

$150 \cdot 100 = 30x$ Multiply.

$\dfrac{15{,}000}{30} = \dfrac{30x}{30}$ Divide.

$500 = x$

30% of 500 is 150.

Try THESE

Solve.

1. 40 is what percent of 50?

2. What percent of 200 is 30?

3. 50% of what number is 4?

4. 7 is 25% of what number?

5. What percent of 75 is 50?

6. $12\frac{1}{2}$% of what number is 8?

Exercises

Solve. Round to the nearest tenth, if necessary.

1. 7 is what percent of 14?
2. 75% of what number is 150?
3. What percent of 30 is 30?
4. 25 is what percent of 125?
5. 350 is 70% of what number?
6. 56 is 14% of what number?
7. What percent of 64 is 24?
8. What percent of $6.50 is $2.60?
9. 1 is what percent of 200?
10. 55 is 20% of what number?
11. 15% of what number is 41?
12. 2.1 is $87\frac{1}{2}$% of what number?
13. $12\frac{1}{2}$% of what number is 79?
14. $33\frac{1}{3}$% of what number is 41?

Problem SOLVING

15. Twenty-four people were invited to a picnic. Only sixteen people came. What percent of those who were invited came to the picnic?

16. A store owner paid $43.20 for a coat. This is 40% of the amount the owner plans to charge for the coat. How much does the owner plan to charge for the coat?

17. On an airplane, 85% of the seats are filled. If 119 seats are filled, how many seats are empty?

18. Adam sold $152 worth of papers at the fair. He was paid 25% of the total sales. How much was he paid?

★19. In a school election, Katie received 55% of the votes, while Jason received 45% of the votes. If 250 students voted, by how many votes did Katie win?

Constructed RESPONSE

20. Mr. Diaz spends 30% of his income on rent. He spends $360 each month on rent.
    a. What is his income each month?
    b. He spends 10% of his monthly income on food, how much does he spend on food each month? Explain.

Test PREP

21. 6 is what percent of 8?
    a. 7.5%   b. 75%   c. 750%   d. 7,500%

22. 3% of what number is 6?
    a. 2   b. 20   c. 200   d. 2,000

23. What number is 5% of 48?
    a. 240   b. 24   c. 2.4   d. 0.24

6.10 Finding Discounts and Sales Tax

Objective: to find discounts, sale prices, and sales tax

An appliance store is having a sale. All of their microwave ovens are discounted by 25%. A **discount** is an amount by which the price of an item is reduced. The discount on each microwave oven is 25%.

The regular price of a microwave oven is $319. Find the discount and the sale price.

The discount is 25% of $319. Find the discount.

$0.25 \cdot \$319 = \$79.75$

The sale price of the oven is $239.25.

Subtract $79.75 from $319 to find the sale price.

$\$319 - \$79.75 = \$239.25$

The appliance store charges sales tax. **Sales tax** is an amount of money that a store charges in addition to the purchase price. The government receives this money. When buying an item, you need to calculate the sales tax and add it to the price of the item.

The sales tax in the state where the appliance store is located is 5%.

Find 5% of $239.25.

$0.05 \cdot 239.25 = 11.9625$ ▷ Round to the nearest hundredth.

The sales tax is $11.96.

To find the final price of the microwave oven, add the amount of the sales tax to $239.25.

$\$239.25 + \$11.96 = \$251.21$

The final price is $251.21.

Try THESE

Find the discount and sale price. Copy and complete the table.

Item	Original Price	Sale	Discount	Sale Price
1. Toy	$8.50	10% off		
2. Chair	$216.00	35% off		
3. Picture	$55.60	25% off		
4. Suit	$129.00	20% off		

Find the sales tax and the final price to the nearest cent. Copy and
complete the table.

Item	Price	Tax	Sales Tax	Final Price
1. Ball	$15.00	6%		
2. Clock	$45.00	3%		
3. Shoes	$53.00	4%		
4. Shirt	$32.00	4.5%		

Problem SOLVING ··

5. At a clearance sale, the price of each item was reduced 40%. The original price of an item was $66.00. What was the sale price?

6. The regular price for a pair of gloves is $6.00. If the gloves are on sale for 15% off, find the sale price.

7. Mr. Garcia bought sunglasses for $6.00 and a hat for $4.75. The sales tax was 6%. How much did Mr. Garcia pay in all?

8. The regular price of a smoke detector is $29.00. Kate buys one at a discount of 10% and pays 6% sales tax. What is the final price?

9. A record store offers a discount of 15% if a customer buys three or more records. Mark wants to buy records that cost $6.97, $10.50, $9.39, and $9.95. Find the total cost.

★10. Carl has $4.00, and Bill has $5.00. Carl said, "I have 20% less than Bill." Bill replied, "I have 25% more than Carl." Who is correct?

Constructed RESPONSE ··································

11. Juanita was calculating 5% of $49.95. Her calculator displayed 24.975. Is this reasonable? If not, explain what mistake Juanita might have made.

Mixed REVIEW ···

Solve.

12. $-5x = 40$

13. $x + 7 = -10$

14. $4x - 1 = -9$

15. $\frac{x}{6} = 2.1$

16. $x - 3.8 = 1.2$

17. $\frac{x}{3} - 6 = -4$

6.11 Problem-Solving Application: Finding Simple Interest

Objective: to find simple interest

When you deposit money in a savings account, the bank pays you **interest** on the money. The amount of money you deposit is called the **principal**. The interest is a percent of the principal.

If you use a credit card, you must pay interest on the amount of the unpaid balance. The **principal** is the amount of the unpaid balance. In order to pay off the credit card balance, you must pay the principal *plus* the interest.

The formula below can be used to estimate how much interest the bank pays on a savings account or how much you must pay to use the credit card.

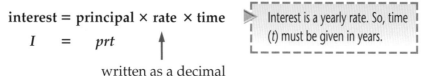

interest = principal × rate × time

$$I \quad = \quad prt$$

↑
written as a decimal

▷ Interest is a yearly rate. So, time (*t*) must be given in years.

Examples

A. Elena deposited $1,250 in a savings account. The interest rate is 7.5% per year. How much interest will she earn in 6 months?

The principal (*p*) is $1,250.
The rate (*r*) is 0.075.
The time (*t*) in years is $\frac{1}{2}$ or 0.5.

$1,250 × 0.075 = $93.75   Round to the nearest cent

$93.75 × 0.5 = $46.875

To the nearest cent, the interest is $46.88.

B. Suppose you have an unpaid balance of $400 on a credit card. The credit card company charges 18% per year. What is the interest charge for 1 month?

The principal is $400.
The rate is 0.18.
The time in years is $\frac{1}{12}$.

$400 × 0.18 = $72

$72 ÷ 12 = $6

↑
months

The interest is $6. The unpaid balance is now $406.

Find the interest to the nearest dollar. All rates are yearly.

1. principal, $400
   rate, 5%
   time, 1 year

2. principal, $1,000
   rate, 8.5%
   time, 1 year

3. principal, $906
   rate, 10%
   time, $\frac{1}{2}$ year

4. principal, $200
   rate, 18%
   time, $\frac{1}{4}$ year

5. principal, $340
   rate, 12%
   time, $\frac{3}{4}$ year

6. principal, $20,000
   rate, 12%
   time, 3 months

Solve ··

Find the interest on each savings account. Then find how much money will be in the account after the given time. Round to the nearest dollar.

1. $1,180 at 5.25% for 6 months

2. $280 at 6% for 1 year

3. $650 at 7.75% for 9 months

4. $2,500 at $8\frac{1}{2}$% for 3 months

★5. $1,040 at $6\frac{1}{2}$% for 4 months

★6. $942 at 6% for 8 months

If you get a loan at a bank, you must pay interest. Find the amount of interest for each loan. Then find the amount that must be repaid.

7. $60 at 8% for 1 year

8. $180 at 19% for 1 year

9. $900 at 9.5% for 1 year

10. $1,400 at $11\frac{1}{2}$% for 1 year

11. $1,150 at 14% for 6 months

★12. $3,000 at 15.75% for 24 months

★13. $5,800 at 17.4% for 4 years

★14. $6,100 at 13.2% for 2 years

15. Quan borrowed $160 from a bank. To repay the loan, she paid the bank $15 a month for 12 months. How much interest did she pay?

★16. Barb has 50% as much money as Betty. Betty has 80% as much money as Sue. Barb has ■% as much money as Sue. Find ■.

17. Maroa invested $3,000 from her summer job in a CD, Certificate of Deposit, at an interest rate of 5%. How many years will it take until there is a total of $4,875 in Maroa's CD?

18. Tim deposited $60 into a savings account with an interst rate of 9%. John invested $65 into an account with an interest rate of 5%. Who will have more money after 5 years? Explain.

Chapter 6 Review

Language and Concepts

Choose the letter of the correct term to complete each sentence.

1. A ratio of two measurements with different units of measure is called a(n) _____.

2. A(n) _____ is an equation that states that two ratios are equivalent.

3. _____ are used to picture things that are too large or too small to be shown in actual size.

4. The _____ 29 out of 100 can be written as 29%.

5. The fraction $\frac{1}{2}$, the decimal 0.5, and 50% are different names for the same _____.

6. You can solve a proportion by finding an equivalent fraction or by using _____.

7. A rate with a denominator of 1 is called a(n) _____.

a. cross products
b. number
c. proportion
d. rate
e. ratio
f. scale drawings
g. unit rate

Skills and Problem Solving

Write each ratio as a fraction in simplest form. Section 6.1

8. 16 out of 24
9. 36:14
10. 18 to 27

Write each of the following as a unit rate. Section 6.2

11. $12 for 3 meals
12. 60 cars in 2 hours
13. $1.28 for 4 pens

Solve each proportion by finding an equivalent fraction or by using cross products. Section 6.3

14. $\frac{4}{5} = \frac{12}{x}$
15. $\frac{4}{9} = \frac{b}{45}$
16. $\frac{6}{3.3} = \frac{2}{s}$
17. $\frac{8}{k} = \frac{32}{8.4}$
18. $\frac{6}{8} = \frac{m}{12}$
19. $\frac{0.3}{4.6} = \frac{n}{6.9}$
20. $\frac{4}{1.5} = \frac{3}{a}$
21. $\frac{12.3}{t} = \frac{2.5}{5}$

Write each expression so that it will be easy to estimate. Section 6.7

22. 25% of 16
23. 50% of 24.2
24. 60% of 15
25. $33\frac{1}{3}$% of 22
26. $37\frac{1}{2}$% of 25
27. 81% of 38

Determine which is the best estimate. Section 6.7

28. 152% of 500   a. 75   b. 750   c. 7,500

29. 75% of 198   a. 1.5   b. 15   c. 150

30. 67% of 24.3   a. 1.62   b. 16.2   c. 162

31. 5.4% of 1,000   a. 5.4   b. 54   c. 540

Estimate each percent. Section 6.7

32. 18 out of 37   33. 15 out of 19

34. 21 out of 60   35. 4 out of 31

36. 9 out of 91   37. 5 out of 26

Solve. Use multiplication or a proportion. Sections 6.8–6.9

38. What number is 28% of 675?

39. $12\frac{1}{2}$% of 400 is what number?

40. Find $33\frac{1}{3}$% of 240.

41. Find 6.5% of 300.

42. What number is 35% of 300?

43. Find 62% of 450.

44. What percent of 40 is 12?

45. 25 is what percent of 75?

46. 140 is what percent of 200?

47. 5.9% of what number is 82.6?

Solve. Sections 6.4–6.6 and 6.10–6.11

48. On a map of South Carolina, 1 cm represents 30 km. On the map, the distance from Charleston to Columbia is 5.6 cm. Find the actual distance.

49. At the same time an 8-foot pole casts a shadow 6 feet long, a monument casts a shadow 426 feet long. How tall is the monument?

50. The price of a vase is $36. If there is a $33\frac{1}{3}$% discount, what is the sale price?

51. A sofa costs $1,074. It is 20% off. The sales tax is 6.5%. Find the final price.

52. Harry invested $600 at an interest rate of 11%. How much money will he have after 1 year? after 2 years? after 5 years?

53. Jon took out a loan for $425. The interest rate was 8.5%. Find the amount of interest for the loan after 2 years. Find the total amount that must be repaid.

54. Greg's Groceries is having a sale on paper towels, 15 rolls for $9.00. The Super Saver also has paper towels on sale, 12 rolls for $7.50. Which grocery store has the better bargain? Explain.

Chapter 6 Test

Write each ratio as a fraction in simplest form.

1. 18 to 32

2. 9:39

3. 36 out of 48

Write each of the following as a unit rate.

4. 25 planes in 5 hours

5. 66 kilometers in 3 hours

6. 75 miles on 3 gallons

Solve each proportion.

7. $\dfrac{4}{h} = \dfrac{10}{12}$

8. $\dfrac{b}{3} = \dfrac{33}{4}$

9. $\dfrac{7}{8} = \dfrac{d}{20}$

10. $\dfrac{10}{3} = \dfrac{0.5}{n}$

On a map of California, 1 cm represents 90 km. Find the actual distance between each pair of cities. The map distance is given.

11. Bakersfield, Riverside, 2.5 cm

12. Crescent City, San Diego, 13.5 cm

Estimate.

13. 52% of 18

14. 75% of 21

15. 33% of 120

16. 5% of 105

Solve.

17. 25% of 800 is what number?

18. What number is 12.5% of 376?

19. What percent of 50 is 35?

20. 16 is what percent of 40?

21. 44 is $33\frac{1}{3}$% of what number?

22. 20% of what number is 1,250?

23. 35% of what number is 7?

24. What percent of 60 is 55?

Solve.

25. A salesperson earns $28 in 8 hours. At the same rate, what does a person earn in 36 hours?

26. The shadow of a tower is 120 feet long. The shadow of a person next to the tower is 4 feet long. If the person is 6 feet tall, how tall is the tower?

27. Sylvia got a loan of $200 at 18% for 4 months. How much will she have to pay in all?

28. Sales tax of 5.5% is added to a purchase of $41.95. Find the amount of tax and the final price.

29. Kyle deposited $400 in a savings account that pays 8% interest. How much interest will he earn in 3 months?

30. At Tom's TVs, the regular price of a television is $499. The television is on sale for 25% off. At Elliot's Electronics, the same TV is $450 and is on sale for 15% off. Where should you buy the TV? Explain.

Compound Interest

When a bank adds interest to a savings account, the interest earned becomes part of the principal. As the principal increases, the account earns more and more interest. Interest on interest is called **compound interest**.

Suppose an account has $100 at the beginning of a year. The yearly interest rate is 6%, and the interest is compounded quarterly (4 times a year). This means interest is figured every 3 months and added to the account. Use the following steps to find out how much money is in the account at the end of each quarter of the year.

	Principal	Interest rate	Quarter of a year
Interest =	$100 ×	0.06 ×	0.25

I = $1.50 is added to the principal the first quarter.

The principal (P) is $100.
Use the formula $I = prt$ to find the interest (I).
Add the interest to the principal.

Calculate the interest for the second quarter. The interest the second quarter is $1.52.

$101.50 × 0.06 × 0.25

How would you calculate the interest for the third and fourth quarters?

Quarter	Principal
1	$101.50
2	$103.02
3	$104.57
4	$106.14

The original amount, $100, increased by $6.14 to $106.14. So, the yearly percent of increase is 6.14%. This rate is called the **annual yield**.

Find the amount of money in each account after 1 year. Then state the annual yield.

1. $100 at 8% compounded quarterly
2. $100 at 12% compounded quarterly
★3. $1,000 at $8\frac{1}{2}$% compounded quarterly
★4. $1,000 at 9% compounded monthly

★5. **Research**
   Check the business section of a newspaper, and compare the annual yield of several different accounts.

Cumulative Test

1. 35% of 40

   a. 5

   b. 14

   c. 54

   d. 75

2. What percent of 50 is 20?

   a. 20%

   b. 40%

   c. 60%

   d. 80%

3. 16 is 25% of which number?

   a. 4

   b. 8

   c. 32

   d. 64

4. Solve. $\frac{m}{7} = 70$

   a. 10

   b. 63

   c. 77

   d. 490

5. How many cookies have to be sold at $0.12 per cookie to collect $48.00?

   a. 4

   b. 40

   c. 400

   d. 4,000

6. Which ratio is equivalent to $\frac{5}{3}$?

   a. 10 to 3

   b. 10 to 6

   c. 10 to 9

   d. none of the above

7. Which situation can be represented by the expression $n - 4$?

   a. Jackie buys n books for $4 each.

   b. Matt gives 4 of his n model cars to Brian.

   c. There are 4 pizzas to be shared by n students.

   d. none of the above

8. Which problem can be solved by the equation $9d = 36$?

   a. Harold made 9 pillows for gifts. Rae made 36 more. How many did Rae make?

   b. If there are 9 cans in a case, how many cans are in 36 cases?

   c. Pam saves $9 a week. How many weeks does it take her to save $36?

   d. none of the above

9. 20% = _____

   a. 0.02

   b. 0.20

   c. 2.00

   d. 20.0

10. If 4,840 square yards = 1 acre, how many acres are in 77,440 square yards?

    a. 16

    b. 121

    c. 160

    d. 1,210

CHAPTER 7

Geometry and Plane Figures

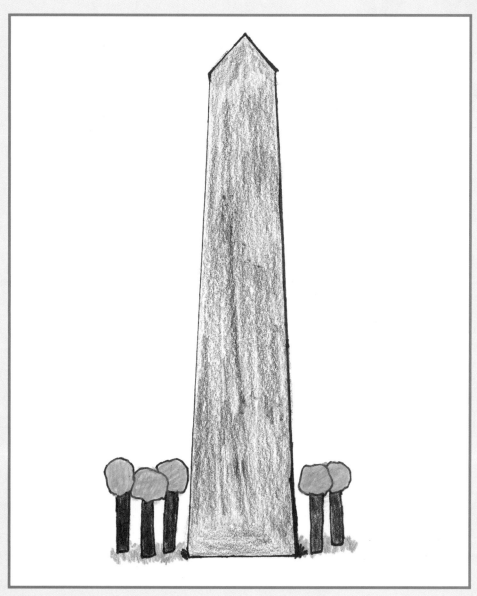

Kathryn Stanley
Calvert Day School

7.1 Angles

Objective: to measure angles

The Vietnam Veterans Memorial is located near the Lincoln Memorial in Washington, DC. Designed by Maya Lin, it is a V-shaped, black granite structure. The memorial lists the names of more than 50,000 Americans who died or are missing in Vietnam. Its shape is a model of an angle.

An **angle** is formed by two **rays** with a common endpoint called the **vertex**. The rays are called the sides of the angle. In the angle shown at the right, rays QP and QR form the sides of the angle PQR. The vertex is point Q.

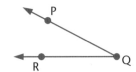

Say: angle PQR

Write: ∠PQR

> You can also name ∠PQR as ∠RQP, ∠Q, or ∠1.

When you measure angles, you measure the space between two rays that meet at a vertex. You can use a **protractor** to measure angles in **degrees**.

- Place the center of the protractor on the vertex of the angle (B) with the straightedge along one ray ($\overrightarrow{BA}$).
- Use the scale that begins with 0 at $\overrightarrow{BA}$. Read where the other ray $\overrightarrow{BC}$ crosses this scale.

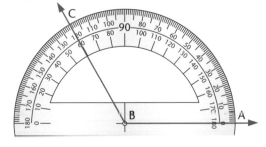

Say: The degree measure of angle ABC is 120.

Write: m∠ABC = 120°

Angles can be classified according to their measure.

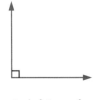

A **right angle** measures 90°.

An **acute angle** measures between 0° and 90°.

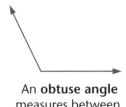

An **obtuse angle** measures between 90° and 180°.

A **straight angle** measures 180°.

Use symbols to name each angle. Then measure each angle.

1.

2.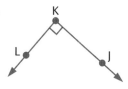

3.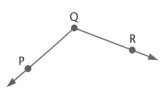

Use a straightedge to draw a representation of each figure.

1. angle T
2. ∠XYZ
3. ∠ABC
4. an acute angle with sides $\overrightarrow{GQ}$ and $\overrightarrow{GC}$ $\overrightarrow{GQ}$ is the symbol for ray GQ.
5. an obtuse angle with vertex K

Classify each angle as *acute*, *obtuse*, or *right*.

6.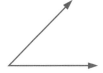

7.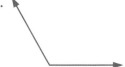

8.

Use a protractor to draw an angle having each measurement.

9. 30°   10. 55°   11. 90°   12. 110°   13. 145°

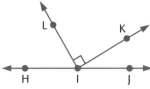

14. Name five angles. Explain why none of the angles can be named ∠I.

15. What is m∠HIL + m∠KIL + m∠JIK?

16. Name a right angle.

17. Name an acute angle.

18. Name an obtuse angle.

19. Name a straight angle.

20. Find the measure of ∠HIK.

21. Find the measure of ∠LIJ.

22. Becky measures an angle that has short sides. She extends each side in a straight line, so she can use a protractor. Marty says she cannot do that because it will make the angle larger. Who is right? Tell why.

7.2 Angle Relationships

Objective: to apply angle relationships

Exploration Exercise

Is there a relationship between lines and angles?

1. Use a straightedge to draw two intersecting lines.
   a. Label the angles 1, 2, 3, and 4.
2. Measure each angle with your protractor.

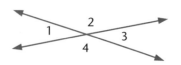

Some pairs of angles have special relationships.

A. Two angles are **adjacent** if they have the same vertex, share a side, and do not overlap. ∠1 and ∠2 are adjacent angles. Can you name some other pairs of adjacent angles?

B. Two angles are **vertical** when they are opposite each other and are formed by two intersecting lines. ∠1 and ∠3 are vertical angles. Vertical angles are congruent, or equal to each other.

C. Two angles are **complementary** if the sum of their degree measures is 90°.

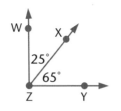

Since 25° + 65° = 90°, ∠WZX and ∠YZX are complementary angles.

Explain why adjacent angles that are complementary always form a right angle.

D. Two angles are **supplementary** if the sum of their degree measures is 180°.

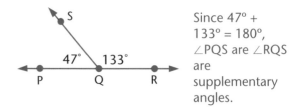

Since 47° + 133° = 180°, ∠PQS are ∠RQS are supplementary angles.

Explain why adjacent angles that are supplementary always form a line.

Examples

A. Find the value of x.

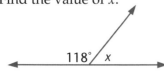

$118° + x = 180°$ Supplementary angles
$x = 62°$ Subtract 118° from both sides.

B. Find the value of y.

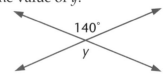

The angles are vertical, therefore they are equal.
The value of y is 140°.

Classify each pair of angles as *complementary, supplementary,* or *neither.*

1.
45°
45°

2.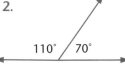
110° 70°

3.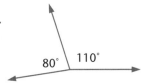
80° 110°

Classify each pair of angles as *complementary, supplementary,* or *neither.*

1.
35°
55°

2.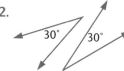
30° 30°

3.
135°
45°

4.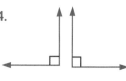

Find the value of *x* in each figure.

5.
25°
x

6.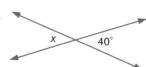
x 40°

7.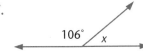
106° x

8.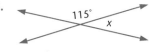
115°
x

9.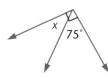
x
75°

10.
72° x

For exercises 11–14, use the figure at the right.

11. Name two pairs of complementary angles.

12. Name three pairs of supplementary angles.

13. Suppose m∠BFC is 65°. What is m∠AFB?

14. Suppose m∠EFD is 58°. What is m∠DFC?

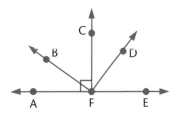

15. Two complementary angles have the same measure. What is the measure of each angle?

★16. If ∠a and ∠b are supplementary and m∠a = x + 50 and m∠b = x + 100, what are the measures of ∠a and ∠b?

Objective: to interpret parallel and perpendicular lines

In the photograph of the Lincoln Memorial, you can see many examples of perpendicular, parallel, and skew lines.

Parallel lines are lines in the same plane that do not intersect. **Perpendicular lines** intersect to form right angles. **Skew lines** are lines in different planes that neither intersect nor are parallel.

> The symbol ⊥ means "is perpendicular to."
> The symbol ∥ means "is parallel to."

Exploration Exercise

Parallel Lines Discovery

1. Use a piece of loose-leaf paper to draw two parallel lines as shown to the right.

2. Draw a **transversal**, a line that intersects the parallel lines.

3. Label the angles as shown in the diagram.

4. Use a protractor to measure all of the angles.

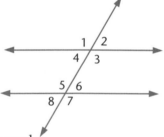

What do you notice about the measures of ∠2 and ∠6? These two angles are called **corresponding angles**. What other angle pairs have the same relationship as ∠2 and ∠6?

What do you notice about the measures of ∠4 and ∠6? These two angles are called **alternate interior angles**. What other angle pair has the same relationship as ∠4 and ∠6?

What do you notice about the measures of ∠1 and ∠7? These two angles are called **alternate exterior angles**. What other angle pair has the same relationship as ∠1 and ∠7?

Angle Relationships

Alternate interior angles	Angles are equal in measure.	∠4 and ∠6, ∠3 and ∠5
Alternate exterior angles	Angles are equal in measure.	∠1 and ∠7, ∠2 and ∠8
Corresponding angles	Angles are equal in measure.	∠2 and ∠6, ∠3 and ∠7, ∠1 and ∠5, ∠4 and ∠8
Vertical angles	Angles are equal in measure.	∠1 and ∠3, ∠2 and ∠4, ∠5 and ∠7, ∠6 and ∠8

Examples

A. If m∠8 = 80°, find m ∠4.

   ∠8 and ∠4 are corresponding angles,
   therefore they are equal.

   m∠4 = 80°

B. If m∠3 = 100°, find m∠5.

   ∠3 and ∠5 are alternate interior angles,
   therefore they are equal.

   m∠5 = 100°

Try THESE

Use the diagram to the right. Lines *l* and *m* are parallel.

1. Name the alternate interior angles.
2. Name the vertical angles.
3. Name the corresponding angles.
4. Name the alternate exterior angles.

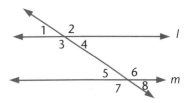

Exercises

Use the diagram to the right to answer questions 1–6. Lines *r* and *q* are parallel.

1. What relationship do ∠5 and ∠1 share?
2. Name three angles that have the same measure as ∠2.
3. If m∠4 = 100°, then m∠6 = _____.
4. If m∠5 = 80°, then m∠7 = _____.
5. If m∠2 = 100°, then m∠3 = _____.
6. If m∠2 = 100°, then m∠8 = _____.

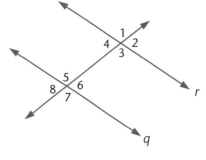

The cube at the right is formed by six squares. The edges of the squares meet at right angles. Describe each pair of segments as *perpendicular*, *parallel*, or *skew*.

7. $\overline{AD}$, $\overline{EH}$

8. $\overline{EH}$, $\overline{AE}$

9. $\overline{CG}$, $\overline{DH}$

10. $\overline{AD}$, $\overline{GH}$

11. $\overline{FG}$, $\overline{HG}$

12. $\overline{AB}$, $\overline{GH}$

Objective: to use a compass and a straightedge to construct lines

L'Enfant's original plan for Washington, DC, was modified by two surveyors, Andrew Ellicott and Benjamin Banneker. A surveyor is a person who determines the form, boundaries, extent, and position of a piece of land. Surveyors need to use specialized tools in their work.

Two important tools in geometry are the **compass** and **straightedge**.

A straightedge is any object that can be used to draw a straight line. A compass is an A-shaped instrument that usually has a metal point and a pencil or lead point. A compass is used to draw circles or parts of circles.

Drawings that are made with only a compass and a straightedge are called **constructions**.

Constructions

A. Construct equal lines.

   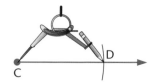

1. Draw a line segment. Label the endpoints A and B.

2. Draw a ray with endpoint C. The drawing of the ray should be longer than $\overline{AB}$.

3. Open your compass to match $\overline{AB}$.

4. Use the same compass setting with the point at C. Draw an arc intersecting the ray at point D.

B. Construct perpendicular lines. *Given:*

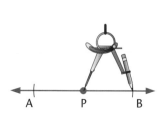 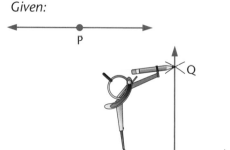

1. With the compass point at P, draw arcs intersecting the line at A and B.

2. Use a large compass setting to draw arcs from A and B that intersect at Q. Draw $\overleftrightarrow{PQ}$. $\overleftrightarrow{PQ} \perp \overleftrightarrow{AB}$.

C. Construct parallel lines.   *Given:*

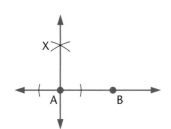

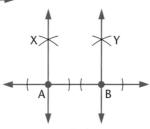

1. Construct a line perpendicular to $\overleftrightarrow{AB}$ at point A. $\overrightarrow{AX} \perp \overrightarrow{AB}$.

2. Construct $\overleftrightarrow{BY}$ perpendicular to $\overleftrightarrow{AB}$. Explain why $\overleftrightarrow{AX} \parallel \overleftrightarrow{BY}$.

Exercises ....

Draw each line. Construct a line perpendicular to each line at the point on the line.

1.

2.

Draw each line. Construct parallel lines through the two points on each line.

3.

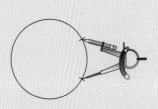

4.

Mind BUILDER

Constructing a Hexagon

Follow these steps to construct a six-sided figure.

    a. First use the compass to draw a circle.

    b. Using the same compass setting, put the metal point on the circle, and draw a small notch on the circle.

    c. Move the compass point to the notch, and then draw another notch along the circle.

    d. Continue doing this until you have six notches.

    e. Use a straightedge to connect the notches in order.

    This six-sided figure is called a hexagon.

Objective: to construct segment and angle bisectors

The Mall in Washington, DC, is the long, straight pathway that leads to the Washington Monument.

If you want to find the halfway point between the Capitol and the Washington Monument, bisect the line segment. **Bisect** means to divide into two **congruent** (same size and same shape) parts.

You can use a compass and straightedge to bisect a line or an angle.

A compass is used to draw a circle or part of a circle called an **arc**. An arc has two endpoints on the circle.

Constructions

A. Bisect a given line segment.

Given: written as segment $\overline{AB}$

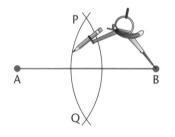

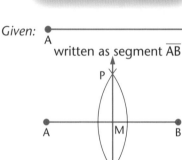

1. Open the compass to more than half the length of $\overline{AB}$, and draw an arc.

2. With the same setting, draw another arc from B. Label the intersection points P and Q.

3. Draw PQ. This line bisects $\overline{AB}$. Point M is called the midpoint of $\overline{AB}$.

B. Bisect a given angle.

Given:

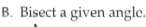

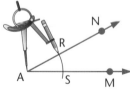

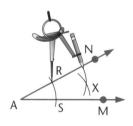

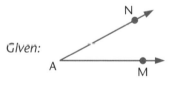

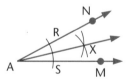

1. Draw an arc from A. Label intersection points R and S.

2. Draw arcs from points R and S intersecting at X.

3. Draw $\overrightarrow{AX}$. This ray bisects /NAM.

Exercises

Trace each figure. Then bisect it.

1.

2.

3.
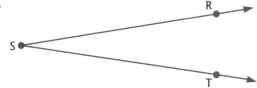

4.

5. Use a protractor to draw a 150° angle. Then use a compass and straightedge to bisect the angle.

Problem SOLVING

6. Using only a compass and a straightedge, draw a line segment. Separate it into four congruent segments.

7. Draw an obtuse angle using only a compass and a straightedge. Separate it into four congruent angles.

8. If an acute angle is bisected, what type of angle is each of the two angles formed?

9. If a right angle is bisected, what type of angle is each of the two angles formed?

10. If an obtuse angle is bisected, what type of angle is each of the two angles formed?

Constructed RESPONSE

11. In general, if any angle is bisected, what type of angle is each of the two angles formed? Explain why.

Objective: to solve problems using a Venn diagram

In a recent survey of middle school students about pizza toppings, it was found that 25 students like pepperoni pizza, 31 like mushroom pizza, and 5 like both pepperoni and mushroom pizza. If 65 students were surveyed, how many like some other topping on their pizza?

You know how many students were surveyed. You know how many like pepperoni pizza and mushroom pizza. You need to find out how many students do not like either topping.

Use a **Venn diagram** to show all possibilities. Find the number of students who like only pepperoni and only mushroom.

Pepperoni 25 – 5 = 20   **Mushroom 31 – 5 = 26**

Pizza Toppings

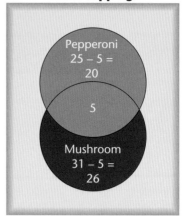

Pepperoni
25 – 5 = 20

5

Mushroom
31 – 5 = 26

The rectangle represents 65 students. One circle represents the students who like pepperoni; the other circle represents the students who like mushroom. The intersection represents the students who like both.

There are 20 students who only like pepperoni, 26 students who only like mushroom, and 5 students who like both.

20 + 26 + 5 = 51   **65 – 51 = 14**

There are 14 students who do not like pepperoni or mushroom.

The total possibilities should be 65.

20 + 26 + 5 + 15 = 65   The answer is correct and reasonable.

Exercises

Use the Venn diagram to answer questions 1–5.

1. How many people play both tennis and golf?

2. What is the total number who play tennis?

3. How many play only golf?

4. How many play golf, tennis, and baseball?

5. How many play golf and baseball?

Sports Played

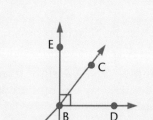

6. During lunch, 125 middle school students were surveyed about what they eat for lunch. There are 36 students who only eat a sandwich for lunch, 25 students who only eat a hamburger for lunch, and 21 students who only eat a piece of pizza for lunch. If 14 only eat a sandwich and a hamburger, and 9 only eat a sandwich and a piece of pizza for lunch, how many only eat a hamburger and a piece of pizza assuming no one eats all three?

7. Of 200 students at Hill Junior High, 68 have blonde hair and 115 have brown eyes. There are 20 students who have blonde hair and brown eyes. How many have blonde hair but not brown eyes?

8. Of 95 families polled, 24 have a red car, 14 have a silver car, and 42 have neither a red car nor a silver car. How many have both a red and a silver car?

Constructed RESPONSE

9. Make a Venn diagram that shows the factors for 20 and 30.

10. Draw a Venn diagram of the whole numbers less than 20. Place the even numbers in Set A and the multiplies of 3 in Set B. Are there any even numbers that are a multiple of 3? Explain.

Mid-Chapter REVIEW

Use the figure at the right to name the following.

1. right angles

2. acute angles

3. obtuse angles

4. adjacent angles

5. complementary angles

6. supplementary angles

7. Find the m∠EBC if m∠CBD = 27°.

8. Find the m∠DBF.

Objective: to classify triangles

Exploration Exercise

How many degrees are in a triangle?

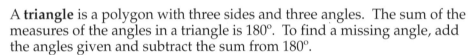

1. Cut out any triangle from a sheet of paper.

2. Label each angle.

3. Tear off each of the three angles.

4. Draw a line, and place point P on the line.

5. Place angles A, B, and C on the line so that their vertices are on point P.

6. The angles of a triangle form a straight line. What is the sum of the measures of the angles?

A **triangle** is a polygon with three sides and three angles. The sum of the measures of the angles in a triangle is 180°. To find a missing angle, add the angles given and subtract the sum from 180°.

Triangles can be classified by sides.

A **scalene triangle** has no congruent sides.	An **isosceles triangle** has two congruent sides.	An **equilateral triangle** (or regular triangle) has three congruent sides.

▷ The matching blue marks indicate congruent parts.

Triangles can also be classified by angles. In every triangle, there are at least two acute angles. You can use the third angle to classify a triangle.

An **acute triangle** has all acute angles (less than 90°).	A **right triangle** has a right angle (90°).	An **obtuse triangle** has an obtuse angle (greater than 90°).

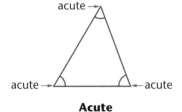

Acute

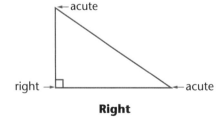

Right

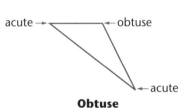

Obtuse

Example

Find the missing angle.

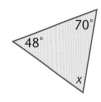

$x + 48° + 70° = 180°$ The sum of the angles is 180°.

$x + 118° = 180°$ Add 48° and 70°.

$x = 62°$ Subtract 118° from both sides.

The missing angle is 62°.

Try THESE ···

Classify each triangle by sides and angles.

1.
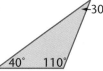

2.

3.

Exercises ···

Find the missing angle measure in each triangle. Then classify each triangle as *acute*, *right* or *obtuse*.

1.

2.

3.

4.

Classify each triangle as *scalene*, *isosceles*, or *equilateral*.

5.

6.

7.

8.

★ 9. Find the third angle of a right triangle if the measure of one of the angles is 25°.

10. Three angles of a triangle measure 65°, 80°, and 35°. Classify the triangle by its angles.

Using graph paper, draw an example of each of the following triangles.

11. scalene   12. isosceles   13. obtuse   14. acute

15. isosceles, right   ★16. scalene, obtuse   ★17. equilateral, acute

State whether each statement is *true* or *false*.

18. All equilateral triangles are acute triangles.

19. Some isosceles triangles are also right triangles.

20. All right triangles are scalene triangles.

21. Some obtuse triangles are equilateral triangles.

Problem SOLVING ·

22. Draw a scalene right triangle with one angle that measures 60°. What are the measures of the other angles?

★23. In an isosceles right triangle the other two angles are congruent. What are their measures?

24. An A-frame house is in the shape of a triangle. Each angle measures 60°. What type of triangle is the frame?

25. A slice of pizza is in the shape of a triangle. Classify the triangle by sides and angles.

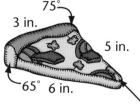

Mind BUILDER

Optical Illusions

A figure that is misleading to a person's sense of sight is called an **optical illusion**. Geometric figures, such as points and lines, can be arranged to create such an image. You should not assume something is true in geometry just by appearance.

Look at the optical illusions below. Make a guess. Then use a ruler to check your guess.

1. Which segment on the upper left forms a straight line with the segment on the lower right?

2. Which segment is the longest?

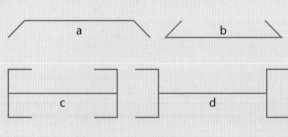

Perspective is the way things look to us. Name two different perspectives of each figure.

3.

4.

Cumulative Review

Replace each ● with <, >, or = to make a true statement.

1. 3.2 ● 32
2. 5.4 ● 0.54
3. 16.0 ● 16
4. 7.63 ● 6.79
5. 0.14 ● 0.41
6. 6.003 ● 6.03

Estimate.

7. $\begin{array}{r} 6.725 \\ + 2.049 \\ \hline \end{array}$
8. $\begin{array}{r} 792 \\ - 435 \\ \hline \end{array}$
9. $\begin{array}{r} 8.16 \\ \times \ 3.9 \\ \hline \end{array}$
10. $\begin{array}{r} 507 \\ \times \ 64 \\ \hline \end{array}$
11. $2.8\overline{)\$12.36}$

Find the value of each expression.

12. 7^2
13. 2^4
14. 12^2
15. 10^3
16. 3^3
17. $5 \times 6 \div 10 + 1$
18. $12 + 6 \div 3 - 5$
19. $7 - 2 \times 8 \div 4$
20. $5^2 - 6 \times 2$
21. $17 - 2^3 + 5$
22. $27 \div 3^2 \times 2$
23. $8 \times (3 + 2)$
24. $(7 + 3) \div 5$
25. $3^3 \times 2 - 5 \times 3$

Compute.

26. -3 + 2
27. 5 − 7
28. -2 • 7
29. 48 ÷ -6
30. 5 • -9
31. -6 + -5
32. -12 − 4
33. -64 ÷ -8

Use the Venn diagram to answer the following questions.

34. How many students have seen only the *Lion King*?

35. How many students have seen *Annie* and *Peter Pan*?

36. How many students have seen *Lion King* and *Peter Pan*?

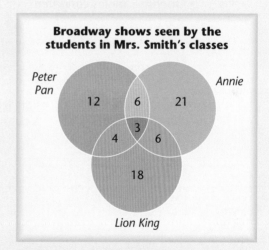

Broadway shows seen by the students in Mrs. Smith's classes

Peter Pan · Annie · Lion King

Solve.

37. Rachel's quiz scores are 25, 20, and 21. Find the average score.

38. What is the measure of an angle that is complementary to a 68° angle?

39. Sarah buys two loaves of bread for $3.56 and a gallon of milk for $2.59. How much change does she receive from $7.00?

40. Miss Moreno is paid $8.25 an hour as a practical nurse. She works a 37.5-hour week. To the nearest cent, how much is she paid for a 7.5-hour day?

Objective: to classify quadrilaterals

Originally, Washington was to be a "ten-mile-square Federal District" that included the town of Alexandria, Virginia. In 1846, the residents of Alexandria convinced Congress to return the city and all land to the west of the Potomac River to the state of Virginia.

A square is a **quadrilateral** because it has four sides. Quadrilaterals are classified using one or more of the following characteristics.

- parallel sides
- congruent sides
- congruent angles

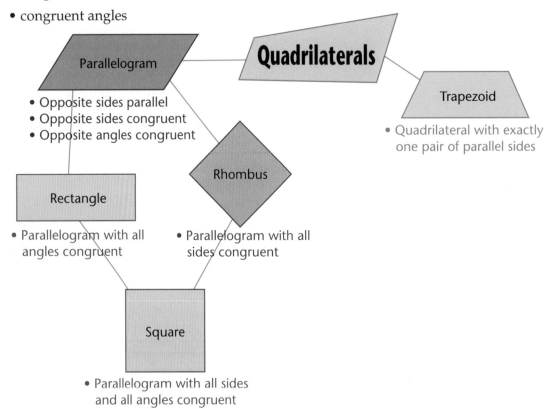

Quadrilaterals

Parallelogram
- Opposite sides parallel
- Opposite sides congruent
- Opposite angles congruent

Trapezoid
- Quadrilateral with exactly one pair of parallel sides

Rhombus

Rectangle
- Parallelogram with all angles congruent

- Parallelogram with all sides congruent

Square
- Parallelogram with all sides and all angles congruent

A square is a **regular polygon**. A regular polygon is a polygon with all sides congruent and all angles congruent.

....

Classify each quadrilateral using the name that best describes it.

1.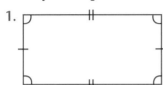

2.

3.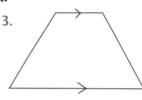

4.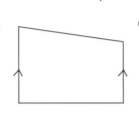

5.

6.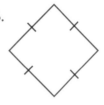

7.

State whether each statement is *true* or *false*.

8. All rectangles are squares.

9. All squares are rectangles.

10. Every rhombus is a rectangle.

11. Every parallelogram is a quadrilateral.

12. Some quadrilaterals are trapezoids.

13. Not every parallelogram is a rectangle.

14. A trapezoid is a regular polygon.

Problem SOLVING ....

15. Why is a trapezoid not a parallelogram?

16. Can a quadrilateral be formed by two triangles? If yes, draw an example.

Test PREP ....

17. Which property is not a characteristic of a parallelogram?

    a. opposite sides are congruent   **b.** all angles are congruent

    c. opposite sides are parallel   **d.** opposite angles are congruent

18. Which quadrilateral has four congruent sides?

    a. trapezoid   **b.** parallelogram

    c. rhombus   **d.** rectangle

7.9 Polygons and Angle Measures

Objective: to find the measures of angles in polygons

Exploration Exercise

The sum of the measures of the angles in a **polygon** is determined by separating the interior of the polygon into triangles. Remember that the sum of the measures of the angles of any triangle is 180°.

1. Complete the chart below.

Polygon	Number of Sides	Number of Triangles	Sum of Measures of Angles
Quadrilateral	4	2	360°
Pentagon			
Hexagon			
Heptagon			
Octagon			
Nonagon			
Decagon			

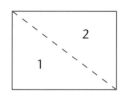

2. Look for patterns in the table. What do you notice about the number of sides and the number of triangles?

3. What formula can you write for the sum of the measures of the angles of a polygon with n sides?

In the exploration above, you discovered that you can use the formula $(n - 2) \cdot 180°$ to find the sum of the measures of the angles in a polygon.

Examples

A. Find the sum of the angles of a 12-sided figure.

n = number of sides = 12

$(12 - 2) \cdot 180 =$

$10 \cdot 180 = 1,800°$

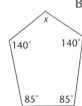

B. Find the missing angle.
This is a pentagon, a 5-sided figure.

$(5 - 2) \cdot 180 = 540°$

$540 - (85 + 85 + 140 + 140) = 90°$

The missing angle is 90°.

Use the formula $(n - 2) \cdot 180$ to find the sum of the measures of the following polygons.

1. 14-sided polygon
2. 20-sided polygon
3. 25-sided polygon

Use the formula to find the sum of the measures of the following polygons.

1. 15-sided polygon
2. 50-sided polygon
3. 100-sided polygon

Find the missing angles.

4.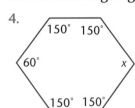

5.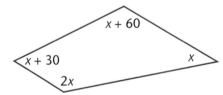

6.

7.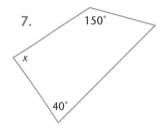

★ 8. Find the value of x, and then find the measure of each angle.

Find the number of sides of a polygon with the following sum of the measures of the angles.

9. sum = 2,700°
10. sum = 16,020°
11. sum = 2,160°

You know the quadrilateral properties and that the sum of the measures of the angles of a quadrilateral is 360°. Use these facts to answer questions 12–15.

12. What is the degree measure of each angle of a square or a rectangle?

13. One angle of a parallelogram measures 30°. Find the measures of the other angles.

14. A rhombus has an angle that measures 122°. What are the measures of the other angles?

★ 15. A trapezoid has two angles that measure 60° each. What are the measures of the other two angles?

7.10 Similar and Congruent Figures

Objective: to solve problems using similar and congruent figures

The United States government designs, engraves, and prints money and stamps at the Bureau of Engraving and Printing. All of the stamps shown have the same shape but are not all the same size.

In geometry, figures that have the same size and shape are **congruent**. Line segments, angles, and figures may be congruent. Figures that have the same shape but different sizes are **similar**. When you reduce or enlarge a figure, the new figure is similar to the original. The figures below show the **corresponding parts** of similar and congruent polygons.

Similar Polygons	Congruent Polygons
△ABC ~ △XYZ	△DEF ≅ △MNO
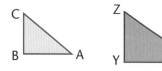	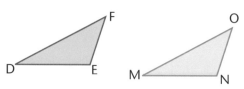
Angles: Corresponding angles are congruent. ∠A ≅ ∠X, ∠B ≅ ∠Y, ∠C ≅ ∠Z	**Angles:** Corresponding angles are congruent. ∠D ≅ ∠M, ∠E ≅ ∠N, ∠F ≅ ∠O
Sides: Measures of corresponding sides are proportional. $$\frac{AB}{XY} = \frac{BC}{YZ} = \frac{AC}{XZ}$$	**Sides:** Corresponding sides are congruent. DE ≅ MN, EF ≅ NO, DF ≅ MO

When naming similar or congruent figures, you must list the letters for the vertices in the same order. The symbol ≅ means "is congruent to," and the symbol ~ means "is similar to."

Examples

A. △RST ≅ △UVW List all the corresponding parts.

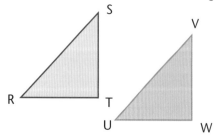

Corresponding sides
ST ≅ VW
RT ≅ UW
RS ≅ UV

Corresponding angles
∠R ≅ ∠U
∠S ≅ ∠V
∠T ≅ ∠W

B. The two rectangles are similar. Find the missing length.

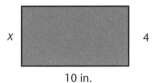

x

4 in.

10 in.

5 in.

To find the value of *x*,
write and solve a proportion.

smaller figure → $\dfrac{5}{10} = \dfrac{4}{x}$ ← **smaller figure**
larger figure → ← **larger figure**

$$5x = 10 \cdot 4$$
$$5x = 40$$
$$x = 8$$

The missing length *x* is 8 inches.

Try THESE ·

Name the corresponding parts.

1.

2.

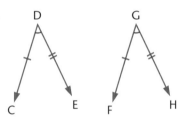

Exercises ·

Answer the following knowing that △MNO ≅ △SQR.

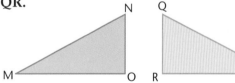

1. Which side of △MNO is congruent to QS?

2. Which angle of △QSR is congruent to ∠M?

3. Which side of △QSR is congruent to MO?

4. Which angle of △MNO is congruent to ∠R?

List the corresponding parts for each pair of congruent figures.

5.

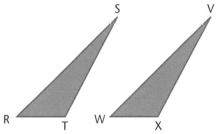

6.

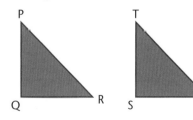

7.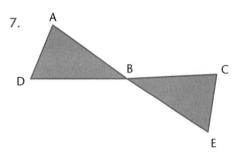

8.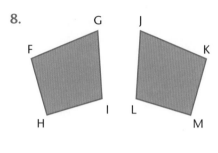

Find the missing length for each pair of similar figures.

9. 4m 2m 9m a

10. d 1.5 m / 2.2 m 3.3 m

11. 1.2 cm 1.4 cm / 3.5 cm s

12.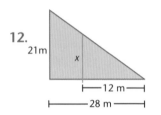
21m / x / 12 m / 28 m

13.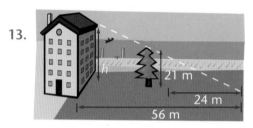
h / 21 m / 24 m / 56 m

14. The width of a photograph is 6 inches. Its length is 10 inches. The photograph is enlarged so that the width is 18 inches. What is the length of the enlarged photograph?

15. An advertising layout measures 4 inches by 12 inches. An enlargement makes the width 6.5 inches. What is the new length?

★16. A 3-inch by 5-inch photograph is enlarged so that its area is 9 times larger. Find the width and length of the enlarged photograph.

Draw the triangles below with the given conditions.

17. Draw △RST with the following conditions:
   - $\overline{RS}$ is 3 cm long.
   - m∠R is 30°.
   - $\overline{ST}$ is 2 cm long.
   - Draw $\overline{RT}$.

18. Let's change the conditions slightly. Draw another triangle with the following conditions:
   - $\overline{RS}$ is 3 cm long.
   - m∠S is 30°.
   - $\overline{ST}$ is 2 cm long.
   - Draw $\overline{RT}$.

19. Compare your triangles from problems 17 and 18. Are they congruent?

Problem Solving

Mrs. O'Grady's Kennel

Mrs. O'Grady buys a square building to use as a dog kennel for very large dogs. She thinks that she can house nine dogs in this kennel in the formation shown below. However, she feels that it would be best if there were a fence separating the dogs. She calls in the fencing company and asks them to build two square fences so that no two dogs share the same area. The fencing company is confused. Can you help?

Extension

Trace the dot pattern at the right. Without lifting your pencil from the paper, draw four line segments that connect all the points.

Objective: to draw solid figures

It is sometimes difficult to visualize three-dimensional objects drawn on paper. Three-dimensional objects are called solids. Probably the most familiar solid is a **cube**.

To draw a three-dimensional figure, it is helpful to use a special kind of dot paper called isometric dot paper. The cube at the right is drawn on isometric dot paper.

Example

Suppose you were given directions to make a solid. The pattern specified what the base, side, and front of the solid looked like.

Base

Side

Front

Use isometric dot paper to complete the drawing.

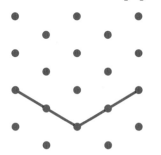

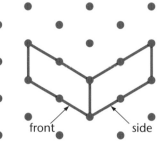
front   side

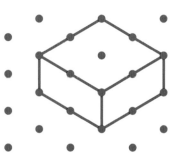

Another Example

Draw a solid given these views.

Base

Side

Front

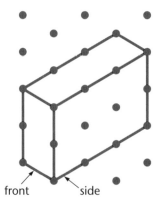
front   side

Determine which figure at the right matches each pattern for the base, side, and front.

1.

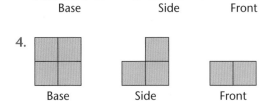

Base   Side   Front

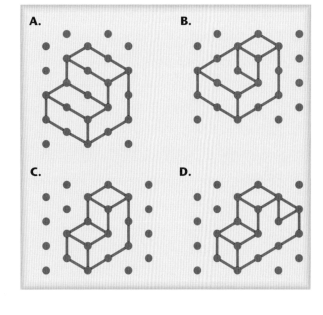

A.

B.

C.

D.

2.

Base   Side   Front

3.

Base   Side   Front

4.

Base   Side   Front

MiXeD REVIEW

Suppose the streets on the map below represent lines or line segments. Find examples of each figure.

5. parallel lines   6. perpendicular lines   7. an obtuse angle

8. adjacent angles   9. supplementary angles   10. a right triangle

11. an acute triangle   12. a square   13. a rectangle

14. a trapezoid

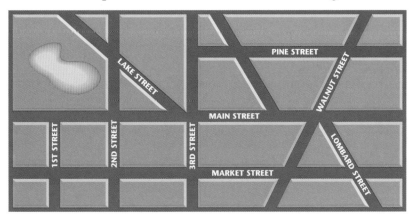

Write *true* or *false*. If *false*, replace the underlined word or phrase to make a true sentence.

1. An angle is formed by two rays with a common endpoint called a <u>vertex</u>.

2. Two angles are <u>supplementary</u> if the sum of their measures is 90°.

3. You can measure angles with a <u>compass</u>.

4. To <u>bisect</u> an angle means to separate it into two congruent parts.

5. <u>Skew</u> lines are lines in the same plane that do not intersect.

6. Figures that have the same size and shape are <u>congruent</u>.

7. A <u>decagon</u> is a polygon with eight sides.

8. Triangles can be classified by sides and <u>angles</u>.

9. A <u>parallelogram</u> is a quadrilateral with two pairs of parallel sides.

10. A square is a <u>quadrilateral</u> because it has four sides.

Skills and Problem Solving

Use the figure at the right for exercises 11–15. Section 7.1

11. Give another name for ∠1.

12. Name the vertex of ∠2.

13. Name the sides of ∠TCE.

14. Measure ∠HCE.

15. Measure ∠ACH.

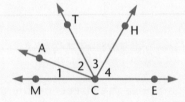

Use the figure at the right for exercises 16–19. Classify each angle as *acute, right,* or *obtuse*. Section 7.1

16. ∠PTS   17. ∠RTS

18. ∠STQ   19. ∠QTR

Use the figure at the right for exercises 20–24. Section 7.2

20. Name an angle complementary to ∠CFD.

21. Name an angle supplementary to ∠DFE.

22. Name an angle adjacent to ∠AFB.

23. Suppose m∠CFD is 40°. What is m∠DFE?

24. What is the m∠BFE?

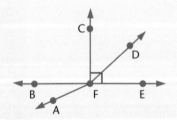

Use the figure at the right for exercises 25–29. Line *l* is parallel to line *m*. **Section 7.3**

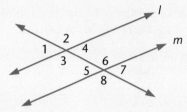

25. Name the alternate interior angles.

26. What relationship do ∠2 and ∠8 share?

27. If m∠1 = 65°, then m∠3 = _____.

28. If m∠6 = 115°, then m∠2 = _____.

29. If m∠1 = 65°, then m∠5 = _____.

Use a compass and straightedge to complete each construction. Section 7.4

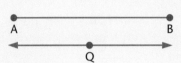

30. Draw the segment at the right. Bisect the segment.

31. Draw the line at the right. Construct a line perpendicular to the line at point Q.

Find the missing angle in each triangle. Classify each triangle as *acute*, *right*, or *obtuse*. Section 7.7

32.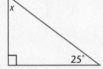

33.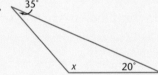

34.

Classify each quadrilateral using the name that best describes it. Section 7.8

35.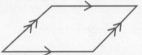

36.

37.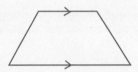

Use the formula to find the sum of the measures of the following polygons. Section 7.9

38. a pentagon

39. an octagon

40. a 12-sided polygon

List the corresponding parts for the congruent polygons. Section 7.10

41.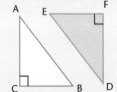

Solve. Section 7.6

42. Of 200 people asked, 115 people said they have a dog, 55 said they have a cat, and 5 said they have both a dog and a cat. How many people have neither a dog nor a cat?

43. There were 185 people asked about their favorite school subject. Of those people, 27 said only math, 55 said only science, and 62 said neither. How many said both, math and science?

Use symbols to name each angle. Then measure each angle and classify it as *acute*, *right*, or *obtuse*.

1.

2.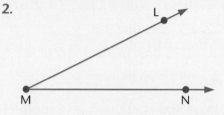

3. What is the measure of an angle supplementary to ∠RST above?

4. What is the measure of an angle complementary to ∠LMN above?

Use the figure at the right to name each of the following.

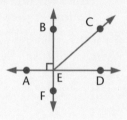

5. right angles

6. acute angles

7. obtuse angles

8. supplementary angles

9. perpendicular lines

10. complementary angles

Use a compass and straightedge to complete each construction.

11. Trace the angle at the right. Bisect the angle.

12. Trace the line at the right. Construct parallel lines through points Y and Z.

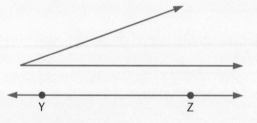

Classify each triangle and quadrilateral. Find the missing angles.

13.

14.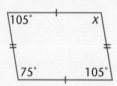

15.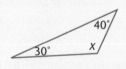

16.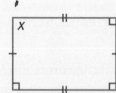

Solve.

17. A rectangular poster has a length of 28 inches and a width of 22 inches. A print of the poster is similar to the original and has a length of 14 inches. What is the width of the print?

Draw a Venn diagram, and solve.

18. In a recent poll of 50 people at an ice-cream store, 25 people liked only vanilla, 28 liked only chocolate, and 8 liked both. How many people did not like either vanilla or chocolate?

Circles

Locate and label a point O any place on your paper. With a ruler, mark off a point 2 centimeters from point O. Going all the way around point O, continue marking ten additional points 2 centimeters from the given point. If all these points were connected, a circle would be formed.

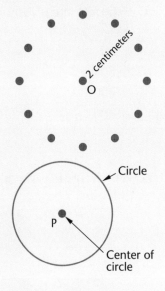

A **circle** is the set of points in a plane that are the same distance from a fixed point. The fixed point is called the **center of the circle**.

A circle is named by its center. The center of the circle at the right is point P.

Say: Circle P

Write: ⊙P

Examples

Special segments in a circle can be identified because of the location of their endpoints.

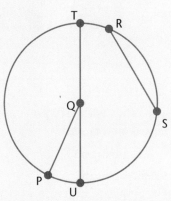

- $\overline{PQ}$ is a radius. The endpoints of this segment are at the center of the circle and any point on the circle.

- $\overline{RS}$ is a chord. Both endpoints of this segment are on the circle.

- $\overline{TU}$ is a diameter. Both endpoints of this segment are on the circle. What makes this segment different from $\overline{RS}$?

State whether each statement is *true* or *false*.

1. Every diameter of a circle is a chord.

2. Every chord of a circle is a diameter.

3. A circle is a simple closed curve.

4. A circle is a polygon.

5. The lengths of all radii in a circle are different.

Cumulative Test

1. Estimate the quotient.
   248.7 ÷ 6.4
   a. 40
   b. 60
   c. 400
   d. 600

2. Find the difference of
   67.32 and 6.518.
   a. 0.224
   b. 2.24
   c. 60.802
   d. 73.838

3. Which two figures can
   also be squares?
   a. circle, quadrilateral
   b. parallelogram,
      trapezoid
   c. rectangle, rhombus
   d. none of the above

4. Which figure is not a
   polygon?

   a.   b.

   c.   d.

5. Which two angles are
   obtuse angles?

   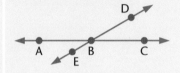

   a. ∠ABD, ∠ABE
   b. ∠ABD, ∠CBE
   c. ∠ABE, ∠CBE
   d. ∠ABE, ∠DBC

6. A roll of stamps costs
   $25.00. How much do 10
   rolls cost?
   a. $2.50
   b. $35.00
   c. $250.00
   d. $275.00

7. What is the shape
   of a stop sign?
   a. hexagon
   b. octagon
   c. pentagon
   d. quadrilateral

8. The measure of ∠HGJ
   is 49°. What is the
   measure of ∠FGJ?
   a. 41°
   b. 90°
   c. 131°
   d. none of the above

   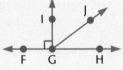

9. A can of tomato soup contains
   12 ounces. How many ounces are there
   in 48 cans?
   a. 4
   b. 36
   c. 60
   d. 576

10. Which inequality is false?
   a. 2.41 > 2.14
   b. 0.38 > 0.29
   c. 4.83 < 3.94
   d. 6.15 < 7.03

CHAPTER 8

Geometry and Measurement

Katherine Kauffman
Calvert Day School

Objective: to give the precision of measurements

Bill mounts his butterfly collection in a display box. He measures the wingspan of a red admiral to find a place for it.

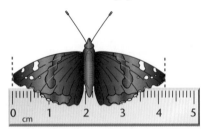

To the nearest centimeter, it measures 4 cm.

To the nearest millimeter, it measures 42 mm.

The more precise measurement is 42 mm.

> *Precision* depends upon the unit of measure used. The smaller the unit of measure, the greater the precision of the measurement.

The difference between the true length and the measured length is called the **error of measurement**. The greatest possible error is 0.5, or one-half the unit of measure. The **relative error** is the greatest possible error divided by the measured value.

The wingspan of the butterfly measured in centimeters can vary no more than 0.5 cm either way. The butterfly is at least 3.5 cm long but less than 4.5 cm long.

More Examples

The examples below list several measurements and their precision.

Measurement	Precision	Greatest Possible Error	Relative Error
A. 4 mm	nearest millimeter	0.5 mm	$0.5 \div 4 = 0.125$ mm
B. 19 m	nearest meter	0.5 m	$0.5 \div 19 = 0.0263$ m
C. 20 m	nearest 10 meters	5 m	$5 \div 20 = 0.25$ m
D. 6.25 cm	nearest 0.01 centimeter	0.005 cm	$0.005 \div 6.25 - 0.0008$ cm

***Try* THESE** ···

Name the more precise measurement in each of the following.

1. 2.300 m, 2 km
2. 457 mm, 46 cm
3. 6.8 m, 68.3 cm
4. 8 m, 790 cm
5. 2.8 km, 2,790 m
6. 355 mm, 35 cm
7. 5 cm, 49 mm
8. 2 m, 1,960 mm
9. 370 m, 0.4 km

Exercises

Give the precision of each measurement.

1. 6 m
2. 17 cm
3. 495 km
4. 1,294 mm
5. 6.7 cm
6. 160 cm
7. 8.3 m
8. 3.06 km
9. 15,000 cm
10. 1,850 km
11. 1,300 mm
12. 9.04 m

★13. Which measure is more precise, 3.4 cm or 34 mm?

Give the shortest and longest true length possible for each measurement.

14. 146 cm
15. 63 mm
16. 182 m
17. 43 km
★18. 10 mm
★19. 360 km

Give the greatest possible error and the relative error for each measurement.

20. 15 mm
21. 362 m
22. 1 km
23. 31 m
★24. 7.8 mm
★25. 8.0 cm

Problem SOLVING

26. Tamara and Ayashe each measure a board that is 15 cm long. Tamara writes 14.6 cm, and Ayashe writes 151 mm. Are both measurements within the greatest possible error? Explain your answer.

★27. If 56.7 represents a number rounded to the nearest tenth, what is the least possible and the greatest possible number that was rounded?

Mind BUILDER

Accuracy

Precision and accuracy are often thought of as being the same thing. However, there is a big difference between the two. Precision tells how close two measurements are when measured with the same instrument. Accuracy tells how closely a measurement agrees with the true measure.

Precision

Accuracy

Look at the dart boards pictured. Precision describes how close together the darts are when they hit the board. Accuracy describes how close the darts come to the center of the board.

1. Can you think of a situation where the accuracy is good and the precision is poor?

2. Can you think of a situation where the accuracy is poor and the precision is good?

Objective: to find the area and perimeter of parallelograms

Recall that the size of a polygon can be indicated in two different ways. One is the **perimeter**, which is the distance around the polygon. The other is **area**, the number of square units that cover the surface.

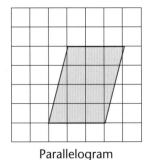

Rectangle   Parallelogram

Exploration Exercise

1. Look at the rectangle to the right. Find the area of the rectangle by counting the units.

2. Look at the parallelogram. Find the area of the parallelogram by counting the units.

3. What is the relationship between the area of the rectangle and the area of the parallelogram?

4. To find the area of a rectangle, you multiply the length by the width. How do you find the area of a parallelogram?

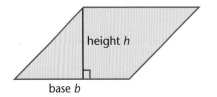

Area = base • height
$A = b • h$

To find the area of a parallelogram, you can multiply the base b and the height h. Any side can be the base. The height is the length of the segment that is perpendicular to the base and extends to the opposite side.

Examples

A. Find the area of the parallelogram.

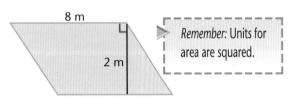

Remember: Units for area are squared.

$A = b • h$
$= 8 \text{ m} • 2 \text{ m}$
$= 16 \text{ m}^2$

B. Find the perimeter of the parallelogram.

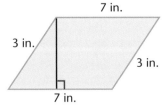

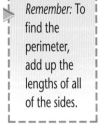

Remember: To find the perimeter, add up the lengths of all of the sides.

$P = 7 \text{ in.} + 3 \text{ in.} + 7 \text{ in.} + 3 \text{ in.}$
$= 20 \text{ in.}$

Label the height and base in each parallelogram.

1. 6 m
4.2 m 3 m

2. $5\frac{1}{3}$ cm
$12\frac{1}{2}$ cm $8\frac{1}{4}$ cm

3. 6 ft
8 ft 15 ft

Exercises •

Find the area and perimeter of each parallelogram.

1. 5 cm
14 cm 12 cm

2. 10.8 ft
2.3 ft 5.1 ft

3. 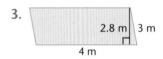 2.8 m 3 m
4 m

4. $15\frac{1}{2}$ in.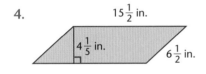
$4\frac{1}{5}$ in. $6\frac{1}{2}$ in.

5. 9 mm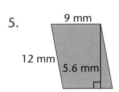
12 mm 5.6 mm

6. 4.1 cm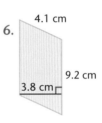
9.2 cm
3.8 cm

Find the area of each parallelogram.

7. base = 12 in.

   height = 7 in.

8. base = 14.5 m

   height = 12.3 m

9. base = $6\frac{2}{3}$ cm

   height = $8\frac{1}{2}$ cm

Problem SOLVING •

10. What is the area of a parallelogram if its base is 30 ft and its height is twice the size of its base?

★11. Two parallelograms have the same area. Do they necessarily have the same base and height? Explain.

Constructed RESPONSE •

12. Jacob is having new carpet put in his living room, which is in the shape of the parallelogram at the right. The carpet costs $5.25 a square foot. How much will it cost him to carpet his living room? Explain.

10 ft
8 ft

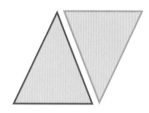

Objective: to find the area and perimeter of triangles

A quilt is made up of a pattern of geometric shapes. The pattern to the right is made up of triangles that form a parallelogram.

Exploration Exercise

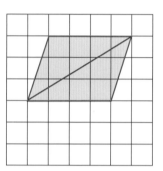

1. Draw a parallelogram on graph paper with a base of 4 and a height of 3.

2. Draw a diagonal.

3. Find the area of the parallelogram.

4. Cut out the parallelogram, and then cut out the triangles.

5. Lay one triangle on top of the other. What do you notice?

6. What is the area of each triangle?

7. The formula for the area of a parallelogram is base • height. Write a formula for the area of a triangle.

The area of each triangle above is $\frac{1}{2}$ the area of the parallelogram. This leads us to the formula for the area of a triangle.

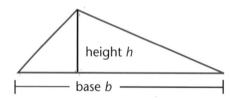

Area is equal to **one-half** times **base** times **height**.

$$A \quad = \quad \frac{1}{2} \quad \bullet \quad b \quad \bullet \quad h$$

Examples

A. Find the area of the triangle.

4 in.

12 in.

$A = \frac{1}{2}bh$

$A = \frac{1}{2} \bullet 12 \bullet 4$

$A = 24 \text{ in.}^2$

The area of the triangle is 24 inches squared.

B. Find the perimeter of the triangle.

14 mm   14 mm

10 mm

$P = 14 + 14 + 10$

$P = 38 \text{ mm}$

> To find the perimeter, add up all of the sides.

The perimeter of the triangle is 38 mm.

C. A triangle has a base of 14 mm and an area of 35 mm². Find the height of the triangle.

$A = \frac{1}{2}bh$

$35 = \frac{1}{2} \cdot 14 \cdot h$ Replace *A* with 35 and *b* with 14.

$35 = 7 \cdot h$ Multiply.

$5 = h$ Divide.

The height of the triangle is 5 mm.

Exercises •

Find the area of each triangle.

1.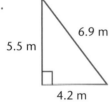
6.9 m
5.5 m
4.2 m

2.
12.8 mm
28.3 mm

3.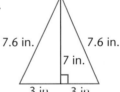
7.6 in.   7.6 in.
7 in.
3 in.   3 in.

Find the missing base or height of each triangle.

4. Area = 110 ft²
   base = 10 ft
   height = _____

5. Area = $35\frac{1}{2}$ cm²
   base = _____
   height = $7\frac{1}{2}$ cm

6. Area = 75.25 in.²
   base = 10.5 in.
   height = _____

Find the perimeter of each triangle.

7.
7 in. $5\frac{1}{2}$ in.
9 in.

8.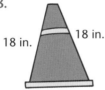
18 in.   18 in.
12 in.

9.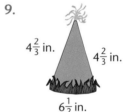
$4\frac{2}{3}$ in. $4\frac{2}{3}$ in.
$6\frac{1}{2}$ in.

Problem SOLVING •

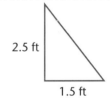
2.5 ft
1.5 ft

10. The base of a triangle is 6 meters long, and its area is 48 square meters. What is the height of the triangle?

11. A kitchen floor is made up of tiles that are in the shape of the triangle to the right. There are 40 tiles on the kitchen floor. What is the area of the floor?

★12. Cut a 4-inch square from paper. Fold it in half so you make a triangle. Now fold the triangle in half. What is the perimeter of the last triangle?

4 in.
4 in.

8.4 Area and Perimeter of Trapezoids

Objective: to find the area and perimeter of trapezoids

Exploration Exercise

1. Draw two trapezoids that are equal to the one shown on the graph paper.

2. Cut out the trapezoids, and put them together to make a parallelogram.

3. Find the area of the parallelogram.

4. What is the area of one trapezoid? (*Remember:* The parallelogram is made up of two equal trapezoids.)

5. If the formula for the area of a parallelogram is base • height, what is the formula for the area of a trapezoid?

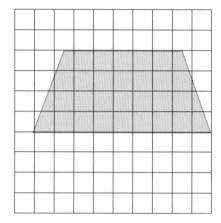

The trapezoid has two bases, b_1 and b_2, and a height, a line that is perpendicular to the bases.

The area of a trapezoid is equal to one-half the sum of the bases times the height.

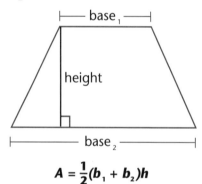

$$A = \frac{1}{2}(b_1 + b_2)h$$

Examples

A. Find the area of the trapezoid.

4 in.

6 in.

7 in.

$A = \frac{1}{2}(b_1 + b_2)h$

$A = \frac{1}{2}(4 + 7)6$

$A = \frac{1}{2}(11)6$

$A = 33$

The area of the trapezoid is 33 square inches.

B. Find the perimeter of the trapezoid.

12 cm

4.5 cm   4.5 cm

8 cm

$P = 4.5 + 12 + 4.5 + 8$

$P = 29$ cm

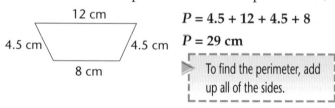

To find the perimeter, add up all of the sides.

The perimeter of the trapezoid is 29 centimeters.

C. A trapezoid has an area of 40 cm². If the bases measure 12 cm and 8 cm, what is the height?

$40 = \frac{1}{2}(12 + 8)h$ Replace A with 40, b_1 with 12, and b_2 with 8.

$40 = \frac{1}{2}(20)h$ Add.

$40 = 10h$ Multiply.

$4 = h$ Divide.

The height of the trapezoid is 4 cm.

Exercises

Find the area of each trapezoid.

1.
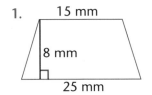
15 mm
8 mm
25 mm

2.
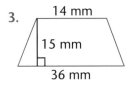
21 m
29 m
10 m

3.
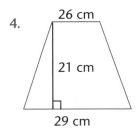
14 mm
15 mm
36 mm

4.
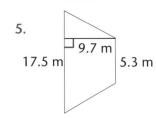
26 cm
21 cm
29 cm

5.
9.7 m
17.5 m
5.3 m

6.
7 m
21 m
21 m

Find the perimeter of each trapezoid.

7.
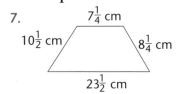
$7\frac{1}{4}$ cm
$10\frac{1}{2}$ cm
$8\frac{1}{4}$ cm
$23\frac{1}{2}$ cm

8.
1.8 m
2.2 m
3.9 m
5.2 m

9.
6.5 in.
12.5 in.
14.8 in.
7.1 in.

Fill in the missing base or height of each trapezoid when given the area.

10. Area = 24 m², base₁ = 5 m, base₂ = 7 m, height = _____

11. Area = 33 in.², base₁ = 4.5 in., base₂ = _____, height = 6 in.

12. Area = 45 in.², base₁ = 15 in., base₂ = 9 in., height = _____

Problem SOLVING

13. A trapezoid's bases are 20 in. and 30 in., and the height is 10 in. What happens to the area of a trapezoid when you double both of the bases? What happens when you double only the height? What happens when you double the bases and the height?

8.5 Problem-Solving Application: Using Measurement

Objective: to solve word problems using measurement

Sharon Hausman planted a flower and vegetable garden for a summer project. She has a plot that is 3 m long and 2,000 cm wide. What is the perimeter and area of the plot?

Notice that one dimension of the plot is given in meters and the other dimension is given in centimeters. To compute with measurements, they must have the same unit of measure.

Rename 2,000 centimeters as meters.

Since there are 100 cm in 1 m, divide by 100. $2,000 \div 100 = 20$ $2,000 \text{ cm} = 20 \text{ m}$

Now you can find the perimeter and area of the plot.

Perimeter = 2(*l* + *w*)   **Area = *lw***

$P = 2(3 + 20) = 46$ $A = 3 \times 20 = 60$

The perimeter of the plot is 46 m.

The area of the plot is 60 m².

Another Example

Diana Hernandez takes pictures and develops her own film. She mixes 60 mL of stop bath with 4 L of water in a tray. How much liquid is in the tray?

Change 4 liters to milliliters.   Add.

4 L = 4,000 mL   Multiply by 1,000.

$$\begin{array}{r} 4,000 \text{ mL of water} \\ + \quad 60 \text{ mL of stop bath} \\ \hline 4,060 \end{array}$$

There are 4,060 mL of liquid in the tray.

Try THESE

Add or subtract.

1. 39.4 km + 14.1 km = ■ km
2. 7.2 cm + 4.3 mm = ■ mm
3. 190 m − 230 cm = ■ cm
4. 49.23 kg − 180 g = ■ kg
5. 9,205 mg + 14 g = ■ g
6. 34.4 kL − 2,200 L = ■ kL

1. Aaron is 1.70 meters tall. Belinda is 181 centimeters tall. How much taller is Belinda than Aaron?

2. Kyle has three 750-mL cans of juice. Will a 2-L container hold all the juice?

3. Mr. Schulz drives 156 km and uses 6 L of gasoline. At that rate, how many liters of gasoline does he need to drive 286 km?

4. Lynn has 2 m of ribbon. She cuts the ribbon into pieces that measure 8 cm in length. How many pieces does she have?

5. A dime has a mass of 2.3 grams. Luisa has a roll of dimes worth $5.00. What is the total mass of the dimes?

6. A 25-liter tank fills at the rate of 500 milliliters per minute. How long does it take the tank to fill?

7. Measure the front cover of this book. Write the length and width to the nearest centimeter and millimeter. Find the perimeter and area in centimeters and millimeters.

8. A tan napkin is 37 centimeters long. A blue napkin is 0.28 meters long. How many centimeters longer is the tan napkin than the blue napkin?

9. A traffic cone is 3 meters tall and has a base of 90 centimeters. What is the area of the traffic cone in centimeters?

10. A picture is 10.16 centimeters by 0.1524 meters. Find the perimeter and area of the picture in centimeters.

Mid-Chapter REVIEW

Give the precision of each measurement.

1. 9.5 m

2. 0.41 mm

3. 2.89 km

Find the area and perimeter of each figure.

4.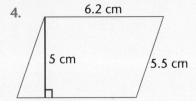
6.2 cm
5 cm
5.5 cm

5.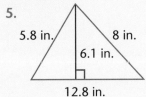
5.8 in.
8 in.
6.1 in.
12.8 in.

6.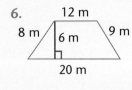
12 m
8 m
6 m
9 m
20 m

Problem Solving

Can You Cover the Checkerboard?

The checkerboard shown below has four rows of four squares and some covering tiles that are exactly the size of two squares. You know that you could use 8 covering tiles to cover all of the squares in the checkerboard, without overlapping. If you removed the upper left-hand and lower right-hand squares and had only 7 tiles, could you cover each square in the checkerboard without overlapping?

Make a drawing to show how it can be done or explain why it cannot be done.

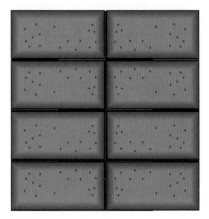

Extension

Pentominoes are shapes that are formed by five adjacent, nonoverlapping squares. Two pentominoes are shown below. How many different pentominoes can you form?

Cumulative Review

Estimate.

1. 3.142
    + 5.638

2. 7,925
    − 2,376

3. 35.7
    × 0.59

4. $38\overline{)465}$

5. $2.6\overline{)0.642}$

Compute.

6. $34.703 - 18.76$

7. $\$34.36 + \$63.78 + \$21.05$

8. 1.67×10

9. $0.42 \times 1{,}000$

10. $3.6 \div 100$

11. $\frac{1}{2} + \frac{5}{8}$

12. $4\frac{1}{3} + 2\frac{4}{9}$

13. $\frac{5}{12} - \frac{1}{3}$

14. $6\frac{5}{6} - 2\frac{3}{4}$

15. $5 \times \frac{7}{10}$

16. $2\frac{1}{3} \times 4\frac{1}{2}$

17. $\frac{8}{15} \div \frac{4}{5}$

18. $5\frac{1}{4} \div 3\frac{3}{8}$

19. $-6 + -17$

20. $-16 - -12$

21. 15×-5

22. -21×-0.1

23. $-72 \div 8$

24. $-48 \div -12$

Solve.

25. What number is 45% of 15?

26. What percent of 40 is 30?

27. 45 is 60% of what number?

28. 8.6% of 65 is what number?

Solve each equation.

29. $0.24 \times m = 15$

30. $n + 26.8 = 100$

31. $k - 2\frac{3}{4} = 5$

32. $\frac{4}{5} = \frac{n}{100}$

33. $x + 3 = -7$

34. $-3y = -21$

35. $5y = -40$

36. $x - 4 = -1$

Solve.

37. A race car traveled 420 miles in 4 hours. Find the unit rate.

38. A set of four tires costs $141.08. What is the cost of one tire?

39. Jon Snider had $300.00 to spend on items for his apartment. He spent $67.45 on a lamp, $139.37 on a chair, and $49.69 on a mirror. How much did he have left?

40. Andy walked around the perimeter of the park four times. The park is 500 feet by 750 feet. What is the total distance he walked?

Objective: to find the area and circumference of circles

Exploration Exercise

1. Trace the circle below on a piece of paper.
2. Cut out the 16 sections.
3. Line up the sections so that they form a parallelogram.
4. What is the measurement of the base and the height?
5. You know that **Circumference** = $2\pi r$ and that the area of a parallelogram is base times height. Write a formula for the area of a circle.

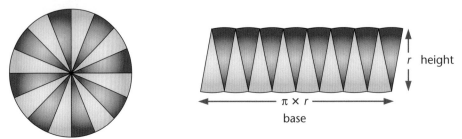

The circular design above was cut apart and rearranged to form a parallelogram. The parallelogram area formula helps us in deriving the formula for the area of a circle.

$$\underbrace{\text{Area}}_{A} \; \underbrace{\text{is equal to}}_{=} \; \underbrace{\text{pi}}_{\pi} \; \underbrace{\text{times}}_{\times} \; \underbrace{\text{radius}}_{r} \; \underbrace{\text{times}}_{\times} \; \underbrace{\text{radius.}}_{r}$$

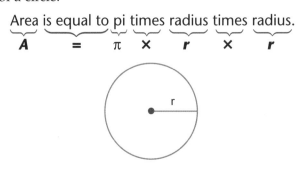

Examples

Find the circumference and area of the circle.

$C = 2\pi r$

$= 2 \bullet 3.14 \bullet 6$

$= 37.68 \text{ m}$

> The **diameter** of the circle is 12, which means the **radius** is 6. The radius is one-half the diameter.

$A = \pi r^2$

$= 3.14 \bullet 6^2$

$= 113.04 \text{ m}^2$

d = 12 m

The circumference is 37.68 m, and the area is 113.04 m².

· ·

Find the radius or diameter of each circle.

1.
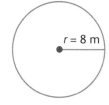
$r = 8$ m

2.
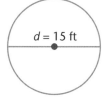
$d = 15$ ft

3.
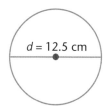
$d = 12.5$ cm

Exercises ·

Find the circumference and area of each circle. Use 3.14 for π. Round to the nearest tenth.

1.

14 m

2.

2.5 in.

3.
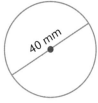
40 mm

4.

21 cm

5.

5.25 in.

6.
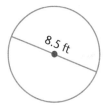
8.5 ft

7. radius = 5.5 ft

8. diameter = 15 mm

9. diameter = 10.5 cm

Find the area of the shaded region.

10.
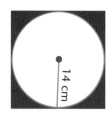
14 cm

11. 12 in.
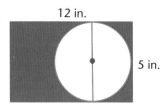
5 in.

12. 9 ft
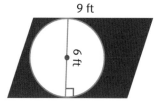
6 ft

Problem SOLVING ·

13. A new cell phone tower was built to allow reception to 52 miles. How many square miles are within the cell tower area?

14. Rachel is baking a cake but does not know if she wants to bake a round or a square cake. Which cake has a larger area, a round 8-inch cake or a square 9-inch cake?

15. Given the circumference of a circle, how can you find the area?

Objective: to find the area of irregular figures

Not all polygons are triangles, parallelograms, rectangles, squares, trapezoids, or circles. Some are a combination of one or more regular shapes. You can still find the area of these figures.

An **irregular figure** is made of triangles, rectangles, circles, and other two-dimensional figures. To find the area of an irregular figure, split the figure into ones you are familiar with and find the area of each figure individually, and then add the areas together.

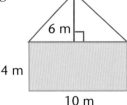

Example

Find the area of the irregular figure.

4 m

■ Step 1: Separate the irregular figure into a triangle and a rectangle.

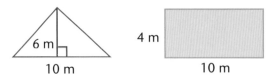

■ Step 2: Find the area of the rectangle and the triangle.

$$A\triangle = \tfrac{1}{2}bh \qquad\qquad\qquad A\square = lw$$

$$= \tfrac{1}{2}(6)10 \qquad\qquad\qquad = (10)4$$

$$= 30 \qquad\qquad\qquad\qquad = 40$$

The area of the triangle is 30 m².
The area of the rectangle is 40 m².

■ Step 3: Add to find the total area.

$$30 \text{ m}^2 + 40 \text{ m}^2 = 70 \text{ m}^2$$

The total area of the irregular figure is 70 m².

Find the area of each irregular figure. Round to the nearest tenth, if necessary.

1.
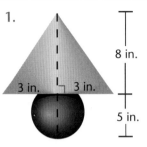
8 in.
3 in. | 3 in.
5 in.

2.
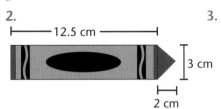
12.5 cm
3 cm
2 cm

3.
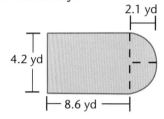
2.1 yd
4.2 yd
8.6 yd

4.
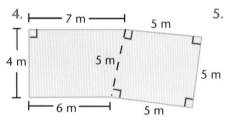
7 m
5 m
4 m
5 m
5 m
6 m
5 m

5.
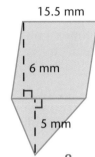
15.5 mm
6 mm
5 mm

6.
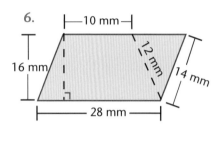
10 mm
16 mm
12 mm
14 mm
28 mm

7.
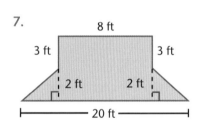
8 ft
3 ft   3 ft
2 ft   2 ft
20 ft

8.
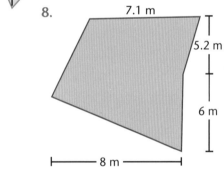
7.1 m
5.2 m
6 m
8 m

9. You plan to replace the floor in the kitchen shown below. What is the area of the floor? Hardwood floor costs $5.50 a foot to be installed. How much will it cost for you to have it installed?

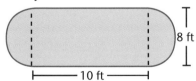
8 ft
10 ft

10. Lois is planting a rose garden in her backyard. What is the area of her rose garden?

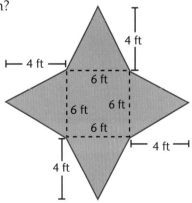
4 ft
4 ft
6 ft
6 ft   6 ft
6 ft
4 ft
4 ft

8.8 Squares and Square Roots

Objective: to find squares and square roots

Consider the two squares below. Find each area.

 5 units

 2.5 units

Area = 5²
= 25 square units

Area = 2.5²
= 6.25 square units

Remember an exponent tells how many times a number, called the **base**, is used as a factor. Squaring a number means using that number as a factor two times.

The opposite of squaring a number is finding the **square root** of the number. Both 2 • 2 and -2 • -2 equal 4. The number 4 has two square roots, 2 and -2. The radical sign $\sqrt{}$ is the symbol for the positive square root.

Say: The square root of 25 is 5.

Write: $\sqrt{25} = 5$

Say: The square root of 6.25 is 2.5.

Write: $\sqrt{6.25} = 2.5$

Examples

A. Find $\sqrt{121}$.

$11^2 = 121$, so $\sqrt{121} = 11$

B. Find $\sqrt{\frac{1}{9}}$.

$\left(\frac{1}{3}\right)^2 = \frac{1}{9}$, so $\sqrt{\frac{1}{9}} = \frac{1}{3}$

Rational numbers, like 25, 6.25, and $\frac{1}{9}$, whose square roots are rational numbers, are called **perfect squares**.

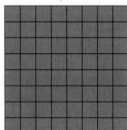

Find the number whose square is 64. Since 8 × 8 or $8^2 = 64$, then the square root of 64 is 8. So, the length of each side is 8 square units.

$\sqrt{64} = 8$

Try THESE

Complete.

1. $4^2 = 16$, so $\sqrt{16} = \blacksquare$

2. $9^2 = 81$, so $\sqrt{81} = \blacksquare$

3. $\left(\frac{1}{7}\right)^2 = \frac{1}{49}$, so $\sqrt{\frac{1}{49}} = \blacksquare$

4. $0.2^2 = 0.04$, so $\sqrt{0.04} = \blacksquare$

Find the square of each number.

1. 24

2. 7

3. 31

4. $\frac{1}{4}$

5. 16

6. $\frac{2}{3}$

7. 27

8. $\frac{3}{8}$

Find each square root.

9. $\sqrt{400}$

10. $\sqrt{1}$

11. $\sqrt{0.16}$

12. $\sqrt{49}$

13. $\sqrt{484}$

14. $\sqrt{\frac{4}{25}}$

15. $\sqrt{10,000}$

★16. $\sqrt{1.21}$

17. What is the square of -6?

18. Find both the square roots of 81.

Problem SOLVING

19. Express 365 as the sum of two consecutive perfect squares.

20. Lupé bought 100 square feet of carpet for her square bedroom. What are the dimensions of her bedroom?

The distance you can see to the horizon in clear weather is given by the formula $d = 1.22\sqrt{h}$. In this formula, d represents the distance in miles, and h represents the height in feet your eyes are from the ground. Use this formula for problems 21–23.

21. How far can you see to the nearest mile if you are at the top of the Sears Tower, 1,454 feet above the ground?

22. Suppose you are flying at 30,000 feet in a commercial airliner. To the nearest mile, how far is the horizon?

23. If you are 6 feet tall, your eyes might be 5.5 feet from the ground. How far can you see to the nearest mile?

★24. The numbers 1, 8, and 27 are called *perfect cubes* because $1^3 = 1$, $2^3 = 8$, and $3^3 = 27$. Name two numbers that are both a perfect square and a perfect cube.

Mixed REVIEW

Divide. Write each quotient in simplest form.

25. $8 \div \frac{1}{2}$

26. $11 \div \frac{2}{3}$

27. $\frac{3}{4} \div \frac{1}{4}$

28. $\frac{3}{5} \div \frac{1}{4}$

29. $\frac{16}{21} \div \frac{2}{7}$

8.9 The Pythagorean Theorem

Objective: to find the missing length in a triangle using the Pythagorean theorem

One of the most important theorems in mathematics is the **Pythagorean theorem**. It describes the relationship that exists among the sides of right triangles. In any right triangle, the side opposite the right angle is called the **hypotenuse**. The other two sides, called the **legs**, form the right angle.

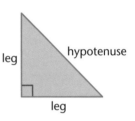

> ### Pythagorean Theorem
>
> In a right triangle, the square of the length of the hypotenuse is equal to the sum of the squares of the lengths of the other two sides.

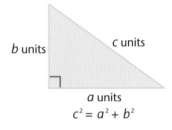

$$c^2 = a^2 + b^2$$

You can use the Pythagorean theorem to find a missing length of a right triangle.

Examples

A. Find the length of the hypotenuse of a right triangle whose legs are 5 cm and 12 cm.

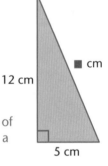

$c^2 = a^2 + b^2$	Use the Pythagorean theorem.
$c^2 = 5^2 + 12^2$	Replace a with 5 and b with 12.
$c^2 = 25 + 144$	
$c^2 = 169$	
$c = \sqrt{169}$	If the square of c is 169, then c is the square root of 169. The length of the hypotenuse is 13 cm. Use a
$c = 13$	calculator to find the square root, if necessary.

B. Find the missing length of the triangle.

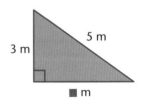

$c^2 = a^2 + b^2$	Use the Pythagorean theorem.
$5^2 = a^2 + 3^2$	Replace b with 3 and c with 5.
$25 = a^2 + 9$	Square 5 and 3.
$16 = a^2$	Subtract 9 from both sides.
$4 = a$	Find the square root.

The leg is 4 m.

Find the length of the missing side of each right triangle. If necessary, round to the nearest tenth.

1.
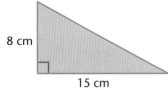
8 cm
15 cm

2.
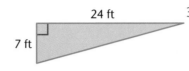
24 ft
7 ft

3.
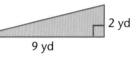
2 yd
9 yd

4.
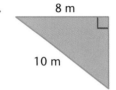
8 m
10 m

5.
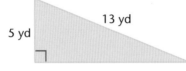
13 yd
5 yd

6.
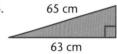
65 cm
63 cm

If *a* and *b* are the measures of the legs of a right triangle and *c* is the measure of the hypotenuse, find each missing measure.

7. $a = 7, b = 24$

8. $a = 24, b = 45$

9. $a = 10, c = 26$

10. $b = 48, c = 50$

11. $a = 9, c = 15$

12. $b = 36, c = 39$

Problem SOLVING

13. Which rectangle has the longer diagonal?

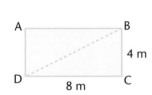

A ___ B
4 m
D ___ C
8 m

Q ___ R
8 m
T ___ S
8 m

14. Find the area and perimeter of the triangle.

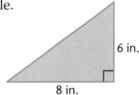

6 in.
8 in.

15. Is a triangle with side lengths of 12 m, 16 m, and 18 m a right triangle? Explain.

16. If xy is the diameter of circle C, then find xy. Find the circumference and area of circle C.

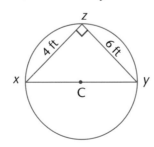

z
4 ft
6 ft
x
C
y

Objective: to solve problems using the Pythagorean theorem

One of the early uses of mathematics was in map making. It was often necessary to find lengths that could not be measured directly. The Pythagorean theorem could be used where right triangles were involved.

For example, find the distance across the lake in the figure shown at the right.

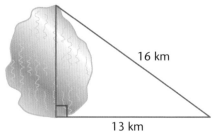

16 km

13 km

You know that a right triangle is formed. You also know the length of the hypotenuse and the length of one of the legs. You need to find the length of the other leg.

Substitute the known values into the Pythagorean theorem. In this case, $c = 16$ and $a = 13$.

$$c^2 = a^2 + b^2$$

$$16^2 = 13^2 + b^2$$

$$256 = 169 + b^2$$

$$256 - 169 = b^2 \quad \text{Subtract 169 from each side.}$$

$$87 = b^2$$

$$\sqrt{87} = b \quad \text{Use a calculator to find the square root.}$$

$$\sqrt{87} \approx 9.3273791$$

The distance across the lake is about 9.3 km.

CHECK Since the hypotenuse of a right triangle is the longest side, you would expect the length of the leg to be less than 16 km. The answer is reasonable.

  ·

Use the Pythagorean theorem to find the missing length for each right triangle.

1. $a = 15$ ft, $c = 17$ ft
2. $a = 40$ in., $c = 41$ in.
3. $b = 80$ m, $c = 89$ m
4. $b = 7$ m, $c = 9$ m
5. $a = 21$ yd, $b = 28$ yd
6. $a = 15$ cm, $b = 36$ cm

Round each answer to the nearest tenth, if necessary.

1. The bottom of a 10-foot ladder is 3 feet from the house. How far above the ground does the ladder touch the house?

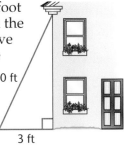

10 ft

3 ft

2. How long is the brace on the gate?

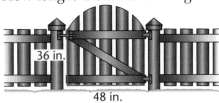

36 in.

48 in.

3. How far above the ground is the kite?

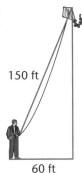

150 ft

60 ft

4. How long are side *a* and side *b*? What is the area and perimeter of triangle ABC?

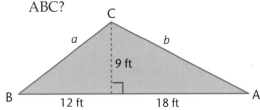

C

a

b

9 ft

B

12 ft

18 ft

A

Make a drawing of each problem. Then solve.

5. Jessica hikes 7 miles due east and then 3 miles due north. How far is she from the starting point?

6. A baseball diamond is a square. The distance from home plate to first base is 90 feet. Find the distance from home plate to second base.

7. The diagonal of a rectangular patio is 12 m long. One side of the patio is 8 m long. What is the length of the other side?

8. The foot of a ladder will be 10 ft from a building. How far must the ladder extend to reach a windowsill 24 ft above the ground?

 Test PREP

9. The length of a leg of a right triangle is 12 m, and the hypotenuse is 20 m. What is the length of the other leg?

   a. 8 m   b. 12 m   c. 23.3 m   d. 16 m

10. An airplane leaves a runway and travels 1,500 ft through the air. It travels a ground distance of 1,200 ft. What is the altitude of the plane at this moment?

    a. 400 ft   b. 350 ft

    c. 1,100 ft   d. 900 ft

    1,500 ft

    altitude

    1,200 ft

Language and Concepts

Choose the letter of the correct term to complete each statement.

1. The _____ is the side of a right triangle opposite the right angle.

2. The _____ of a circle is the distance around the circle.

3. The _____ is the greatest possible error divided by the true length.

4. The _____ of a circle is a line segment from the center of a circle to any point on the circle.

5. The opposite of squaring a number is the _____ of a number.

6. The _____ of a circle is a line segment through the center of a circle with endpoints on the circle.

a. square root

b. relative error

c. radius

d. circumference

e. hypotenuse

f. diameter

Skills and Problem Solving

Name the more precise measurement. Section 8.1

7. 43 m or 43.2 m

8. 390.4 cm or 3.9 m

9. 0.5 m or 50.1 cm

10. 56.5 km or 56 km

Find the area and perimeter of each figure. Sections 8.2–8.4

11.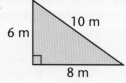

12.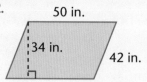

13.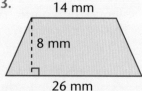

14.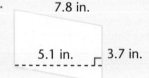

15.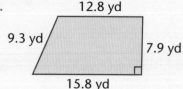

16.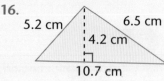

Find the missing base or height for each polygon. Sections 8.2–8.4

17. triangle area = 48 m^2

    base = _____

    height = 8 m

18. trapezoid area = 60 in.^{2}

    base$_1$ = 3 in.   base$_2$ = 9 in.

    height = _____

Find the area and circumference of each circle. Use 3.14 for π. Round to the nearest tenth. Section 8.6

19.
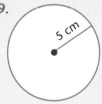
5 cm

20.

21 in.

21.
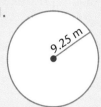
9.25 m

Find the square of each number. Section 8.8

22. 12

23. 5.3

24. $\frac{2}{3}$

25. 4.25

Find each square root. Section 8.8

26. $\sqrt{64}$

27. $\sqrt{255}$

28. $\sqrt{\dfrac{9}{25}}$

29. $\sqrt{1.44}$

Find the length of the missing side of each right triangle. If necessary, round to the nearest tenth. Section 8.9

30.
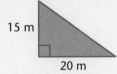
15 m
20 m

31.
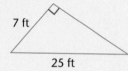
7 ft
25 ft

32.
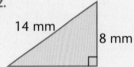
14 mm
8 mm

Solve. Sections 8.1–8.2, 8.5, and 8.10

33. A city block is 225 meters long on each side. Eduardo jogs around the block four times. How many kilometers does he jog?

34. A finished car off the assembly line measures 508 cm. Another car measures 5.2 m. Which is the more precise measurement?

35. How long must a ladder extend if it is 2.5 feet from a house and needs to reach a window that is 20 feet from the ground?

36. How far above the ground is the tethered hot air balloon?

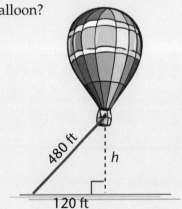
480 ft
h
120 ft

Find the area and perimeter of each figure.

1.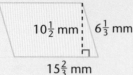
$10\frac{1}{2}$ mm $6\frac{1}{3}$ mm
$15\frac{2}{3}$ mm

2.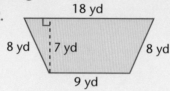
18 yd
8 yd   7 yd   8 yd
9 yd

3.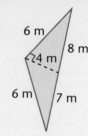
6 m   8 m
4 m
6 m   7 m

4.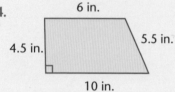
6 in.
4.5 in.   5.5 in.
10 in.

5.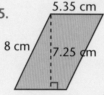
5.35 cm
8 cm   7.25 cm

6.
9 ft
$7\frac{1}{4}$ ft $6\frac{1}{2}$ ft
9 ft

Find the area and circumference of each circle. Use 3.14 for π. Round to the nearest tenth.

7.
8.5 m

8.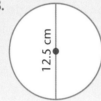
12.5 cm

9.
35 yd

Find each square root.

10. $\sqrt{25}$ **11.** $\sqrt{144}$ **12.** $\sqrt{400}$ **13.** $\sqrt{\dfrac{25}{36}}$ **14.** $\sqrt{0.009}$

Find the measure of each missing side.

15.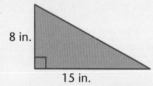
8 in.
15 in.

16.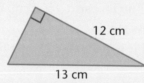
12 cm
13 cm

17.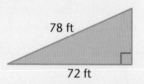
78 ft
72 ft

Solve.

18. Find the length of the diagonal of a rectangle whose length is 8 m and width is 5 m.

19. Juan walks 4 blocks due north then 3 blocks due west. What is the shortest distance from his starting point?

20. The diameter of a basketball hoop is 16.5 inches. What is the circumference? Round to the nearest tenth.

21. On a test, students were asked to measure a pencil. Becky gave a measurement of 21.5 cm, and Brad gave a measurement of 215 mm. Who gave a more precise measurement? Explain.

Change of Pace

The Golden Ratio

A **golden rectangle** is considered to be most pleasing to the eye. In a golden rectangle, the ratio of width to length is about 0.618034. This special ratio is called the **golden ratio**.

Many famous buildings, such as the Parthenon in Greece, and some paintings by Leonardo da Vinci and many other artists appear to be framed in the golden rectangle.

In 1753, the Scottish mathematician Robert Simson discovered an interesting relationship between the golden ratio and a sequence called the **Fibonacci sequence**.

The first eleven terms of the Fibonacci sequence are:

1, 1, 2, 3, 5, 8, 13, 21, 34, 55, 89

> Tell how to get the next term of the Fibonacci sequence. What is the next term?

For problems 1–4, refer to the Fibonacci sequence.

1. Compute these ratios to the nearest ten thousandth. Describe these numbers in terms of the golden ratio.

   a. $\dfrac{8}{13}$ b. $\dfrac{13}{21}$ c. $\dfrac{21}{34}$ d. $\dfrac{34}{55}$ e. $\dfrac{55}{89}$

2. Trace this number line. The points for $\dfrac{8}{13}$ and $\dfrac{13}{21}$ in problem 1 are already graphed. Graph the three remaining points. Describe the graph.

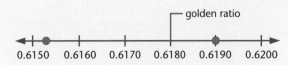

3. Find the next four terms of the Fibonacci sequence. Compute four more ratios like those in problem 1.

4. On your number line, graph the four ratios from problem 3. Describe the graph of these points.

5. **Research**
   Find out ways in which the golden ratio and the Fibonacci sequence appear in nature.

1. Find the square root.

$\sqrt{169}$

  a. 11

  b. 12

  c. 13

  d. none of the above

2. $2 \times (3 + 2) \times 4^2 =$ _____

  a. 38

  b. 128

  c. 160

  d. none of the above

3. $-9 + 16 =$ _____

  a. -25

  b. -7

  c. 7

  d. 25

4. Find 16% of 320.

  a. 0.512

  b. 5.12

  c. 51.2

  d. 512

5. Find the value of c.

  a. 13 cm

  b. 20 cm

  c. 169 cm

  d. none of the above

16 cm c 12 cm

6. What is the formula for the perimeter P of a square with sides of length s?

  a. $P = s^2$

  b. $P = 2s$

  c. $P = 4s$

  d. none of the above

7. Sam Cowan has dimes and nickels in his pocket. The 13 coins have a total value of $1.10. He has more dimes than nickels. How many of each coin does Sam have?

  a. 7 dimes, 5 nickels

  b. 8 dimes, 6 nickels

  c. 9 dimes, 4 nickels

  d. none of the above

8. If Peggy doubles her age, the product is the age of her mother. If Peggy's mother is 46, how old is Peggy? Which equation can be used to solve the problem given above?

  a. $2 + a = 46$ b. $2a = 46$

  c. $\frac{2}{a} = 46$ d. $\frac{a}{2} = 46$

9. The trapezoid has an area of 1,131 in.^{2}. What is the height of the trapezoid?

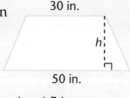

30 in.

h

50 in.

  a. 15.7 in.   b. 6.5 in.

  c. 83.8 in.   d. 26 in.

10. Nicole earns $6.00 for each lawn she mows. She mows 3 lawns one weekend and 2 the next. How much does she earn in all?

Ralph multiplies $6 by 3 and $6 by 2, and then adds the products. What is another way to solve the problem?

  a. multiply 6 by the product of 3 and 2

  b. multiply 6 by the sum of 3 and 2

  c. multiply the sums 6 + 3 and 6 + 2

  d. none of the above

Three-Dimensional Figures

Daniel Nickerson
Salisbury, NC

Objective: to classify three-dimensional figures

A **solid** is a three-dimensional figure that has length, width, and depth and encloses part of a space. Some examples are a basketball, an ice-cream cone, or a box.

Solids

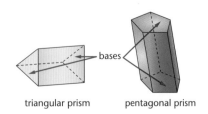

triangular prism   pentagonal prism

A **prism** is a solid with two parallel congruent bases that are shaped like polygons. The other faces of the prism are shaped like parallelograms.

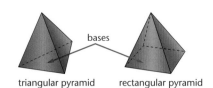

triangular pyramid   rectangular pyramid

A **pyramid** is a solid with one base that is shaped like a polygon. The other faces of the pyramid are triangular.

A **cylinder** is a solid that has two parallel congruent circular bases.

A **cone** is a solid with a circular base and one vertex.

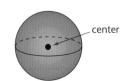

A **sphere** is a solid with all points the same distance from a given point called the center.

Three-dimensional figures are made up of faces, edges, and vertices. A **face** is the polygon that makes up a solid. An **edge** is the intersection of the two faces in a three-dimensional figure. A **vertex** is the point where the edges of a three-dimensional object intersect.

Examples

A. Classify the solids represented by the object.

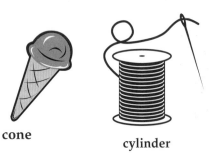

cone

cylinder

B. Count the number of faces, edges, and vertices in the cube below.

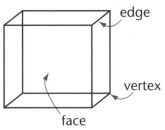

It has 6 faces, 12 edges, and 8 vertices.

....

Classify each solid.

1.

2.

3.

4.

Exercises ....

Classify the solid represented by the object. Be specific.

1.

2.

3.

4.

Count the number of faces, edges, and vertices. Classify each solid.

5.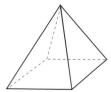

6.

7.

Problem SOLVING ....

8. Make a drawing of a hexagonal prism and an octagonal prism.

9. Is the statement "A rectangular prism has one base" true or false? Support your answer.

Mind BUILDER

More About Solids

Solve.

1. Copy and complete the table.

2. What is the sum of F and V for a triangular prism? How does this compare to E?

Polyhedron	Number of Faces (F)	Number of Vertices (V)	Number of Edges (E)
Triangular prism	5	6	9
Rectangular prism	■	8	12
Pentagonal prism	■	■	15
Hexagonal prism	■	■	■
Octagonal prism	■	■	■

vertex
edge
face

3. What is the sum of F and V for a pentagonal prism? How does this compare to E?

4. A polyhedron has 14 faces and 24 vertices. How many edges does it have?

5. Write a formula to show the relationship between the number of faces, vertices, and edges.

Objective: to find the surface area of prisms

Teresa is building a jewelry box. The box is in the shape of a rectangular prism. She wants to know how much paint she will need to cover the jewelry box. She needs to find the surface area of the jewelry box. The **surface area** (*S*) of a solid is the sum of the areas of all the faces.

Surface Area of a Prism

The surface area of a prism is the sum of the area of its faces.

$$S = 2lw + 2lh + 2wh$$

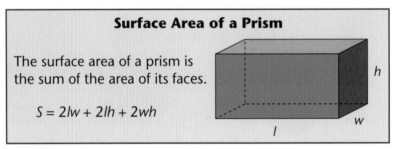

Example

Find the surface area of the rectangular prism.

Sometimes it is helpful to make a pattern, or net, of the polyhedron so the area of each face can be found more easily.

front	$9 \times 10.5 = 94.5$
back	$9 \times 10.5 = 94.5$
top	$4 \times 9 \quad = 36$
bottom	$4 \times 9 \quad = 36$
sides	$\begin{cases} 4 \times 10.5 = 42 \\ 4 \times 10.5 = 42 \end{cases}$

$$2(94.5 + 36 + 42) = 345$$

The surface area is 345 cm².

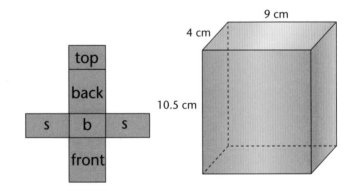

Try THESE

Find the surface area of each rectangular prism.

1. 24 m, 3 m, 2 m

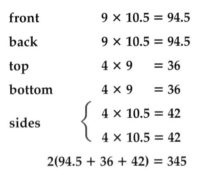

2. 3 in., 2 in., 4 in.

Exercises

Find the surface area of each rectangular prism.

1.
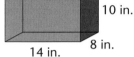
10 in.
14 in. 8 in.

2.
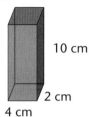
10 cm
2 cm
4 cm

3.
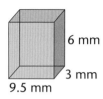
6 mm
3 mm
9.5 mm

4.
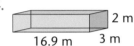
2 m
16.9 m 3 m

5.
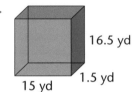
16.5 yd
1.5 yd
15 yd

6.

$4\frac{3}{4}$ ft
$1\frac{1}{2}$ ft
$\frac{1}{2}$ ft

Problem SOLVING

7. A tube of paint will cover 24 square inches. How many tubes are needed to paint Teresa's jewelry box that measures 10 inches by 4 inches by 10 inches?

8. Find the surface area of a cube with a side length of x ft. Write your answer in terms of x.

Constructed RESPONSE

9. Taylor is wrapping a gift in a box that is 20 inches by 15 inches by 5 inches. She has 900 square inches of wrapping paper. Does she have enough paper to wrap the gift? Explain.

Test PREP

10. Find the surface area of the rectangular prism.
    a. 24 m²
    b. 18 m²
    c. 52 m²
    d. 64 m²

    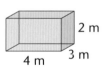
    2 m
    4 m 3 m

11. The surface area of a cube is 54 cm². What is the length of one side?
    a. 3 cm
    b. 6 cm
    c. 9 cm
    d. 12 cm

Objective: to find the surface area of cylinders and cones

Exploration Exercise

1. Cut out paper to cover a can. You should have three pieces, the top, bottom, and side.

2. Lay the three pieces of paper on the table. What is the shape of the papers that cover the top and bottom? What is the shape of the paper that covers the side of the can?

3. What is the relationship between the length of the paper that covers the side and the circumference of the top and bottom?

4. Use the pieces to find the surface area of the can.

This exploration leads to the surface area formula for a cylinder.

Surface Area of a Cylinder

The surface area of a cylinder is the sum of the area of the curved surface and the areas of the circular bases.

$$S = 2\pi rh + 2\pi r^2$$

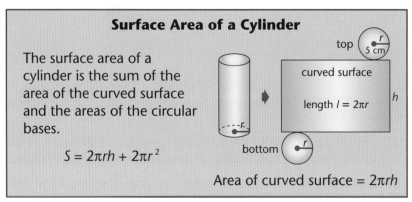

Area of curved surface = $2\pi rh$

We can also find the surface area of a cone. Remember that a cone is a solid with a circular base and one vertex.

Surface Area of a Cone

The surface area of a cone is the sum of the area of the circular base and the area of its curved surface.

$$S = \pi r^2 + \pi rs$$

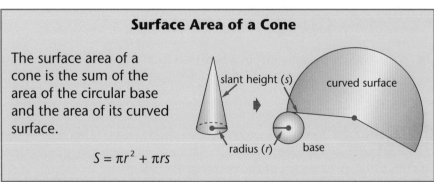

Example

Find the surface area of the cylinder below.

$S = 2\pi rh + 2\pi r^2$	Surface area of a cylinder
$= 2\pi(3)(5) + 2\pi(3)^2$	Replace r with 3 and h with 5.
$= 2(3.14)(3)(5) + 2(3.14)(3)^2$	Replace π with 3.14.
$= 150.72$	

The surface area is about 150.72 m².

Find the surface area. Use 3.14 for π.

1.
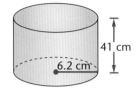

2. 2 cm
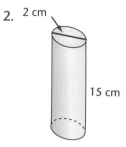

3.
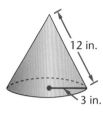

4.
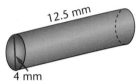

5.
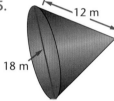

6.
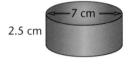

Problem SOLVING

7. The height of a cylindrical milk tank is 1.4 m. The radius is 0.4 m. Find the surface area.

8. A traffic cone has a radius of 0.5 ft and a slant height of 3 ft. What is its surface area?

★ 9. The surface area of a cylinder is 376.80 cm². The radius of the cylinder is 5 cm. What is the height of the cylinder? Use 3.14 for π.

Constructed RESPONSE

10. Pat has a cylinder with a radius of 4 in. and a height of 6 in. Kelly has a cylinder with a radius of 6 in. and a height of 4 in. Do the cylinders have the same surface area? If not, which one has a larger surface area? Explain.

MIXED REVIEW

Find the area of each figure.

11. 3 m
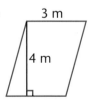
4 m

12.

4.25 in.

13.
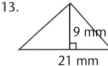
9 mm
21 mm

14. 12 mm
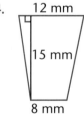
15 mm
8 mm

The Creative Cube Company

The Creative Cube Company constructs cubes from small unit cubes.
One day, Cathy carelessly dropped the large cubes into a container of paint.

She wondered how many of the unit cubes would be painted on three
faces, two faces, one face, and no faces. She took the large cubes apart and
counted the cubes in each category. Suppose she has a cube whose
dimensions are $10 \times 10 \times 10$. How many are painted on three faces, two
faces, one face, and no faces?

Extension

Suppose the cube's dimensions are $n \times n \times n$. How many are painted on
three faces, two faces, one face, and no faces?

Cumulative Review

Estimate.

1. $9,129 + 3,889$

2. $7.2 - 4.783$

3. $47.2 \cdot 19$

4. $8,894 \div 192$

5. $26.3 \div 1.7$

6. $36.25 \div 2.5$

Solve.

7. $2\frac{1}{4} + 6\frac{5}{6}$

8. $3\frac{1}{2} - 1\frac{3}{5}$

9. $\frac{2}{3} \cdot 19$

10. $6\frac{4}{9} + 5\frac{1}{3}$

11. $3\frac{2}{3} \div 3\frac{3}{4}$

12. $2\frac{3}{5} \cdot 1\frac{1}{8}$

13. $5\frac{7}{9} - 3\frac{1}{3}$

14. $5 \div 3\frac{1}{2}$

Solve each equation.

15. $n - 6.2 = 14.8$

16. $15t = 22.5$

17. $\dfrac{r}{0.3} = 165$

Evaluate each expression if $x = 4$, $y = 2.5$, and $z = -2$.

18. xy

19. y^2

20. $x + z$

21. $x - z$

Solve each proportion.

22. $\dfrac{10}{a} = \dfrac{8}{6}$

23. $\dfrac{b}{5} = \dfrac{68}{8}$

24. $\dfrac{7}{8} = \dfrac{d}{40}$

25. $\dfrac{4}{5} = \dfrac{0.6}{f}$

Find the missing length for each pair of similar figures.

26.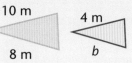

27.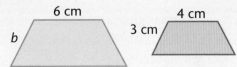

Solve.

28. What number is 63% of 22?

29. What percent of 80 is 8?

30. Chloe bought a pair of jeans that cost $26. They were discounted 25%. How much did she pay for the jeans?

31. Carpet for a rectangular living room costs $17.50 a square yard. If the room is 18 feet by 15 feet, find the cost of the carpet for the entire room.

9.4 Volume of Prisms and Cylinders

Objective: to find the volume of prisms and cylinders

Volume is the amount of space that a solid figure contains. Volume is measured in cubic units, such as a cubic inch (in.^{3}) or cubic centimeter (cm^3).

You can find the volume of prisms and cylinders. Remember that a prism is a solid figure that has two parallel congruent sides, called bases. A prism can be classified by the shape of its bases. The most common type of prism is a rectangular prism.

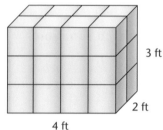

The prism to the right measures 4 ft by 2 ft by 3 ft. To find its volume we can fill it with cubes. It has three layers, each with 4×2, or 8 cubes. Since there are three layers, the volume is $(4 \times 2) \times 3$, or 24 ft^3.

Volume of a Rectangular Prism

The volume V of a rectangular prism can be found by multiplying the area of the base by the height.

$$V = Bh \text{ or } V = lwh$$

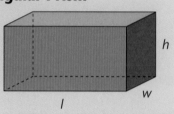

You can also find the volume of cylinders. The main difference between a rectangular prism and a cylinder is the base. A circle is the base of a cylinder, and to find the area of a circle, you multiply π by the radius squared. This leads to the volume formula for a cylinder.

Volume of a Cylinder

The volume of a cylinder can be found by multiplying the area of the base by the height.

$$V = Bh \text{ or } V = \pi r^2 h$$

Example

Suppose the radius of the base of a cylinder is 20 cm and its height is 70 cm. Find the volume.

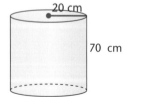

$V = Bh$ The base is a circle. Its area is πr^2.

$V = \pi r^2 h$

$V = 3.14 \cdot 20^2 \cdot 70$ Use a calculator.

The volume is about 87,920 cm^3.

· ·

Find the volume of each prism.

1. area of base: 12 m²
   height: 3.5 m

2. area of base: 7.5 m²
   height: 14 m

3. area of base: 16 ft²
   height: 4.2 ft

Find the volume of each cylinder.

4. radius: 2 m
   height: 8 m

5. radius: 3.2 m
   height: 10.5 m

Find the volume of each solid figure. Use 3.14 for π. Round to the nearest whole number.

6.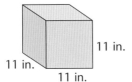

11 in.
11 in.
11 in.

7.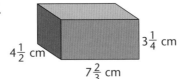

$3\frac{1}{4}$ cm
$4\frac{1}{2}$ cm
$7\frac{2}{3}$ cm

8.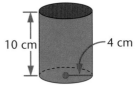

10 cm
4 cm

9.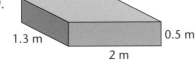

1.3 m
0.5 m
2 m

10.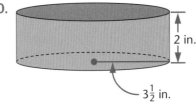

2 in.
$3\frac{1}{2}$ in.

Problem SOLVING ·

Solve. Use 3.14 for π. Round to the nearest whole number.

11. The base of a rectangular cake pan has an area of 117 in.². It has a volume of 292.5 in.³. What is the height of the cake pan?

12. Each edge of a 1-meter cube is 100 centimeters long. How many 1-centimeter cubes are in a 1-meter cube?

13. A flowerpot is cylindrical. The radius of the base is 14 cm. The height is 25 cm. What is the volume of the flowerpot?

14. Make a chart showing the heights and diameters of cans of food in your kitchen cupboard. What is the volume of the most common size?

★ 15. Find the volume and surface area of the solid on the right.

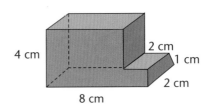

4 cm
2 cm
1 cm
2 cm
8 cm

9.5 Volume of Pyramids and Cones

Objective: to find the volume of pyramids and cones

A pyramid is a solid figure in which all the faces, except one, intersect at a point called the **vertex**. The face that does not intersect at the vertex is called the base. A cone is similar to a pyramid. It has a circular base and a vertex.

In the figures below, the pyramid and prism have the same base and height, and the cone and cylinder have the same base and height. You can see that the volume of the pyramid is less than the volume of the prism. The volume of the cone is less than the volume of the cylinder.

The volume of a cone or pyramid can be found as follows:

$V = \frac{1}{3} \times B \times h$ B is the measure of the base area.
h is the measure of the height.

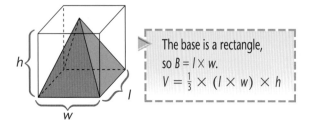

The base is a rectangle,
so $B = l \times w$.
$V = \frac{1}{3} \times (l \times w) \times h$

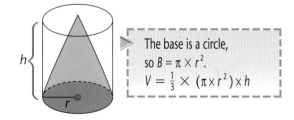

The base is a circle,
so $B = \pi \times r^2$.
$V = \frac{1}{3} \times (\pi \times r^2) \times h$

Examples

A. Find the volume of a pyramid whose length is 4 m, width is 3 m, and height is 6 m.

$V = \frac{1}{3} \times (l \times w) \times h$

$= \frac{1}{3} \times 4 \times 3 \times 6$

$= \frac{1}{3} \times 4 \times 3 \times 6$

$= 24 \text{ m}^3$

The volume of the pyramid is 24 m³.

B. Find the volume of a cone whose radius is 5 cm and height is 8 cm.

$V = \frac{1}{3} \times (\pi \times r^2) \times h$

$= \frac{1}{3} \times 3.14 \times 5^2 \times 8$

$= \frac{1}{3} \times 3.14 \times 25 \times 8$

$= 209.3 \text{ cm}^3$

The volume of the cone is about 209.3 cm³.

Find the volume of each pyramid. Round answers to the nearest whole number.

1. area of base: 15 ft²
   height: 7 ft

2. area of base: 24 cm²
   height: 5 cm

3. area of base: 10 ft²
   height: 0.3 ft

Find the volume of each cone. Round answers to the nearest whole number.

4. radius: 5 ft
   height: 16 ft

5. radius: 4 m
   height: 11 m

6. radius: 4.2 m
   height: 10.3 m

Find the volume of each solid figure. Use 3.14 for π. Round to the nearest whole number.

7.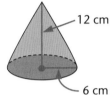
   12 cm
   6 cm

8.
   8 in.
   3 in.

9.
   4 cm
   2 cm
   3 cm

10.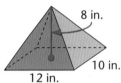
    8 in.
    10 in.
    12 in.

11.
    5 ft
    12 ft

12.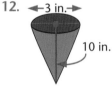
    3 in.
    10 in.

Solve. Round each answer to the nearest whole number.

13. A cone-shaped funnel has a radius of 4 in. and a height of 7 in. Find the volume of the funnel.

★14. Find the volume of the triangular prism.
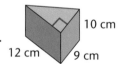
10 cm
12 cm
9 cm

Mid-Chapter REVIEW

Find the volume of each solid figure. Round to the nearest whole number.

1. cone
   area of base: 25.8 cm²
   height: 7 cm

2. pyramid
   area of base: 31.9 m²
   height: 14.6 m

Find the surface area and volume of each solid figure. Round to the nearest whole number.

3. rectangular prism
   length: 2.5 in.
   width: 3 in.
   height: 7 in.

4. cylinder
   radius: 2 m
   height: 2.5 m

9.6 Problem-Solving Application: Using Volume

Objective: to solve problems using volume

One of the most famous accounts of problem solving is credited to Archimedes, a mathematician and inventor who lived around 200 B.C. He worked for Hiero, a king of Sicily. Hiero suspected that the goldsmith had not made his new crown of pure gold. He asked Archimedes to investigate.

Archimedes needed to find the volume of the new crown. The problem was that the crown had an irregular shape. Legend has it that while getting into a bathtub, Archimedes noticed that the water level rose. He reasoned that the difference in the water level would be equal to the volume of his body. He then reasoned that he could find the volume of the crown in the same manner.

Once he found the volume of the crown, he compared its weight to the weight of an equal amount of pure gold. "Eureka!" The goldsmith had cheated the king.

You may never be asked to solve a problem like this, but there will be many problems that require a knowledge of volume.

Example

A cylinder fits exactly in a cube 10 cm on each edge. How much empty space is between the cylinder and the cube?

The volume of empty space can be found by subtracting the volume of the cylinder from the volume of the cube.

Volume of Cube	Volume of Cylinder
$V = 10^3$	$V = \pi \times r^2 \times h$ Estimate: $3 \times 25 \times 10 = 750$
$= 1,000 \text{ cm}^3$	$= \pi \times 5^2 \times 10$
	$= 3.14 \times 25 \times 10$
	$\approx 785 \text{ cm}^3$

> Making an estimate is an important step.

The volume of the cylinder is about 785 cm^3.

The volume of the empty space is approximately $1,000 - 785$, or 215 cm^3.

1. An aquarium is shaped like a rectangular prism. Its length is 30 cm, its width is 45 cm, and its height is 35 cm. Find the volume of the aquarium.

2. A storage silo is a cylinder. The radius of the base is 3 m. The height of the silo is 15 m. Find the volume of the silo.

Solve ···

1. How much water is needed to fill a circular swimming pool that is 22 ft in diameter and 5 ft deep?

2. Each edge of a cube is 5 in. If the dimensions are doubled, find the volume.

3. A pipe is 100 feet long and has an inside diameter of 0.5 feet. Find the number of cubic feet of oil that it can hold.

4. A rectangular piece of marble measures 4 ft by 7 ft by 0.5 ft. If 1 ft^3 of marble weighs 180 lb, how much does the piece of marble weigh?

5. The Great Pyramid in Egypt is approximately 150 yards tall. Each side of its square base is 252 yards long. Find the volume of the Great Pyramid.

6. A cone-shaped paper cup is 4 inches deep and has a diameter of 3 inches. How many of these cups can be filled with one gallon of lemonade? One gallon is equivalent to 231 inches cubed.

7. Find the approximate year in which the Great Pyramid was built. Locate it on the number line below.

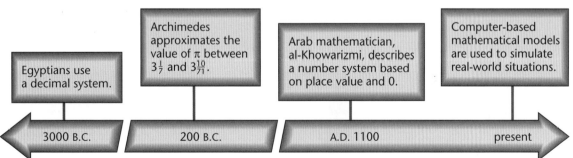

| Egyptians use a decimal system. | Archimedes approximates the value of π between $3\frac{1}{7}$ and $3\frac{10}{71}$. | Arab mathematician, al-Khowarizmi, describes a number system based on place value and 0. | Computer-based mathematical models are used to simulate real-world situations. |

| 3000 B.C. | 200 B.C. | A.D. 1100 | present |

Language and Concepts

Write *true* or *false*. If false, replace the underlined word or phrase to make a true sentence.

1. A <u>pyramid</u> is a solid figure that has two parallel congruent bases.

2. The bases of a cylinder are two parallel congruent <u>circles</u>.

3. A <u>cone</u> is a solid with a circular base and one vertex.

4. You can use the formula $V = Bh$ to find the volumes of prisms and <u>pyramids</u>.

5. The value of π is <u>exactly</u> 3.14.

6. A shoe box is an example of a <u>cone</u>.

7. You can use the formula $S = 2\pi rh + 2\pi r^2$ to find the surface area of a <u>cylinder</u>.

8. <u>Surface area</u> is the amount of space that a solid figure contains.

Skills and Problem Solving

Classify the solid represented by the object. Section 9.1

9.

10.

11.

Find the surface area of each figure. Use 3.14 for π. Round to the nearest whole number. Sections 9.2–9.3

12.
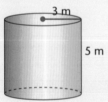

13.
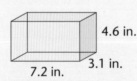

14.
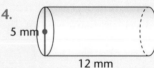

15.
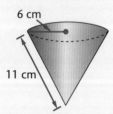

16.
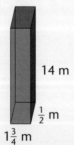

17.
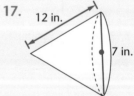

Find the volume of each figure. Use 3.14 for π.   Round to the nearest whole number. Sections 9.4–9.5

18. prism

    area of base: 16 in.²

    height: 5 in.

19. cylinder

    radius: 2 in.

    height: 3.5 in.

20. cone

    radius: 3 in.

    height: 4 in.

21. pyramid

    area of base: 42 cm²

    height: 8 cm

22.

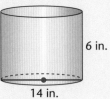

6 in.

14 in.

23.

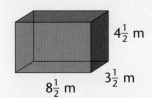

$4\frac{1}{2}$ m

$8\frac{1}{2}$ m

$3\frac{1}{2}$ m

24.

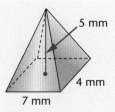

5 mm

4 mm

7 mm

25.

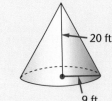

20 ft

9 ft

Solve. Sections 9.2 and 9.6

26. How much wrapping paper is needed to wrap a rectangular gift box that is 18 in. long, 10 in. wide, and 3 in. tall?

27. Two cans of soup cost the same amount. Can A has a radius of 2 in. and a height of 7.5 in. Can B has a radius of 4 in. and a height of 5 in. Which can has a greater volume and is therefore the better buy?

28. A paint can is 12 in. high with a radius of 4.5 in. How much paper is needed to make a label for the paint can?

29. A rectangular prism has a volume of 100m³. If the length is 5 m and the height is 20 m, what is the width?

30. Find the height of a cylinder that has a volume of 843.12 ft³ and a radius of 6 ft.

Chapter 9 Test

Classify the solid represented by the object.

1.

2.

3.

Find the surface area of each figure. Use 3.14 for π. Round to the nearest whole number.

4.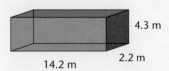
4.3 m
2.2 m
14.2 m

5.
8 ft
6 ft

6.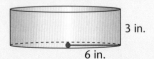
3 in.
6 in.

7.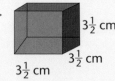
$3\frac{1}{2}$ cm
$3\frac{1}{2}$ cm
$3\frac{1}{2}$ cm

Find the volume of each figure. Use 3.14 for π. Round to the nearest whole number.

8.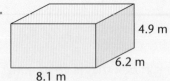
4.9 m
6.2 m
8.1 m

9.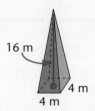
16 m
4 m
4 m

10.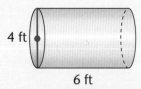
4 ft
6 ft

11.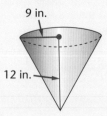
9 in.
12 in.

Solve.

12. The volume of a fish tank is 2,400 in.^{3}. If the length is 20 in. and the height is 10 in., what is the width?

13. A cone-shaped funnel has a diameter of 4 in. and a height of 6 in. Find the volume.

14. The edge of one cube is 2 cm. The edge of another cube is 4 cm. Find the ratio of the surface areas. Find the ratio of the volumes.

15. How are the formulas for the volume of a cone and pyramid similar?

Change of Pace

Density

The **density** of a substance is the mass per unit of volume. To find the density, divide the mass in grams by the volume in cubic centimeters.

$$\text{density} = \frac{\text{mass(g)}}{\text{volume (cm}^3)}$$

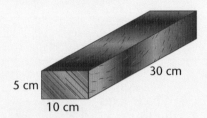

The mass of the block of wood is 1.1 kg or 1,100 g. The volume is $5 \times 10 \times 30$, or 1,500 cm³. Divide 1,100 by 1,500 to find the density.

mass $\longrightarrow$
volume $\longrightarrow$ $\dfrac{1,100}{1,500} \approx 0.7 \dfrac{g}{cm^3}$ $\longleftarrow$ density

How can you find the volume of an object that has an unusual shape? When an object is placed in water, some of the water is *displaced*, or moved. If the object is completely underwater, its volume in cubic centimeters is equal to the number of milliliters of water displaced. This is because 1 mL of water has a volume of 1 cm³.

The volume of the rock shown at the right is 22 cm³. Do you see why? If the mass is 40 g, what is the density?

mass $\longrightarrow$
volume $\longrightarrow$ $\dfrac{40}{22} \approx 1.8 \dfrac{g}{cm^3}$ $\longleftarrow$ density

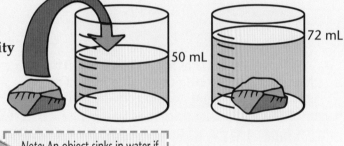

▷ *Note:* An object sinks in water if the density is greater than 1.

Solve. Round each result to the nearest tenth.

1. The mass of a piece of aluminum is 650 g and the volume is 240 cm³. Find the density.

2. The mass of a copper penny is 3.1 g and the volume is 0.35 cm³. Find the density.

3. The density of water is 1.0. Find the mass of 32 mL of water.

4. The density of pure gold is 19.3. Find the mass of 10 cm³ of gold.

5. An empty bottle has a mass of 340 g. When filled with water, the mass is 725 g. How many milliliters does the bottle hold?

6. A bottle contains 480 mL of corn oil and has a mass of 604 g. The empty bottle has a mass of 160 g. Find the density of the corn oil.

Cumulative Test

1. Solve. $\dfrac{5}{8} = \dfrac{x}{100}$

   a. $x = 160$

   b. $x = 62.5$

   c. $x = 75$

   d. none of the above

2. If m∠1 = 35°, what is m∠2?

   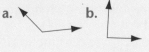

   a. 35°

   b. 45°

   c. 55°

   d. 65°

3. What does the drawing represent?

   a. angle

   b. line

   c. line segment

   d. ray

4. Which pair of figures is similar but not congruent?

   a.   b.

   c.   d. none of the above

5. Which angle measures about 85°?

   a.   b.

   c.   d. none of the above

6. Which solid figure does the drawing represent?

   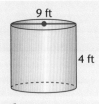

   a. cone

   b. cylinder

   c. parallelogram

   d. rectangular prism

7. The Pine City Zoo has several giraffes. The Midland Zoo recently purchased half as many giraffes. Which statement gives the same information?

   a. Midland has as many giraffes as Pine City.

   b. Midland has twice as many giraffes as Pine City.

   c. Pine City has half as many giraffes as Midland.

   d. Pine City has twice as many giraffes as Midland.

8. The Primms want to buy carpet for their living room. It is 18 feet long and 15 feet wide. How many square yards of carpet must they buy?

   a. 30

   b. 90

   c. 270

   d. none of the above

9. The diameter of a milk storage tank is 9 ft long. It is 4 ft high. What is its volume? Round to the nearest tenth.

   a. 56.5 ft³

   b. 113.1 ft³

   c. 254.3 ft³

   d. 1,017.9 ft³

10. Chris can save $5 per week if she earns about $25 per week. Suppose Chris earns $25, $10, $38, and $27 over a period of 4 weeks. Which is a reasonable conclusion?

    a. Chris does not save $5 per week.

    b. Chris earned an average of $25 per week over the 4-week period.

    c. Chris saves $5 per week.

    d. none of the above

Probability

Nigel Lewis
Surrey, England

Objective: to find the probability of events

Rita and Dora are playing "Buckorama." Each girl rolls a blue number cube and a red number cube on her turn. To win, Rita needs to roll a sum of 7. One possible winning outcome is shown below.

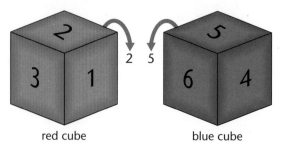

red cube   blue cube

A listing of all possible outcomes is called a **sample space**. The sample space for a roll of two number cubes is shown in this table.

1,1	1,2	1,3	1,4	1,5	1,6
2,1	2,2	2,3	2,4	2,5	2,6
3,1	3,2	3,3	3,4	3,5	3,6
4,1	4,2	4,3	4,4	4,5	4,6
5,1	5,2	5,3	5,4	5,5	5,6
6,1	6,2	6,3	6,4	6,5	6,6

Each of these rolls has a sum of 7.

> 4,3 and 3,4 are two different outcomes.

An **event** is a specific outcome. Suppose the event is a sum of 7. The probability that Rita will roll a sum of 7 is found as follows:

$$P(\text{sum of 7}) = \frac{6}{36} \leftarrow \text{number of successful outcomes}$$
$$\leftarrow \text{number of possible outcomes}$$

means the probability of rolling a sum of 7

> **Probability** is the ratio of the number of ways an event can occur to the number of possible outcomes.

The probability for a sum of 7 is $\frac{6}{36}$ or $\frac{1}{6}$.

Rita will either roll a sum of 7 or not roll a sum of 7. These events are called **complementary events**. Complementary events are two events that include all possible outcomes.

The probability of an event ranges between 0 and 1. It is impossible for an event to occur when the probability is 0, and it is certain to occur when the probability is 1.

Try THESE •

Find each probability. Refer to the sample space listed above.

1. $P(6, 1)$
2. $P(2, 4)$
3. $P(\text{sum of 3})$
4. $P(\text{sum of 8})$
5. $P(\text{sum of 0})$
6. $P(\text{sum greater than 1})$

Exercises

Two number cubes are rolled. Find the probability of each event.

1. P(both numbers are odd)
2. P(both numbers are the same)
3. P(a 1 on the red cube)
4. P(an even sum)
5. P(a sum greater than 10)
6. P(a sum of 7 or 11)
7. P(*not* a sum of 7)
8. P(the number on the red cube is less than the number on the blue cube)

Find the probability of spinning each of the following.

9. $P(7)$
10. P(*not* a 7)
11. P(a multiple of 2)
12. P(a blue number)
13. P(a number greater than 4)
14. P(a number less than 5)
15. P(a factor of 12)

Problem SOLVING

16. Suppose you have a bag of red, blue, and yellow marbles. If the probability of picking a red marble is $\frac{1}{6}$ and the probability of picking a yellow marble is $\frac{1}{2}$, what is the probability of picking a blue marble?

★17. Charlotte has 25 pennies, 15 nickels, 18 dimes, and 10 quarters in her piggy bank. She chooses one coin at random.

   a. What is the probability she chooses a dime?

   b. What is the probability she chooses a coin greater than a penny?

18. A bag contains yellow and blue marbles. The probability of randomly picking a yellow marble is 25%, and the probability of randomly picking a blue marble is 75%. Determine the number of yellow and blue marbles in the bag if there is a total of 16 marbles in the bag.

Constructed RESPONSE

19. Hallie is trying to win the grand prize on a game show. Should she try her luck by spinning a wheel labeled from 1 to 6 and hope she gets a 5, or should she roll two dice and hope she gets the same number on both dice? Explain.

Mixed REVIEW

Compute.

20. $\frac{1}{2} + \frac{1}{3}$

21. $1 - \frac{1}{6}$

22. $\frac{1}{4} \times \frac{3}{4}$

23. $\frac{1}{4} + \frac{1}{8} + \frac{3}{8}$

24. $0.5 + 0.25$

25. $1 - 0.75$

26. 0.5×0.5

27. $\frac{1}{4} \times 0.5$

10.2 Tree Diagrams

Objective: to find probabilities using tree diagrams

What are the chances that a family with three children will have two girls? First you need to list how many outcomes are possible. Then count how many outcomes include exactly two girls.

BBB	**BGB**	**GBB**	**GGB** ✔	There are 8 possible three-children families.
BBG	**BGG** ✔	**GBG** ✔	**GGG**	There are 3 possible families with exactly two girls.

The probability that a family of three children has exactly two girls is $\frac{3}{8}$.

Another Example

You can also use a **tree diagram** to list all possible outcomes. A tree diagram uses branches to show all possible outcomes.

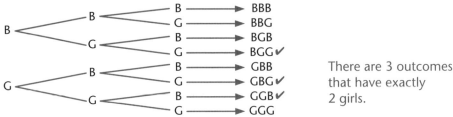

There are 3 outcomes that have exactly 2 girls.

The tree diagram shows 8 possible outcomes.

$2 \times 2 \times 2 = 8$ possible outcomes

└── possible outcomes each time

Try THESE ··

A penny and dime are tossed at the same time. Use the tree diagram to find each probability.

Penny Dime   Outcomes

H ─< H ⟶ HH
      T ⟶ HT
T ─< H ⟶ TH
      T ⟶ TT

1. HH

2. HT

3. TT

4. HH or HT

5. *not* TH

6. *no* heads

7. at least one tail

Exercises ··

Draw a tree diagram to show the possible outcomes. Then write the number of possible outcomes.

1. a choice of peach or apple pie with a choice of tea, coffee, or milk

2. a choice of chocolate or vanilla frozen yogurt with a choice of butterscotch, strawberry, or fudge topping.

3. tossing a coin and rolling an odd number on a number cube

4. a choice of a tan or black raincoat with a choice of red, yellow, or blue rain boots with a choice of a green or blue umbrella

A penny, a nickel, and a dime are tossed at the same time. Find the probability for each of the following.

5. at least two tails

6. exactly two tails

7. exactly one head

8. at least one head

9. *no* tails

10. exactly one tail

11. tails on the dime

★12. *not* all heads

★13. exactly four tails

Problem SOLVING ··

14. Three number cubes are rolled. How many outcomes are possible?

15. Mieko has 5 blouses, 3 skirts, and 3 scarves. How many outfits are possible?

★16. A drawer contains two blue socks and four black socks. Suppose one sock is chosen at random, and then another is chosen without replacing the first one. What is the probability that both socks chosen are black?

Mind BUILDER

Pascal's Triangle

Toss one coin. There are 2 possible outcomes. Toss two coins. There are 4 possible outcomes. Toss three coins. There are 8 possible outcomes. Toss four coins. How many possible outcomes are there?

one Head (H)   one Tail (T)
1   1

all H   one H, one T   all T
1   2   1

all H   two H, one T   one H, two T   all T
1   3   3   1

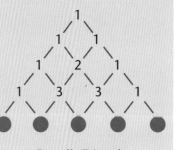

Pascal's Triangle

> The pattern formed is known as *Pascal's Triangle.*

Copy Pascal's Triangle as shown above.

1. Replace the circles in the last row with numerals.

2. Write the next six rows of Pascal's Triangle.

★3. When three coins are tossed, there are $1 + 3 + 3 + 1$, or 8, possible outcomes. Compute the number of possible outcomes for 8 coins.

10.3 Counting Principle

Objective: to find the probability of an event using the counting principle

Marie is going to summer camp. She needs to choose the activities she will participate in while at summer camp. The morning sessions are swimming, tennis, and arts and crafts. The afternoon sessions are sailing, ping-pong, badminton, and volleyball. Marie needs to pick an activity for the morning and afternoon session. How many different morning/afternoon sessions are possible?

You can make a tree diagram to find all of the possible outcomes.

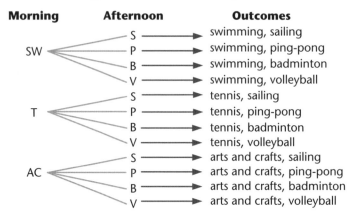

You can also find the number of session possibilities by multiplying. If you multiply the number of morning session activities (3) by the number of afternoon session activities (4), you get the number of possible outcomes (12).

Fundamental Counting Principle

The fundamental counting principle is used to find the total number of possible outcomes of an event.

If event A can occur in m ways and for each of these ways, an event B can occur in n ways, then events A and B can occur in $m \bullet n$ ways.

Examples

A. You have 6 shirts to choose from in your closet and 5 pairs of pants. How many different outfits can you put together?

shirts • pants = total outfits

$$6 \bullet 5 = 30$$

There are 30 total outfits.

B. Find the total number of outcomes when tossing a penny, rolling a number cube, and tossing a quarter.

penny • number cube • quarter

$$2 \bullet 6 \bullet 2 = 24$$

There are 24 outcomes.

Exercises

Find the total number of outcomes.

1. In your closet, you can choose from 6 pairs of pants, 8 shirts, 4 pairs of shoes, 3 coats, 2 scarves, and 2 hats.

2. When making a sandwich you can choose from white, wheat, rye, pumpernickel, or sourdough bread; ham, turkey, or roast beef; and Swiss, Cheddar, Munster, American, or Colby cheese.

3. In an ice-cream shop, you can choose from 25 flavors, 3 kinds of cones, and 4 kinds of sprinkles.

Problem SOLVING

4. Amanda and Annie were asked to find the total number of outcomes when choosing from 3 colors and 2 shapes. Who completed the problem correctly and why?

> **Amanda**
> $3 \cdot 2 = 6$ outcomes

> **Annie**
> $3 + 2 = 5$ outcomes

5. The number of ways that both events A and B can occur is 24. If event B can occur in 3 ways, in how many ways can event A occur?

★6. In a competition, 4 figure skaters will skate in a randomly assigned order. Why can't you evaluate the product $4 \times 4 \times 4 \times 4$ to find the number of possible orders in which the skaters can skate?

★7. Students in a high school are assigned four-digit identification numbers. If no numbers are repeated, how many identification numbers can be created? Remember, digits are whole numbers from 0 to 9.

Constructed RESPONSE

8. What are the advantages of solving a probability problem using the fundamental counting principle versus a tree diagram? Give an example.

Test PREP

9. A bakery sells round or square cakes that are chocolate, vanilla, or carrot with cream cheese or strawberry frosting. How many possibilities does the bakery offer?

   a. 7   b. 12   c. 10   d. 9

10. You can choose from 2 math classes, 4 English classes, and 3 science classes. How many possibilities do you have for your schedule?

    a. 12   b. 9   c. 18   d. 24

10.4 Permutations

Objective: to use permutations to solve problems

Exploration Exercise

1. Form a line with yourself and two friends or family members.

2. Line up in a different order.

3. How many ways can you line up? *Remember:* Anyone can be in the front, anyone can be in the middle, and anyone can be in the back.

4. How many people can be first in line? Once the line leader is chosen, how many people can be second in line? After the first and second person are chosen, how many people can be last in line?

The above exploration is an example of a **permutation**. A permutation is an arrangement in which order is important.

You can use the fundamental counting principle to find the number of ways three people can line up.

Position	Position 1	Position 2	Position 3
Number of people	3 people	2 people	1 person

There are 3 • 2 • 1, or 6 ways for them to line up. 3! is the symbol for 3 • 2 • 1. Read 3! as "three factorial."

If 6 people are lining up, how many ways can they line up?

Evaluate. 6! = 6 • 5 • 4 • 3 • 2 • 1

$\qquad$ **6! = 720**

Example

Five students run a race. In how many different orders can they finish the race?

$\qquad$ First place: 5 students can win

$\qquad$ Second place: 4 students are left to win

$\qquad$ Third place: 3 students are left to win

$\qquad$ Fourth place: 2 students are left to win

$\qquad$ Fifth place: 1 student is left to win

5! = 5 • 4 • 3 • 2 • 1

$\quad$ = 120

There are 120 different orders the students can finish the race.

Evaluate.

1. 4!

2. 2!

3. 6!

4. 8!

5. $(5 - 3)!$

6. $5! + 2!$

7. $3! \cdot 4!$

8. $(3 + 4)!$

Problem SOLVING ··

9. How many ways can six books be arranged on a shelf?

10. There are eight girls competing in an ice-skating competition. In how many ways can they finish in first, second, and third place?

11. How many ways can a president and a vice president be selected from a class of twelve?

12. How many ways can seven students line up for a class picture?

13. How many ways can you arrange the letters in the word *math*?

14. How many ways can a coach arrange a softball roster with nine players?

15. There are twenty-five people competing in a race. In how many ways can they finish in first and second place?

16. At a banquet, the head table seats five people. How many ways can the president, vice president, and secretary be seated?

17. How many three-scoop ice cream cones can be made from fifteen flavors?

Test PREP ··

18. How many ways can you choose first, second, and third place from fifteen contestants?

    a. 42　　　　b. 210　　　　c. 2,730　　　　d. 24

19. How many ways can the letters of the word *computer* be arranged?

    a. 5,040　　　b. 36　　　　c. 40,320　　　　d. 18,320

MIXED REVIEW ··

20. What is 20% of 15?

21. What percent of 80 is 36?

22. 32.3 is 19% of what number?

23. 11 is 10% of what number?

24. What is 155% of 68?

25. What percent of 25 is 80.5?

Objective: to solve problems using combinations

The student council at Arlington Junior High is having a pizza sale to raise money. They are offering four different toppings: mushrooms, pepperoni, onion, and sausage. If the price of the pizza includes two different toppings, how many different pizzas must the student council make?

We can make a list of the possibilities. **MP, MO, MS, PO, PS, OS**

There are six different pizzas that the student council can make. The toppings are not arranged on the pizza, so order is not important. This is called a **combination**. A combination is a grouping in which order is not important. Putting mushrooms and pepperoni on a pizza is the same as putting pepperoni and mushrooms on a pizza.

Combinations are related to permutations. To calculate a combination, you must first understand permutations and factorials.

Examples

A. Given four pizza toppings, how many combinations of two toppings are possible?

Above you used a list to determine the answer. You can also calculate the answer.

■ Step 1: Find the number of permutations when choosing 2 toppings from 4 toppings.

There are 4 • 3 permutations of 2 pizza toppings chosen from 4.

■ Step 2: Find the number of permutations when arranging 2 toppings.

There are 2! ways to combine the 2 toppings.

■ Step 3: Divide.

$$\frac{4 \cdot 3}{2!} = \frac{12}{2} = 6$$

There are 6 ways a person can select 2 toppings at a time from 4 toppings.

B. How many ice cream combinations are there when choosing three flavors from five flavors?

There are 5 • 4 • 3 permutations of ice cream flavors chosen from 5.

There are 3! ways to combine the flavors.

$$\frac{5 \cdot 4 \cdot 3}{3 \cdot 2 \cdot 1} = \frac{60}{6} = 10$$

There are 10 combinations of 5 ice cream flavors chosen 3 at a time.

State whether each example is a *permutation* or *combination*. Then solve the problem.

1. 6 books in a row on a shelf

2. a team of 5 selected from 8

3. a 4-person committee selected from 7 people

4. a batting order with 5 people

5. 2 of 5 students elected to student council

6. 4-digit numbers formed from the digits 1, 3, 5, and 7

Evaluate.

7. $\dfrac{5 \bullet 4 \bullet 3}{3 \bullet 2 \bullet 1}$

8. $\dfrac{6 \bullet 5}{2 \bullet 1}$

9. $\dfrac{12 \bullet 11 \bullet 10}{3 \bullet 2 \bullet 1}$

Problem SOLVING

10. Suppose the student council decided to sell plain pizza, with all four toppings, or any combination of the four toppings. How many different pizzas are possible? Complete the chart below as you answer this question.

Number of Toppings	Plain (Zero)	One	Two	Three	Four	Total
Number of Combinations	?	?	?	?	?	?

11. Suppose you have five toppings to choose from. Make a table similar the one above. How many different pizzas are possible?

Constructed RESPONSE

12. Explain the similarities and differences between a permutation and a combination.

Mind BUILDER

More About Pascal's Triangle

Pascal's Triangle is a triangular array of numbers used in the study of probability. The numbers also reveal information about combinations.

1. Explain how the combinations in problems 10–11 are related to Pascal's Triangle.

2. Suppose the student council had six possible toppings for their pizza. Use Pascal's Triangle to predict how many different pizzas are possible.

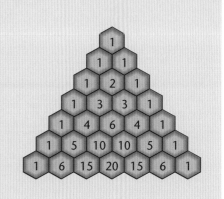

The True-False Test

Lee forgot to study for her geography quiz, but she wasn't too worried because the quiz had only five true-false questions. Suppose she guessed all of the answers. What are the chances that she passed with four or five correct answers?

Extension

Suppose Lee's quiz had ten true-false questions. What are the chances that she guessed all ten answers correctly?

Cumulative Review

Solve.

1. 2,491
   + 609

2. $26.89
   − 4.98

3. 8.92
   − 2.617

4. $42.86
   + 0.94

5. 207 × 5

6. 4,370 × 5

7. 6)2,706

8. 5)197

Express each number in scientific notation.

9. 4,300

10. 7,000,000

11. 63,400

12. 972

Write each fraction in simplest form.

13. $\frac{5}{20}$

14. $\frac{4}{14}$

15. $\frac{9}{18}$

16. $\frac{15}{21}$

17. $\frac{15}{27}$

18. $\frac{8}{32}$

Compute.

19. $\frac{13}{15} + \frac{2}{15}$

20. $4 - \frac{1}{10}$

21. $2\frac{2}{3} - \frac{1}{6}$

22. $7\frac{9}{10} + 4\frac{3}{20}$

23. $\frac{2}{3} \times 18$

24. $\frac{1}{2} \times \frac{2}{5}$

25. $\frac{8}{9} \times \frac{3}{10}$

26. $\frac{7}{8} \div \frac{1}{2}$

Write each fraction as a decimal. Round each result to the nearest hundredth.

27. $\frac{1}{4}$

28. $\frac{5}{8}$

29. $\frac{2}{3}$

30. $\frac{1}{9}$

31. $\frac{3}{7}$

32. $\frac{7}{20}$

Find the missing angle in each figure.

33.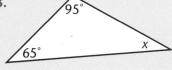

34.

35.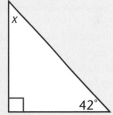

Solve.

36. How many times would you have to hike a 7-mile trail in order to hike a total of at least 100 miles?

37. Tickets to the play cost $2.00 each. A ticket to the concert costs $1\frac{1}{2}$ times as much. What is the difference in cost?

10.6 Theoretical and Experimental Probability

Objective: to gain a better understanding of theoretical and experimental probability

Did you listen to a weather forecast before you started school today? Do you think it will rain? Everyday weather forecasters make predictions based on information they have collected.

Let's try to make a prediction. Your teacher will give you an envelope containing 100 slips of paper, some red and some blue. Don't peek inside! This experiment will help you predict how many slips of paper are red.

Exploration Exercise

1. Draw one slip of paper, record its color, and replace it in the envelope. Do this ten times.

2. Repeat this procedure for twenty, thirty, forty, and fifty draws.

3. Complete the chart. The term relative frequency means what fraction of the time was a red slip of paper drawn. Express this as a decimal.

Number of draws	10
Number of reds	ⅠⅠⅠⅠ
Number of blues	卌 Ⅰ
Relative frequency of drawing red	$\frac{4}{10} = 0.4$

This is only a sample.

4. The **experimental probability** is an estimate based on the relative frequency you obtained. Based on your information after ten draws, what was the experimental probability of drawing a red slip of paper? after twenty draws? after fifty draws?

5. Predict how many red slips of paper are in your envelope.

Exercises

Copy and complete the graph using the information from the chart you created on p. 250. Then answer each question about the graph.

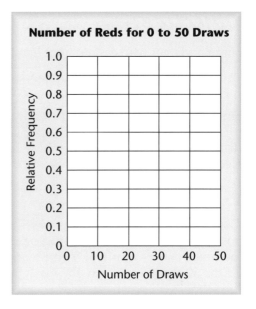

Number of Reds for 0 to 50 Draws

1. On the vertical scale, why do the numbers range from 0 to 1?

2. Do the points of your graph seem to cluster around one frequency? Why?

3. Estimate the relative frequency after 60 draws and after 100 draws.

4. The **theoretical probability** of choosing red is:

$$P(\text{event}) = \frac{\text{number of ways the event can occur}}{\text{number of possible outcomes}}$$

↑ choosing red

Now, open the envelope and determine the theoretical probability of choosing red. Sometimes this is referred to as odds. You found the odds of choosing a red slip from the envelope.

Problem SOLVING

5. Write a sentence that describes the relationship between the experimental probability and the theoretical probability.

6. Suppose your envelope has 100 slips of paper, all red. What is $P(\text{red})$? Suppose the envelope has 100 slips of paper, all blue. What is $P(\text{red})$?

7. Make an envelope containing 100 slips of paper, some red, some blue, and some yellow. Ask someone to predict how many of each color are in the envelope.

Mid-Chapter REVIEW

A number cube is rolled. Find the probability of each event.

1. $P(2)$ 2. $P(\text{odd number})$ 3. $P(8)$ 4. $P(\text{greater than } 0)$

Solve.

5. Margo has a choice of three different skirts and three different blouses. Find the number of possible outfits.

6. A menu offers the choice of orange, grapefruit, or tomato juice and waffles or pancakes. Draw a tree diagram to represent the possibilities.

7. How many ways can nine books be stacked in a pile?

Objective: to use samples to make predictions

Have you ever read a statement like the following in the newspaper?

> **Nearly two-thirds of Americans approve of the job the president is doing.**

Since it is impossible to ask the entire population, the news reporter probably asked a sample of the population. People use information from samples to predict everything from the winner in a presidential election to how many students will buy a school pennant.

> A good sample is:
> • taken randomly
> • representative of the larger group

Example

The Spencer Spirit Club plans to sell school pennants. They need to know how many to order. Spencer Junior High has 825 students. The club members ask a **sample** of 50 students whether they will buy a pennant. Of the 50 students, 21 say they will buy one. About how many students in the school will buy pennants?

1. READ The school has 825 students. Also, 21 out of 50 students in the sample will buy a pennant. You need to predict, or estimate, how many students in the school will buy pennants.

2. PLAN The sample should represent the whole school. Since $\frac{21}{50}$ of the sample will buy a pennant, estimate that $\frac{21}{50}$ of 825 will buy a pennant.

3. SOLVE Estimate $\frac{2}{5}$ of 825. $\frac{21}{50} \approx \frac{2}{5}$

$\frac{1}{5}$ of 825 = 165

$2 \times \frac{1}{5} = 2 \times 165$, or 330

About 330 students are likely to buy pennants.

4. CHECK Less than half of the students in the sample said they would buy a pennant. The school has about 800 students, and half of 800 is 400. It seems reasonable that about 330 students will buy pennants.

· ·

State whether each of the locations given would be a good place to find a representative sample for the poll given. Explain why or why not.

Poll	Location
1. number of pets	apartment building
2. favorite sandwich	shopping center
3. favorite color of car	state fair
4. number of movies seen	movie theater
5. favorite singing group	record shop
6. number of bedrooms	suburban development

Solve ·

Solve. Use the results of the survey at the right. Suppose the sample is a good random sample of 230 students.

1. How many students are in the sample?

2. What is the probability that a student supports Brunner?

3. Estimate how many of the 230 students support Brunner.

4. What is the probability that a student supports Marshall?

5. Estimate how many of the 230 students support Marshall.

6. What is the probability that a student supports Kavali?

7. Estimate how many of the 230 students support Kavali.

8. Describe a situation in which this sample would not be representative of the group of 230 students.

Whom do you support for class president?

Brunner	13
Kavali	9
Marshall	8

10.8 Independent and Dependent Events

Objective: to find the probability of independent and dependent events

A **compound event** consists of two or more simple events. In this lesson, you will find probabilities in this form:

P(event A *and* event B) 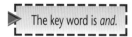 The key word is *and*.

Chris collects coins as a hobby. She tosses a dime twice. Find the probability that both tosses result in heads, $P(HH)$. You can find $P(HH)$ by using a tree diagram or by multiplying.

Look at the tree diagram. The sample space has 4 outcomes. In one of the outcomes, both tosses result in heads.

So, $P(HH) = \frac{1}{4}$.

1st Toss	2nd Toss	Outcomes
H	H	HH
	T	HT
T	H	TH
	T	TT

You can use multiplication. On the first toss, $P(H) = \frac{1}{2}$. $P(H)$ on the second toss is also $\frac{1}{2}$. Since $\frac{1}{2} \times \frac{1}{2} = \frac{1}{4}$, you can conclude that $P(HH) = \frac{1}{4}$.

$$P(HH) = P(H) \times P(H)$$
$$= \frac{1}{2} \times \frac{1}{2}$$
$$= \frac{1}{4}$$

Another Example

Chris has three of her dimes in a bag. One was minted in 1920. Two were minted in 1925.

Suppose she draws two dimes out of the bag without replacing the first. What is P(1925 and then 1925)?

1st Draw	2nd Draw	Outcomes
1920	1925	1920 and 1925
	1925	1920 and 1925
1925	1920	1925 and 1920
	1925	1925 and 1925
1925	1920	1925 and 1920
	1925	1925 and 1925

From this tree diagram, P(1925 and then 1925) is $\frac{2}{6}$ or $\frac{1}{3}$.

$$P(1925 \text{ and then } 1925) = P(1925) \times P(1925)$$
$$= \frac{2}{3} \times \frac{1}{2}$$
$$= \frac{2}{6} \text{ or } \frac{1}{3}$$

On the second draw, $P(1925) = \frac{1}{2}$. This assumes that the first dime drawn was a 1925 and was *not* replaced.

In the first example, the events are **independent** because neither affects the other. In the second example, the events are **dependent** because the first draw affects the second draw.

Try THESE

Find each probability. Refer to the examples on p. 254.

1. P(TT)
2. P(TH)
3. P(*not* HH)
4. P(1920 and then 1925)
5. P(1925 and then 1920)
6. What is P(1925 and then 1925) if the first coin is replaced?

Exercises

Dimes are drawn from the six shown. Find each probability.

1st dime is *not* replaced	1st dime *is* replaced
1. P(1924 and then 1924)	4. P(1920 and then 1920)
2. P(1920 and then 1920)	5. P(1925 and then 1924)
3. P(1925 and then 1925 and 1925)	6. P(1924 and then 1924 and 1924)

A bag contains 4 white, 3 blue, and 5 red marbles. Find the probability of each event if the marbles are replaced.

7. a red marble, then a white marble
8. a blue marble, then a red marble
9. 2 white marbles in a row
10. 3 red marbles in a row

Problem SOLVING

11. Kim's drawer contains three navy socks and six black socks. Which of the methods of picking two socks will have a greater probability of picking two navy socks? Explain your reasoning.

    Method 1: You randomly choose a sock from the drawer, but you don't replace it. Then, you randomly choose another sock.

    Method 2: You randomly choose a sock from the drawer and replace it. Then, you randomly choose another sock.

Test PREP

12. You flip a coin and roll a number cube. Find the probability of getting heads and rolling an even number.

    a. $\frac{1}{2}$ b. $\frac{1}{4}$ c. $\frac{1}{8}$ d. 1

13. You flip a coin three times. Find the probability of getting heads, tails, heads.

    a. $\frac{1}{2}$ b. $\frac{1}{4}$ c. $\frac{1}{8}$ d. 1

Objective: to solve problems using a simulation

You were lucky enough to get tickets for the basketball game. It is an exciting game. Your team is losing by one point when Miguel steps to the foul line.

- ▪ **If he misses the foul shot, your team loses.**
- ▪ **If he makes the foul shot, he gets one point and another try.**
- ▪ **If he makes the second shot, your team wins the game.**

Suppose Miguel has a record of making a basket two out of every three tries. What is the probability that your team wins the game?

One way to solve this problem is to do a **simulation**, that is, act it out. Construct a spinner similar to the one shown at the right. Spin the spinner, and record the results for twenty-five trips to the foul line.

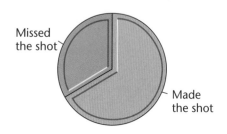

Missed the shot

Made the shot

Calculate the relative frequency for zero, one, and two points. For your simulation, what is the experimental probability that Miguel scores two points and wins the game?

Simulating the event can help you find the theoretical probability of an event occurring.

Try THESE ··

Suppose Jake had gone to the foul line instead of Miguel. Jake has a record of making one basket out of every two tries.

1. How would you modify the spinner to simulate this situation?

2. Find the probability that Jake makes two baskets.

Solve ··

1. Suppose you spin this spinner twice and record the sum. Predict which sum will occur most frequently. Test your prediction with a simulation.

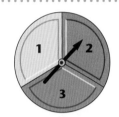

Use the Venn diagram on the right to solve problems 2–3.

2. Suppose you randomly chose a student from Mrs. Carr's class. What is the probability that he or she owns both a cat and a dog?

3. How many students own a cat, a bird, and a dog?

4. A dance class stands equally spaced in a circle and then counts off. If student number 10 is directly opposite student number 23, how many students are in the class?

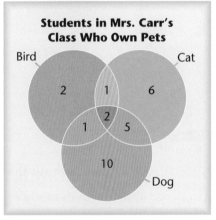

Students in Mrs. Carr's Class Who Own Pets

Use the figure on the right to solve problems 5–6.

5. Suppose a sky diver parachutes onto a square field that is 1 mile by 1 mile. Estimate the probability that the diver will have a dry landing.

★ 6. Suppose the pond was a circular pond with a radius of $\frac{1}{8}$ mile. Find the probability of a dry landing.

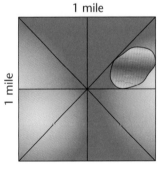

1 mile

1 mile

Language and Concepts

Choose the letter of the correct term or symbol to complete each sentence.

1. The result of some activity or experiment is called a(n) _____.

2. A(n) _____ is a list of all possible outcomes.

3. In a(n) _____ sample, every member has an equal chance of being chosen.

4. An event that cannot occur has a probability of _____.

5. An event that will certainly occur has a probability of _____.

6. A(n) _____ is used to show all possible outcomes.

7. An arrangement in which order is important is called a(n) _____.

8. A selection of objects in which order is not important is called a(n) _____.

9. The symbol for $4 \times 3 \times 2 \times 1$ is 4!, which is read "four _____."

10. It is usually impossible to survey an entire _____.

a. 0
b. 1
c. combination
d. factorial
e. outcome
f. permutation
g. population
h. probability
i. random
j. sample
k. sample space
l. tree diagram

Skills and Problem Solving

Answer each question about the spinner. Section 10.1

11. If you spin the spinner once, how many outcomes are possible?

12. What is the probability that the spinner stops on red?

13. What is the probability that the spinner does not stop on blue?

14. What is the probability that the spinner stops on green?

15. What is the probability that the spinner stops on red or blue?

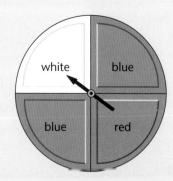

Draw a tree diagram to show the possible outcomes. Section 10.2

16. tossing the coin and spinning the spinner

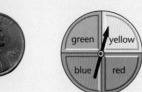

17. spinning each spinner once

Use the fundamental counting principle to find the total number of outcomes. Section 10.3

18. You have a choice of cherry, peach, or apple pie with or without ice cream.

19. When painting you have a choice of 2 different canvases, 5 colors of paint, and 4 different brushes.

State whether each example is a *permutation* or *combination*. Then solve. Sections 10.4–10.5

20. a committee of 3 selected from 5

21. 5 books in a row on a shelf

Evaluate. Section 10.4

22. $3!$

23. $4!$

24. $(4 - 2)!$

25. $(7 - 6)!$

Solve. Sections 10.4–10.5

26. In how many ways can four students be elected president, vice president, secretary, and treasurer?

27. In how many ways can a committee of three be selected from four volunteers?

A bag contains 7 green marbles, 8 yellow marbles, and 5 blue marbles. Find the probability of each event if the marbles are *not* replaced. Section 10.8

28. P(green marble, then green marble)

29. P(blue marble, then yellow marble)

30. P(blue marble, then blue marble, then blue marble)

Solve. Use the results of the survey at the right. Suppose the sample is a good random sample of 550 people. Section 10.7

31. How many people are in the sample?

32. What is the probability that a person prefers Marvel?

33. Estimate how many of the 550 people prefer Marvel.

34. What is the probability that a person prefers Alive?

35. Estimate how many of the 550 people prefer Alive.

36. What is the probability that a person prefers Shine?

37. Estimate how many of the 550 people prefer Shine.

Which brand of soap do you prefer?

Alive	43
Sudsy	19
Shine	22
Marvel	26

Chapter 10 Test

Suppose you roll two number cubes. Find the probability of each event.

1. P(a sum of 2)
2. P(*not* a sum of 7)
3. P(a sum of 16)

Solve.

4. You have a choice of oatmeal or cereal and a choice between skim, 2%, or whole milk. Draw a tree diagram to show the possible outcomes. Find the probability of choosing oatmeal with whole milk.

5. On Monday, Rosa's Restaurant has a special price on spaghetti or ziti. You can get marinara, meat, or Alfredo sauce on it as well as Parmesan or Romano cheese on it. How many different pasta dishes are possible?

6. Marge had to place eight photographs on the bulletin board. How many ways can Marge arrange the photographs in a row?

7. Suppose you want to order a burger with two toppings. You can choose from cheese, bacon, onions, lettuce, and tomatoes. How many burgers are possible?

8. A closet has five brown shoes and six black shoes. Two shoes are chosen at random without replacement. What is the probability that the shoes are both black?

9. A bag of paper clips has four yellow paper clips, three red paper clips, and five silver paper clips. One is chosen then replaced, and then another is chosen. What is the probability of choosing a red paper clip and then a silver paper clip?

10. There are 30 runners participating in a marathon. How many ways can runners place first, second, and third?

11. A bucket contains 14 blue, 8 red, and 5 white balls. You randomly choose 1 ball, put it back in the bucket, and then randomly choose another ball. Are events A and B below independent or dependent? Explain. What is the probability of event A then event B?

    Event A: Choose a blue ball first.

    Event B: Choose a white ball second.

12. A baking company tests the quality of its bread by taking a random sample of 20 loaves each hour. In one sample, 3 loaves were overweight and 4 were underweight. Suppose the company bakes 8,000 loaves a day. How many do you predict will be underweight? How many will be overweight?

13. A survey to determine favorite radio stations was conducted in a local mall. Suppose there are 120,000 people in the listening range of these stations. About how many do you predict listen to KRZY?

Favorite Radio Stations	
KALM	28
KOOL	32
KRZY	34
none	11

Photographic Sampling

Samples can be used to estimate the size of a population. For example, the photograph below shows many birds. An estimate of the total number of birds in the population may be made as follows.

- Divide the photo into sections.
- Count the number of birds in one section.
- Multiply this number by the number of sections.

This product is one estimate of the number of birds in the population.

1. Make another estimate using a different section.

2. Use the same method to estimate the number of cars in the photograph below.

Cumulative Test

1. How many outcomes are possible when two number cubes are rolled?
   a. 6
   b. 36
   c. 12
   d. none of the above

2. There are 8 red, 6 blue, and 2 white buttons in a sack. What is the probability of choosing a blue button?
   a. $\frac{1}{8}$
   b. $\frac{1}{7}$
   c. $\frac{3}{8}$
   d. $\frac{1}{2}$

3. A number cube is rolled. What is the probability of rolling a number less than 7?
   a. 0
   b. $\frac{1}{2}$
   c. $\frac{1}{6}$
   d. 1

4. Solve.
   $$\frac{x}{3} + 6 = 10$$
   a. 10
   b. 12
   c. $\frac{4}{3}$
   d. 9

5. Solve.
   $$x + 3 = -5$$
   a. 8
   b. -8
   c. 15
   d. -15

6. What type of angle does the ramp form with the ground?

   a. acute
   b. right
   c. obtuse
   d. both a and b

7. The peaches in a basket can be separated into equal groups of 4 or 14. What is the least number of peaches that could be in the basket?
   a. 18
   b. 56
   c. 28
   d. 112

8. The wall of a building is 36 blocks high. If each block is 9 inches high, how many feet high is the building?
   a. 4
   b. 324
   c. 27
   d. none of the above

9. A bag contains 5 red marbles and 10 blue marbles. What is the probability of choosing 2 blue marbles if you do not replace your first choice?
   a. $\frac{1}{3}$
   b. $\frac{4}{9}$
   c. $\frac{3}{7}$
   d. $\frac{2}{3}$

10. One can of corn weighs 16 ounces. What is the weight of eight cans of corn? Which problem is solved using the same operation used to solve the problem given above?
    a. A book costs $3.95, and an album costs $8.95. How much more does the album cost?
    b. How many eggs are there in 30 dozen?
    c. If Mr. Lane drove 21,000 miles last year, how many miles did he average each month?
    d. none of the above

Displaying and Analyzing Data

Angela Latona
Naples, FL

Objective: to find the mean, median, mode, and range of a data set

Jack asked members of his class how many hours they spend on homework each week. Their responses are below.

| 5 | 7 | 10 | 6 | 8 | 8 | 7 | 6 | 8 | 8 |

We can find the mean, median, mode, and range of the data above.

The **mean** is the sum of the numbers in the data divided by the number of items in the data set. It is sometimes referred to as the average.

To find the average, divide the sum of hours by the number of students.

$$\frac{5+7+10+6+8+8+7+6+8+8}{10} = \frac{73}{10} \qquad \frac{73}{10} = 7.3$$

The mean is 7.3 hours.

The **median** is the middle number when the data are listed in order from least to greatest.

Arrange the data in order from least to greatest.

5, 6, 6, 7, 7, 8, 8, 8, 8, 10

$$\frac{7+8}{2} = \frac{15}{2} = 7.5$$

There are two middle numbers; the median in this case is the mean of these two numbers.

The median is 7.5 hours.

The **mode** is the number or item that appears most often in a data set.

8 hours appears most often.

The mode is 8 hours.

Mean, median, and mode are sometimes called **measures of central tendency**. Measures of central tendency are numbers that represent the center of a data set.

The **range** is the difference between the greatest and the least number in a data set.

The least number of hours is 5.
The greatest number of hours is 10.
$$10 - 5 = 5$$

The range is 5 hours.

List each set of data from least to greatest. Then find the mean, median, mode, and range. Round to the nearest tenth, if necessary.

1. 3, 6, 7, 9, 9, 10

2. 71, 84, 87, 87

3. 52, 53, 58, 64, 64, 74, 74, 74

4. 88, 88, 109, 110, 111, 123, 124

5. 2.3, 1.7, 2.9, 1.8, 3, 3.1, 2.5

6. 0.12, 0.13, 0.14, 0.15, 0.12, 0.11

7. Replace one of the members of the set 14, 18, 21, 13 so that the median of the numbers in the resulting list is 17.

8. Insert another member in the set 9, 12, 17, 15, 13 so that the median of the numbers in the resulting list is 14.

9. Insert another member in the set 18, 12, 15, 12 so that the mean in the new list is 16.

10. Replace one of the members in the set 2, 4, 6, 5, 4 so that the mean of the numbers in the new list is 5.

Problem SOLVING

11. The table to the right shows the scores for Mrs. Yang's science test. Find the mean and the median for the test scores.

Mrs. Yang's Class

| 85 | 96 | 77 | 83 | 70 | 91 | 86 | 88 |
| 85 | 93 | 82 | 85 | 72 | 93 | 75 | 89 |

12. The heights, in inches, of the members of a junior high basketball team are given.

67, 72, 73, 64, 70, 68, 74, 68, 65, 66

Explain why finding the mode would not be meaningful.

★ 13. Is it possible for the mean, median, and mode of a data set to be the same number? If so, give an example.

Constructed RESPONSE

14. Maggie's scores so far on her English tests are 85, 72, 80, and 83. If she earns a 100 on the next test, how are the mean, median, and mode of her test scores affected? Explain.

Test PREP

15. What measure describes the average of a set of data?

   a. median   b. mean   c. mode   d. range

16. The median of the data set 6, 4, 5, 1, 6, 3, 2 is _____.

   a. 2   b. 3   c. 4   d. 5

11.2 Frequency Tables and Line Plots

Objective: to use data to make a frequency table and line plots

Rosita asked some of her classmates how much time they listen to the radio each day (to the nearest $\frac{1}{2}$ hour). Then she marked a tally for each in a table and counted the tallies in each row.

Time Spent Listening to Radio		
Hours	**Tally**	**Frequency**
0	ꓕꓕꓕꓕ ꓕꓕꓕꓕ ꓲ	11
$\frac{1}{2}$	ꓕꓕꓕꓕ ꓲꓲꓲ	8
1	ꓕꓕꓕꓕ ꓕꓕꓕꓕ ꓲꓲꓲ	13
$1\frac{1}{2}$	ꓕꓕꓕꓕ ꓕꓕꓕꓕ	10
2	ꓕꓕꓕꓕ ꓕꓕꓕꓕ ꓕꓕꓕꓕ	15
$2\frac{1}{2}$	ꓕꓕꓕꓕ ꓲ	6
3	ꓲꓲꓲꓲ	4

67 total

> The numbers in the first column should include a range for all of the data. It should be separated into equal intervals.

> The number of tallies are counted and displayed in the frequency column.

> Tally marks are used to show how many people chose each category.

This method of organizing data is called a **frequency table**. A frequency table is a graph that allows us to interpret data and create graphs from data. The mode is 2, and the range is 3.

Another way to organize data is by using a **line plot**. A line plot is a picture of information on a number line. On the line plot below, an **x** is used to indicate the number of books each student reads.

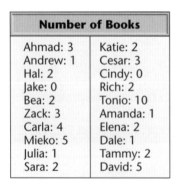

Number of Books	
Ahmad: 3	Katie: 2
Andrew: 1	Cesar: 3
Hal: 2	Cindy: 0
Jake: 0	Rich: 2
Bea: 2	Tonio: 10
Zack: 3	Amanda: 1
Carla: 4	Elena: 2
Mieko: 5	Dale: 1
Julia: 1	Tammy: 2
Sara: 2	David: 5

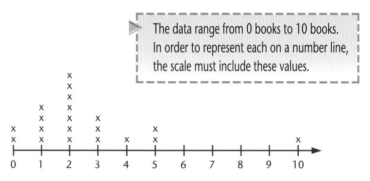

> The data range from 0 books to 10 books. In order to represent each on a number line, the scale must include these values.

You can analyze data more easily in a line plot than from the table.

- From this line plot, we can see that the mode is 2.

- The number 10 is an **outlier**. An outlier is a piece of data that lies far away from most of the other pieces of data.

- There is a **cluster** of data between 1 and 3. A cluster is an area on a line plot which seems to contain many numbers in the data set.

··

State the scale you would use to plot each set of data.

1. 25, 28, 40, 42, 55, 70

2. 4, 4.5, 5, 6.3, 6.8, 7.3

3. 122, 180, 198, 260, 310, 425

4. 5, 7, 2, 9, 7, 3, 1, 8, 20

The frequency table at the right gives the length (to the nearest 10 seconds) of a sample of television commercials.

5. How many commercials are in the sample?

6. What is the mode of the data?

7. What is the range of the data?

Lengths of TV Commercials		
Length	Tally	Frequency
10	卌 l	6
20	卌 卌 l	11
30	卌 卌 卌 lll	18
40	卌 llll	9
50	l	1
60	卌	5

··

8. The data below are the ages of those who recently attended a movie.

   > 18, 17, 19, 67, 56, 32, 34, 45, 46, 19, 25, 16,
   > 33, 30, 41, 7, 9, 25, 8, 51, 43, 55, 42, 17, 67,
   > 58, 30, 18, 22, 24, 25, 26, 29, 22, 26

   a. Construct a frequency table of the ages (to the nearest 10 years).

   b. Identify the range and mode of the data.

9. Recently, some early editions of books written by Samuel Clemens (Mark Twain) sold for the following prices: $2,200, $160, $450, $330, $325, $1,600, $800, $130, $180, $65, $420, $100, $110, $110, $150, $60, $70, $50. Make a line plot of the prices. Describe the range, mode, cluster, and outlier.

··

10. The data below give the heights (to the nearest 5 centimeters) of a sample of students at a junior high school.

    > 155 150 160 145 150 160 165
    > 145 155 160 180 165 160 155
    > 150 160 165 150 155 145 160
    > 155 140 145 155 145 155 165

    Make a frequency table and a line plot of the data. Compare and contrast the frequency table and the line plot. Is one a better representation of the data than the other? Explain.

11.3 Stem-and-Leaf Plots

Objective: to construct and read stem-and-leaf plots

Student	Grade
Doug	85
Rebecca	94
Bradley	75
Justine	88
Allison	64
Tami	72
Mick	91
Montega	63
Christy	75
Wanda	87

Mrs. Gomez just graded her classes' history tests. The table at the right shows the grades she entered into her grade book. She can organize the grades in a stem-and-leaf plot.

A **stem-and-leaf plot** is a graph to organize data that displays all numbers in the data set by place value. Numbers in the data set are ordered when a stem-and-leaf plot is completed. The greatest place value is used for the stem, and the next greatest place value forms the leaves.

You can make a stem-and-leaf plot from the data above.

1. **Find the stems.** The stems are in the tens place value. The lowest grade is 63, and the highest grade is 94. This means the stems will range between 6 and 9. Make a vertical list of the stems with a line to their right.

Stem	Leaf
6	
7	
8	
9	

2. **Put the leaves on the plot.** The leaves are in the ones place value. Record each data on the graph by pairing the units digit, or leaf, with the correct stem. For example, 63 is plotted by placing the units digit 3 to the right of the stem 6.

Stem	Leaf
6	4 3
7	5 2 5
8	5 8 7
9	4 1

3. **Arrange the leaves so that they are ordered from least to greatest.** You also need to include an explanation of the data.

Stem	Leaf
6	3 4
7	2 5 5
8	5 7 8
9	1 4

6|3 = 63

Try THESE

Use the stem-and-leaf plot above to answer the following questions.

1. How many students are in Mrs. Gomez's history class?

2. What is the median of the data?

3. What does 7|5 represent?

4. What is the mode of the data?

5. Write a sentence that describes the information from the plot.

Make a stem-and-leaf plot for each set of data.

1. Weights of turkeys (in pounds): 12, 14, 23, 10, 14, 16, 9, 21, 8, 25, 15

2. Heights of students (in inches): 58, 45, 63, 51, 70, 65, 62, 54, 71, 42, 55

3. The ages of people who attended a movie: 15, 40, 28, 23, 16, 18, 21, 22, 16

4. Number of points scored in a football game: 21, 23, 7, 31, 14, 33, 20, 10, 17, 28, 34, 35

The table at the right shows the distances people commute to work every day (in miles).

5. Make a stem-and-leaf plot of the data in the table.

6. What is the range of the data?

7. What is the median of the data?

8. What is the mean of the data?

9. Into what interval (stem) do most of the data fall?

10. Write a sentence that describes the information from the plot.

Commute (in miles)					
12	20	8	32	25	15
30	17	24	52	22	36
14	7	15	18	4	25

Use the stem-and-leaf plot at the right for exercises 11–16.

11. What is the range of the data?

12. Are there any clusters or gaps in the data?

13. What is the median of the data?

14. What is the mode of the data?

15. Into which interval (stem) do most of the data fall?

★ 16. Describe the distribution of the data in the plot.

Stem	Leaf
5	4 5
6	0 6 9
7	2 3 4 5 5
8	1 2 8 9
9	5 6

5|4 = 54

17. Look at the stem-and-leaf plot to the right. Describe the errors and correct them.

Stem	Leaf
0	5 7 3
1	2 6 8 7
2	5 3 6 7

1. Find the mean, median, mode, and range of the data set.

   7, 12, 15, 4, 23, 15, 25, 9

2. Make a frequency table and line plot for the data below.

   4, 6, 3, 5, 0, 1, 5, 4, 6, 6, 7

3. Make a stem-and-leaf plot for the data below.

   48, 37, 54, 56, 55, 39, 31, 42, 43, 45

Peggy's Postal Problem

Peggy went to the post office to buy 7 postage stamps. The postal clerk gave her 7 stamps, in the formation below.

Peggy wondered, "How many ways can a postal clerk sell 7 postage stamps that are still attached?"

Can you find 20 different ways? Be careful not to use the same figure that has been rotated.

Extension

Draw each of the 20 formations, using graph paper.

Compute.

1. $\begin{array}{r} 2{,}492 \\ +\ \ 609 \\ \hline \end{array}$

2. $\begin{array}{r} \$41.83 \\ -\ 12.91 \\ \hline \end{array}$

3. $\begin{array}{r} 9.53 \\ -\ 3.191 \\ \hline \end{array}$

4. $\begin{array}{r} 7{,}684 \\ +\ \ 324.6 \\ \hline \end{array}$

5. $\begin{array}{r} 207 \\ \times\ \ \ 9 \\ \hline \end{array}$

6. $\begin{array}{r} 4{,}370 \\ \times\ \ \ \ 5 \\ \hline \end{array}$

7. $\begin{array}{r} 59 \\ \times\ 0.7 \\ \hline \end{array}$

8. $\begin{array}{r} 42.1 \\ \times\ \ \ 6 \\ \hline \end{array}$

9. $6\overline{)2{,}706}$

10. $8\overline{)6.4}$

11. $5\overline{)\$10.15}$

12. $12\overline{)7.2}$

13. $7\frac{1}{3} + 9\frac{3}{4}$

14. $\frac{2}{3} \times 19$

15. $7\frac{9}{10} - 4\frac{3}{20}$

16. $9\frac{1}{8} \div 2\frac{7}{8}$

Solve each equation. Check your solution.

17. $3.24 + n = 5.08$

18. $k - 24 = 5\frac{1}{3}$

19. $\frac{x}{4} = 3.9$

20. $5m = 75$

Draw an example of each figure.

21. hexagon

22. right triangle

23. rhombus

24. quadrilateral with two pairs of parallel sides

25. triangle with no congruent sides

Write each fraction in simplest form.

26. $\frac{5}{20}$

27. $\frac{4}{14}$

28. $\frac{9}{18}$

29. $\frac{15}{21}$

30. $\frac{15}{27}$

31. $\frac{8}{32}$

Write each fraction as a decimal. Round each result to the nearest hundredth.

32. $\frac{1}{4}$

33. $\frac{5}{8}$

34. $\frac{2}{3}$

35. $\frac{1}{9}$

36. $\frac{3}{7}$

37. $\frac{7}{20}$

Solve.

38. Janice ran 6 miles on Monday, 8 miles on Tuesday, and 10 miles on Thursday. How many miles did she run on average each day?

39. A gallon of milk costs $2.80. A gallon of ice cream costs $2\frac{1}{2}$ times as much. How much more does the ice cream cost?

40. Pizzas for a party cost $24.10, and the rest of the food costs $10.60. The decorations cost $6.95. Is the total cost for food greater or less than $35.00?

41. A sack of 40 potatoes has a mass of 4.7 kilograms. Find the average mass of a potato in grams to the nearest 10 grams.

Objective: to construct and read box-and-whisker plots

Juan is writing about the climate of the United States for a science project. As part of his research, he finds data on the mean daily temperatures in two U.S. cities, Miami and Denver. The data are in the table on the right.

Mean Daily Temperature		
Month	**Miami**	**Denver**
January	68	29
February	69	33
March	72	40
April	76	48
May	80	57
June	82	68
July	84	73
August	84	72
September	82	62
October	79	51
November	74	38
December	70	30

A **box-and-whisker plot** can be constructed with the range, median, and quartiles. A box-and-whisker plot is a graph that helps to visualize how data are arranged. A box is drawn around the quartile values, and whiskers are extended from each quartile to the extreme points.

A box-and-whisker plot is divided into sections. The median divides the data into two sections. These sections can be divided into **quartiles**. The **lower quartile** is the median of the bottom half. The **upper quartile** is the median of the top half.

You can use the information from the table above to make a box-and-whisker plot of the mean daily temperatures for Denver.

1. Order the data from least to greatest.

2. Find the median, the lower quartile, the upper quartile, and the extremes, the least and greatest data.

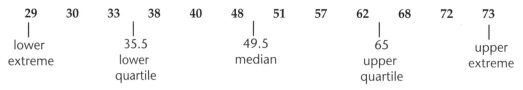

3. Draw a number line that includes all the data points. Mark dots for the median, quartiles, and extremes above the number line.

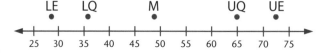

4. Draw a box around the quartile values. Draw a vertical line through the median value. Draw whiskers from each quartile to the extreme data points.

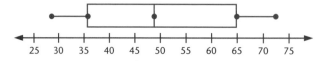

Look at the data set to the right to solve problems 1–7.

| 25 | 8 | 10 | 35 | 5 | 45 | 40 | 30 | 20 |

1. Make a box-and-whisker plot of the data.

2. What is the lower quartile?

3. What is the upper quartile?

4. What is the lower extreme?

5. What is the upper extreme?

6. What is the range of the data?

7. What is the median?

Make a box-and-whisker plot for each set of data.

8. 6, 7, 1, 3, 9, 3, 2, 5, 4, 8

9.

Stem	Leaf
5	2 3 6 7
6	1 1 8
7	0 3 7
8	5 7 5|2 = 52

10. Draw a box-and-whisker plot for the mean daily temperatures of Miami shown on p. 272. Compare and contrast this plot to the box-and-whisker plot for Denver.

11. Compare the box-and-whisker plots shown at the right. What is similar about the data? What is different?

12. What information is easier to find on a box-and-whisker plot than on a stem-and-leaf plot? What information is more difficult to find?

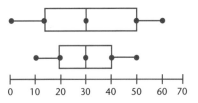

Percentile

On various nationwide tests, a **percentile** is used to describe a score. For example, the eighty-second percentile is the point at or below which 0.82 of the scores fall.

Suppose your test score is 85. Your score is at the seventy-fifth percentile. This means that 0.75 $\left(\text{or } \frac{3}{4}\right)$ of the scores are at or below your score.

Test Scores

96	←	99th percentile
86		
85	←	75th percentile
80		
78	←	50th percentile
74		
73	←	25th percentile
65		

Solve. Use the list above.

1. Suppose your score is 78. At what percentile is your score?

2. Suppose your score is 96. At what percentile is your score?

3. Add 86, 67, 82, and 93 to the list. What score is at the seventy-fifth percentile?

4. Suppose your score is 73. At what percentile is your score?

11.5 Bar Graphs and Histograms

Objective: to construct and read bar graphs and histograms

School Play Attendance	
Grade	**Students**
6	25
7	42
8	31
9	18

The Arts School recently put on a play. The table to the right shows the number of students from each grade that attended the play. We can use the information in the table to create a bar graph. A **bar graph** is a way to represent data using horizontal or vertical bars to represent quantities.

To make a bar graph:

1. Draw vertical and horizontal axes.

2. Choose a scale.

3. Label the axes.

4. Draw bars.

5. Give the graph a title.

Mr. Hughes surveyed his students to find out how much time they spent sleeping at night. The results are shown in the frequency table to the right. Notice that the data have been grouped into half-hour intervals. It is useful to show the data in a **histogram**. A histogram shows how data are distributed using intervals.

Time Spent Sleeping	
Hours	**Frequency**
$7-7\frac{1}{2}$	6
$7\frac{1}{2}-8$	8
$8-8\frac{1}{2}$	10
$8\frac{1}{2}-9$	7
$9-9\frac{1}{2}$	5

To make a histogram:

1. Draw horizontal and vertical axes.

2. Label the axes.

3. Draw bars to represent the frequency of the intervals.

4. Give the graph a title.

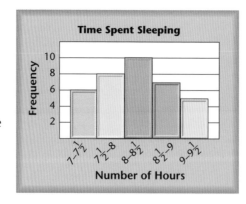

Use the histogram shown on p. 274.

1. Find the mode of the data.
2. Find the range of the data.
3. Find the median of the data.
4. Describe how much time students spent sleeping.

Exercises

Use the histogram at the right for exercises 1–6.

1. What kind of data is graphed in the histogram?
2. In what interval was the data collected?
3. What does each interval represent?
4. For what interval is the frequency the greatest?
5. How many students were asked?
6. How many students spent more than 3 hours studying?
7. Use the table below of the population of the world's largest cities to make a bar graph.

Largest Cities	
City	**Population (in millions)**
Tokyo, Japan	34
Mexico City, Mexico	18
New York, U.S.	18
San Paulo, Brazil	17
Bombay, India	16
Los Angeles, U.S.	12

Problem SOLVING

Use the frequency table to the right to solve problems 8–10.

8. Construct a histogram using the data in the table.
9. Find the mean and median of the histogram.
10. How many total players have hit more than 55 home runs in a season?
11. Compare and contrast bar graphs and histograms.
12. Write a survey question. Ask a group of people your question. Make a histogram to display the results of the survey.

50 Home Run Club		
Home Runs	**Tally**	**Frequency**
65–70	II	2
60–64	III	3
55–59	IIII II	7
50–54	IIII IIII IIII I	16

Objective: to solve problems by drawing a graph

Tai is doing research for a health project. He wants to find if there is a definite difference between the amount of sugar in cereals advertised for kids and adults.

He visited the grocery store and made a list of cereals. **K** means the cereal is for kids; **A** means the cereal is for adults. Then he listed the number of grams of sugar contained in each of them.

What kind of graph should Tai use to compare the two kinds of cereal?

Grams of Sugar in Cereals		
K1: 12	K13: 3	K23: 13
K2: 10	K14: 13	A18: 3
A1: 0	K15: 10	A19: 3
A2: 0	A9: 2	A20: 0
K3: 6	K16: 13	A21: 5
K4: 6	K17: 14	A22: 3
A3: 2	K18: 2	A23: 10
A4: 14	A10: 12	K24: 11
A5: 3	K19: 11	K25: 17
A6: 4	A11: 5	K26: 3
K5: 11	K20: 15	A24: 0
K6: 7	K21: 11	A25: 6
K7: 9	K22: 11	A26: 0
K8: 1	A12: 5	A27: 6
A7: 5	A13: 7	A28: 5
K9: 10	A14: 6	A29: 3
K10: 12	A15: 12	K27: 13
K11: 11	A16: 6	A30: 3
A8: 9	A17: 11	A31: 2
K12: 11		

1. READ You know the amount of sugar in each cereal. You need to find a graph that will make it easy to compare the data.

2. PLAN You might choose a histogram, line plot, stem-and-leaf plot, or box-and-whisker plot. Since there are many data, a box-and-whisker plot would be appropriate.

3. SOLVE Separate the data into two sets. Make a box-and-whisker plot for each set of data.

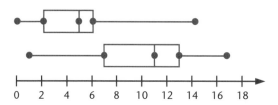

From the plot, you can see that the two sets of data have about the same range, 14 and 16. But, it is obvious that the median for the kid's cereal, 11, is much higher than the median for the adult's cereal, 5.

4. CHECK One way to check the answer is to find the mean for each set. The mean for the adult's cereal is 7 grams; the mean for the kid's cereal is 10 grams. The data on the box-and-whisker plot is reasonable.

··

1. Make a box-and-whisker plot for each set of data given below. Write a sentence that compares the life spans of the two sets of animals.

Maximum Recorded Life Span			
Fish	**Age (years)**	**Birds**	**Age (years)**
Abalone	13	Canary	24
Goldfish	30	Chicken	30
Halibut	40	Duck	20
Herring	19	Hummingbird	8
Mackerel	15	Ostrich	50
Salmon	13	Parakeet	25
Trout	41	Sparrow	20
Tuna	7	Swan	29
		Turkey	12
		Vulture	41

Solve ··

1. Make a stem-and-leaf plot for the data below. What is the median, mode, and range?

   Number of points scored in a girl's basketball game:

   61, 73, 91, 65, 84, 71, 72, 84, 90, 65, 72, 66

2. Five students earned the following amounts of money: $7.00, $16.00, $7.50, $8.00, $6.75. Find the mean and median. Which is a better indication of the money earned by each student? Explain.

3. Collect data on a topic that interests you. Using the data, decide on an interval and make a frequency table and a histogram for the data.

4. Make a bar graph for the data set below.

Animal Life Span	
Box turtle	100 years
Asian elephant	40 years
Grizzly bear	25 years
Horse	20 years
Gorilla	20 years
Lion	15 years

Objective: to recognize when graphs and data are misleading

You have seen that statistics is a useful tool for organizing and presenting data. It is important to use **statistics** in a proper manner and to recognize abuses and misuses of statistics.

Example

Tom decided to make bar graphs that showed his math grades for each grading period. Graphs A and B show Tom's grades. Although they display the same data, each graph gives a different impression.

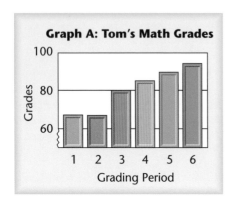

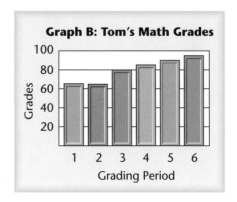

Try **THESE** ···

Answer each question based on the graphs above.

1. What is the range in Tom's math grades?

2. What is the vertical scale on each graph?

3. What is the purpose of the broken line at the bottom of Graph A?

4. Which graph would Tom probably show his parents to emphasize his improvement?

5. What causes the graphs to appear different?

Use Graphs C and D for problems 1–4.

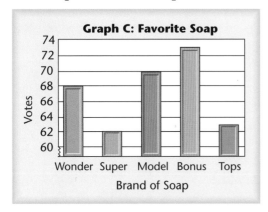

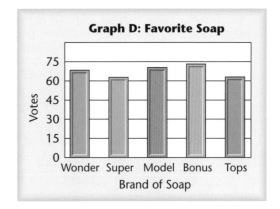

1. Which graph shows a definite favorite?

2. What is the difference between the number of votes of the top two brands of soaps?

3. Compare the range on the vertical scales. How does this affect the two graphs?

4. Why would Bonus soap prefer Graph C? Why would Super soap prefer Graph D?

5. Salaries for a company that employs six people are shown.

    $15,000; $21,000; $18,000; $18,000; $20,000; $85,000

    Would you quote the mean or median to a person who is thinking of working for the company? If you were thinking of working for this company, which measure would be more important?

6. Use the data in the table on the right to construct two bar graphs. For one graph, label the vertical axis from 0 to 100. For the other graph, use 40 to 60. How do the graphs differ? When might one be more useful than the other?

★7. Find a graph in a magazine or newspaper. Redo the graph so that the data will appear to show different results.

The Westlake Company	
Month	**Total Sales (thousands)**
January	45
February	40
March	30
April	50
May	45
June	50
July	60

Language and Concepts

Choose the letter of the correct term to complete each statement.

1. The _____ of a set of data is the middle number when the numbers are arranged in numerical order.

2. The difference between the greatest and least values of a set of data is called the _____.

3. The _____ of a set of data is the number or item that appears most often.

4. The _____ of a set of data is affected by the extreme values of the data.

5. In a histogram, the width of the rectangular region represents the _____ of the data.

6. In a histogram, the height of the rectangular region represents the _____ of the data.

7. A number in a set of data that is much higher or lower than the rest of the data is the _____.

8. A(n) _____ is a way to display data that organizes all numbers in the data set by place value.

9. You can construct a(n) _____ if you know the median, quartiles, and extreme values of the data.

10. _____ separate the data into four parts.

a. box-and-whisker plot
b. frequency
c. interval
d. mean
e. median
f. mode
g. outlier
h. quartiles
i. range
j. stem-and-leaf plot

Skills and Problem Solving

The table shows test scores for a class of students. Use the table to solve problems 11–15. Sections 11.1 and 11.5

11. How many students are in the sample?

12. What is the mode of the scores?

13. What is the range of the scores?

14. What is the median of the scores?

15. Make a histogram of the scores.

Test Scores		
Score	**Tally**	**Frequency**
18–20	$\cancel{||||}$	5
16–17	$\cancel{||||}$ ||||	9
14–15	$\cancel{||||}$	5
12–13	|||	3
10–11			1
8–9	||	2

Use the data set on the right to solve problem 16. Section 11.2

16. Construct a frequency table.

Favorite Subject

M	E	S	M	H	S	H	M	M	E	S	H
H	E	S	M	E	S	M	S	M	E	H	S

Use the data set below to solve problem 17. Section 11.2

7, 8, 6, 7, 5, 6, 4, 5, 2, 12, 5, 7, 6, 4, 2, 1

17. Make a line plot. Identify any clusters, gaps, or outliers.

Use the data set below to solve problem 18. Section 11.3

15, 7, 26, 5, 32, 16, 19, 24, 16, 3, 5, 36

18. Make a stem-and-leaf plot.

Use the data on the right to solve problems 19–20. Section 11.4

19. Make a box-and-whisker plot.

20. Describe the plot. Are there any outliers?

Money Spent on Groceries Weekly

$50	$65	$45	$85	$62	$60	$58	$69
$71	$51	$63	$48	$90	$65	$50	$64

Use the data on the right to solve problems 21–24. It shows the number of cars Sid has on his used car lot. Section 11.5

21. Make a histogram of the data.

22. In which interval is the median?

23. In which interval is the mode?

24. How many cars does Sid have on his lot?

Sid's Used Cars	
Price	**Frequency**
$5,000–$5,999	6
$6,000–$6,999	5
$7,000–$7,999	9
$8,000–$8,999	12
$9,000–$9,999	4
$10,000–$10,999	6

Use the graphs on the right to answer questions 25–27. The graphs represent seasonal sales for a coffee shop. Section 11.7

25. Which graph shows more consistency in sales throughout the year?

26. What is the difference between the sales from the top two seasons?

27. Compare the range on the two scales. How does it affect the two graphs?

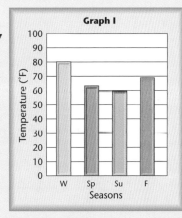

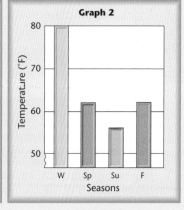

Chapter 11 Test

Use the data below to find the following. Round to the nearest tenth.

14, 17, 13, 16, 14, 14, 15, 19, 35, 17, 16

1. range   2. mode   3. median   4. mean

Use the frequency table to find each of the following.

5. sum of the frequencies

6. mode

7. median

8. mean (to the nearest tenth)

Scores on a 5-Point Quiz		
Score	**Tally**	**Frequency**
2	JHT	5
3	IIII	4
4	JHT I	6
5	JHT III	8

The frequency table shows the number of hours of TV that a sample of middle school students watch a week.

9. Draw a histogram of the data.

10. In which interval is the median?

11. In which interval is the mode?

12. Explain why it would be difficult to display the data on a line plot.

Hours of Watching TV	
Number of Hours	**Frequency**
0–4	3
5–8	4
9–12	16
13–16	15
17–20	20
21–24	19
25–28	13
29–32	5

Below are the ages of the people who attended a gymnastics meet. Use this data to solve problems 13–16.

12, 17, 15, 14, 19, 17, 13, 16, 15, 16, 17, 18, 24, 23, 28, 45, 48, 36, 12, 23, 15, 14, 13, 15, 17, 18, 19, 15, 15, 16, 16, 16, 16, 17

13. Make a stem-and-leaf plot.

14. What is the range of the data?

15. Mark the median on the stem-and-leaf plot.

16. Which age group was more widely represented?

17. Company A and Company B manufacture flashlight batteries. Ten batteries from each company were selected and tested to see how many hours they would last. The results of the test are shown below. From which company would you purchase batteries? Why? Use a box-and-whisker plot to help answer the question.

Hours of Life from Flashlight Batteries
Company A: 8, 15.5, 14, 14, 24, 19, 16.7, 15, 11.4, 16
Company B: 18, 14, 15.8, 9, 12, 16, 20, 16, 13, 15

Change of Pace

Scatter Plots

Scatter plots show how two things are related. Terry Wilder wants to know if there is a relationship between the grades earned on a test and the time spent studying for the test. He collected the data presented in the chart.

Student	Study Time	Test Score
Doug	10 min	65
Rebecca	15 min	68
Bradley	75 min	87
Justine	60 min	92
Allison	45 min	73
Tami	90 min	95
Mick	60 min	83
Montega	30 min	77
Christy	120 min	98

Make a scatter plot as follows. Plot the point that represents a study time of 10 minutes and a score of 65.

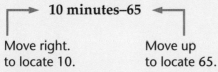

Move right.
to locate 10.

Move up
to locate 65.

Plot the remaining data points.

Solve. Use the scatter plot above.

1. How many students had a grade of 85 or better?

2. How many students studied less than 1 hour?

3. What does the scatter plot tell you about the relationship between the grade scored on the test and the time spent studying?

Draw a scatter plot for the following data. Then tell how the two groups of data are related.

4.

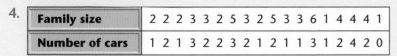

Family size	2 2 2 3 3 2 5 3 2 5 3 3 6 1 4 4 4 1
Number of cars	1 2 1 3 2 2 3 2 1 2 1 1 3 1 2 4 2 0

Explain how you think each of the following things may be related.

5. outside temperature, heating bill

6. sales per salesperson, years of experience per salesperson

7. test score, height of student

8. miles per gallon, weight of car

9. height, weight

10. amount of fertilizer, crop yield

Cumulative Test

1. Alma's quiz scores are 85, 80, 93, 100, and 80. To the nearest whole number, find the mean.
   a. 80
   b. 85
   c. 88
   d. none of the above

2. Find the upper quartile for the data below.
   340, 430, 420, 225, 295, 310
   a. 295
   b. 325
   c. 420
   d. none of the above

3. Estimate the product of 19 and 3.1.
   a. 6
   b. 16
   c. 22
   d. 60

4. Complete the sequence.
   1, 2, 4, 8, ■, ■, ■
   a. 4, 2, 1
   b. 12, 17, 23
   c. 16, 32, 64
   d. none of the above

5. Solve.
   $2x + 1 = 10$
   a. 2
   b. $4\frac{1}{2}$
   c. $5\frac{1}{2}$
   d. 18

6. Which data set has a median of 16?
   a. 16, 21, 26, 29, 32
   b. 0, 4, 7, 10, 16, 16
   c. 4, 15, 18, 20, 23
   d. 0, 8, 10, 22, 26, 31

7. Between what two data points is the middle one-half of the data?

   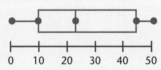

   a. 0, 50
   b. 10, 45
   c. 10, 25
   d. 25, 45

8. What is the value of $0.4st$ when $s = 4.3$ and $t = 5.55$?
   a. 1.72
   b. 9.546
   c. 10.25
   d. 23.865

9. Maria works 4.5 hours a day. She earns $4.05 an hour. How many weeks will it take her to earn $500? What information is needed to solve the problem?
   a. daily wages
   b. days worked each week
   c. hourly wages
   d. All the needed information is given.

10. The points you scored in the last seven basketball games are listed below. Which statement about the data is false?

    11, 15, 6, 10, 7, 22, 6
    a. The range is 11.
    b. The median is 10.
    c. The mode is 6.
    d. The mean is 11.

Functions and Coordinate Graphing

Ellen Brooks
Calvert Day School

Objective: to graph points on the coordinate plane

Numbers are graphed on the number line. **Ordered pairs** of numbers, such as (2, 4), (-1, 5), and (3, -8), are graphed on the **coordinate plane**. The coordinate plane has two perpendicular number lines. Each number line is called an **axis**. The horizontal axis is the *x*-axis, and the vertical axis is the *y*-axis. The axes (plural of *axis*) intersect at the **origin**, labeled *O*.

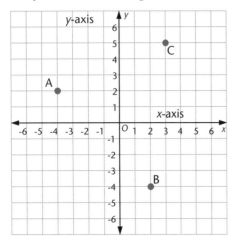

Every **point** in the coordinate plane has two **coordinates**. The **first coordinate** is a number on the horizontal axis. The **second coordinate** is a number on the vertical axis. The two coordinates form an ordered pair.

What is the ordered pair for point A at the left?

Point A is above -4 on the *x*-axis.

(-4, 2)

Point A is across from 2 on the *y*-axis.

What are the ordered pairs for points B and C?

The ordered pairs (-5, 3) and (0, -6) can be graphed as shown below. Start at the origin.

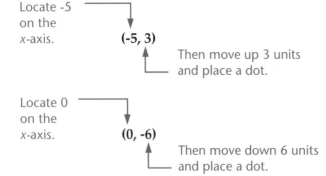

Locate -5 on the *x*-axis.

(-5, 3)

Then move up 3 units and place a dot.

Locate 0 on the *x*-axis.

(0, -6)

Then move down 6 units and place a dot.

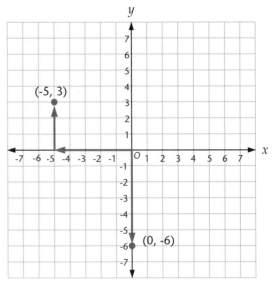

─────────────────────────────

Try THESE •

On graph paper, draw coordinate axes. Then graph each ordered pair. Label each point with the given letter.

1. A(-5, 0)   2. B(-3, -2)   3. C(5, -5)   4. D(6, 3)

....

On graph paper, draw coordinate axes. Then graph each ordered pair.
Label each point with the given letter.

1. E(2, 6)
2. F(-2, 5)
3. G(1, -4)
4. H(-6, 5)
5. I(-6, 1)
6. J(4, 1)
7. K(0, -3)
8. L(7, 7)

Find the ordered pair for each point on the
coordinate plane.

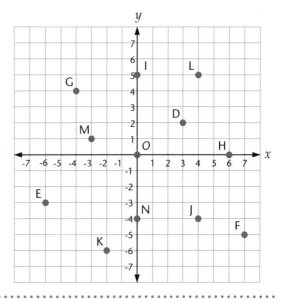

9. D
10. E
11. F
12. G
13. H
14. I
15. J
16. K
17. L
18. M
19. N
20. O

★21. What is true of points that have the same first
coordinate?

★22. What is true of points that have the same
second coordinate?

....

Solve. Use graph paper.

23. Graph the following ordered pairs and
connect the points in order: (5, 3), (3, 4),
(1, 3), (2, 1), (4, 1), and (5, 3). Identify the
geometric figure.

24. Graph the following ordered pairs and
connect the points in order: (1, 1), (1, 5),
(3, 3), (5, 5), and (5, 1). Identify the letter
of the alphabet.

25. Graph (-1, -3) and (-3, -7) and draw a
line that connects the points. Then find
the ordered pair for another point on
the line segment.

★ 26. The ordered pairs for three vertices of a
parallelogram are (0, 0), (2, 2), and (8, 2).
Find the ordered pair for the other
vertex.

....

27. The ordered pairs for three vertices of a square are (3, 1), (5, 3), and (3, 5). Find the
ordered pair for the other vertex. Explain why you chose this point using your
knowledge of squares.

12.2 Problem-Solving Application: Using Graphs

Objective: to solve problems using a graph

Graphs of functions can be useful in solving problems. For example, Kelly made the following graph to show her weekly earnings.

Example

Kelly knows that her base salary as a sales clerk in a sporting goods store is $200. She also receives a commission of 10% on all sales. The equation $y = 0.10x + 200$ describes the relationship between sales in dollars and Kelly's total earnings.

The first number on the y-axis is $210 to save space. Kelly will earn $200 per week even if she does not sell anything. Therefore, 0 on the y-axis is actually $200.

The graph shows Kelly's total earnings based on the amount of sales.

Kelly's sales amount was $100. What are her total earnings? Locate $100 on the x-axis. Now go up until you reach the line representing $y = 0.10x + 200$. Then go across to the left and read the total earnings. Kelly's total earnings will be $210. Kelly's sales amount is $600. What are her total earnings?

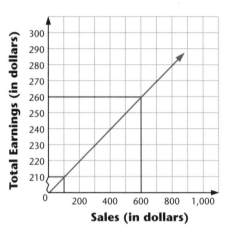

Try THESE

Use the graph at the right to answer questions 1–4.

1. How many eggs are required for 6 servings of egg creole?

2. How many eggs are required for 8 servings of egg creole?

3. How many servings of egg creole will 12 eggs make?

4. How many servings of egg creole will 15 eggs make?

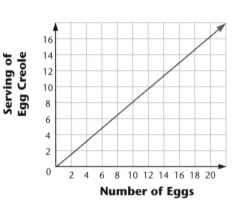

· ·

The graph at the right shows the height of a baseball after it has been thrown into the air. The height depends on the number of seconds since the baseball was thrown.

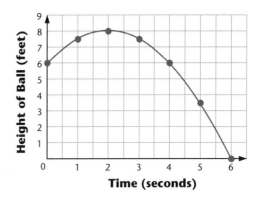

1. How high is the baseball after 1 second?

2. How high is the baseball after 4 seconds?

3. What is the greatest height the baseball reaches after the throw?

4. How many seconds after the baseball is thrown does it reach its highest point?

5. How many seconds after the baseball is thrown does it hit the ground?

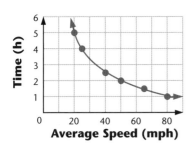

The graph at the left shows the time it takes to travel 100 mi at various speeds. The time it takes depends on the average speed.

6. How long does it take to travel 100 mi at an average speed of 55 mph?

7. How long does it take to travel 100 mi at an average speed of 40 mph?

8. What should your average speed be if you want to travel 100 mi in 2 h?

The graph at the right shows how the distance you are from home is related to the time you have been riding your bike.

9. Suppose after you have been on your bike for 5 minutes, you realize that you have forgotten your math homework. You need to return home to get your homework. Draw a graph that represents this trip to school.

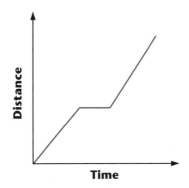

· ·

Compute.

10. 3 − -4

11. -2 + 7

12. -4 • 7

13. -3 • 9

14. -6 + -2

15. 24 ÷ -8

16. -5 • -6

17. -4 − 7

12.3 Translations

Objective: to translate polygons on a coordinate plane

Study the triangle shown on the coordinate plane at the right. It has vertices at points A(1, 1), B(2, 4), and C(4, 1).

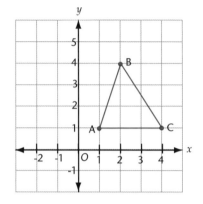

This triangle can be moved around the coordinate plane. When we translate a polygon, we slide the polygon along the coordinate plane. Every point on the polygon is moved the same distance and in the same direction in a **translation**.

Example

Translate triangle ABC 2 units left and 1 unit up.

2 units left—subtract 2 from each *x*-coordinate ($x - 2$)

1 unit up—add 1 to each *y*-coordinate ($y + 1$)

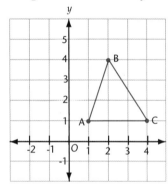

$$A(1, 1) \longrightarrow (1 - 2, 1 + 1)$$
$$A'(-1, 2)$$

$$B(2, 4) \longrightarrow (2 - 2, 4 + 1)$$
$$B'(0, 5)$$

$$C(4, 1) \longrightarrow (4 - 2, 1 + 1)$$
$$C'(2, 2)$$

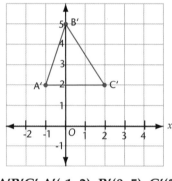

△ABC A(1, 1), B(2, 4), C(4, 1)   △A′B′C′ A′(-1, 2), B′(0, 5), C′(2, 2)

Translation Tips

Move left—Subtract from *x*-coordinate   **Move right**—Add to *x*-coordinate

Move down—Subtract from *y*-coordinate   **Move up**—Add to *y*-coordinate

---

Try THESE

Give the new coordinates for the translated points.

1. D(5, 3) move 3 units right and 2 units down
2. E(-1, 4) move 2 units right and 4 units down
3. F(-2, 1) move left 2 units
4. G(7, -1) move up 4 units

1. Translate △DEF 3 units right and 5 units down. Graph △D'E'F'.

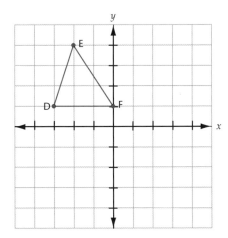

2. Translate parallelogram MNOP 2 units left and 2 units up. Graph M'N'O'P'.

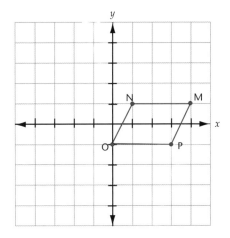

3. Draw a triangle that has vertices at S(1, 1), T(2, -3), and U(4, 0). Draw the translation of △STU up 3 units. Then write the coordinates of the new triangle.

4. Draw a rectangle that has vertices at A(-1, 4), B(2, 4), C(2, 2), and D(-1, 2). Draw the translation of rectangle ABCD right 3 units and down 3 units. Then write the coordinates of the new rectangle.

Problem SOLVING ··

5. △GHI has vertices at G(1, 1), H(3, 2), and I(1, 4). The translated triangle has vertices at G'(3, 4), H'(5, 5), and I'(3, 7). Describe the translation.

Constructed RESPONSE ···

★6. When a triangle is translated, is it congruent to the original triangle? Explain.

7. Draw a rectangle with vertices A(0, 0), B(0, 4), C(3, 4), and D(3, 0). Find the length, width, and area of the rectangle. Then translate the rectangle 3 units down. Find the length, width, and area of the new rectangle. Explain your findings.

Test PREP ···

8. Point A(x, y) is translated 3 units left and 2 units up. What rule describes this translation?
   a. $(x + 3, y + 2)$ b. $(x - 3, y + 2)$ c. $(x + 3, y - 2)$ d. $(x - 3, y - 2)$

9. Point M(4, 3) is translated 2 units right and 5 units down. Which point is a translation of M?
   a. $(2, -2)$ b. $(6, 8)$ c. $(2, 8)$ d. $(6, -2)$

Objective: to reflect polygons on a coordinate plane

Exploration Exercise

1. Draw △ABC A(1, 1), B(2, 4), and C(4, 1).

2. Multiply each *x*-coordinate by -1.

3. Graph the new coordinates. This is △A′B′C′.

4. Fold the graph paper in half at the vertical axis.

5. What do you notice about the two triangles?

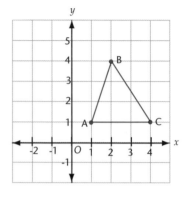

6. Draw △DEF D(1, 1), E(2, 4), and F(4, 1).

7. Multiply each *y*-coordinate by -1.

8. Graph the new coordinates. This is △D′E′F′.

9. Fold the graph paper in half at the horizontal axis.

10. What do you notice about the two triangles?

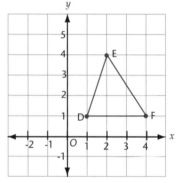

A **reflection** is a transformation that is a flip with respect to an axis of the coordinate plane.

> When reflecting about the *y*-axis, multiply each *x*-coordinate by -1.
> When reflecting about the *x*-axis, multiply each *y*-coordinate by -1.

Example

Reflect △DEF about the *x*-axis.

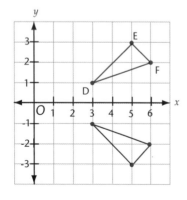

D(3, 1) ⟶ (3, 1 • -1) ⟶ D′(3, -1)

E(5, 3) ⟶ (5, 3 • -1) ⟶ E′(5, -3)

F(6, 2) ⟶ (6, 2 • -1) ⟶ F′(6, -2)

△D′E′F′ is a reflection of △DEF about the *x*-axis.

1. Reflect △MNO over the *y*-axis.

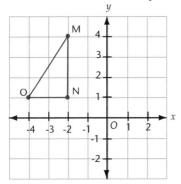

2. Reflect rectangle GHIJ over the *x*-axis.

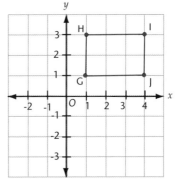

3. Graph the triangle that has vertices at L(-2, -1), M(-4, -2), and N(-1, -3). Reflect the triangle about the *x*-axis. Graph and label the new triangle.

4. Graph the triangle that has vertices at P(-3, 2), Q(-1, 1), and R(0, 4). Reflect the triangle about the *y*-axis. Graph and label the new triangle.

Problem SOLVING ···

★ 5. When a triangle is reflected, is it congruent to the original triangle? Explain.

6. Graph the triangle that has vertices at D(1, 2), E(3, 5), and F(5, 2). Reflect the triangle about the *x*-axis. Then reflect the triangle about the *y*-axis. Graph and label the new triangle.

7. Draw one triangle with vertices (2, 1), (3, 4), and (4, 1) and a second triangle with vertices (-4, 1), (-3, 4), and (-2, 1). Describe two different transformations that could move the first triangle onto the second.

Objective: to rotate figures

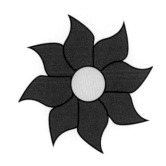

Look at the flower to the right. Can you move the flower in a counterclockwise direction and see the same flower?

If you rotate the flower, you will see the same image. A **rotation** is a transformation that turns a figure about a fixed point, the **center of rotation**, at a given angle and in a given direction. In this lesson, all images will be rotated counterclockwise.

A figure that can be rotated 180° or less about its center and line back up with itself is said to have **rotational symmetry**. The flower above has rotational symmetry.

Examples

A. Does the sun have rotational symmetry?

Yes, it lines up as you rotate it.

B. Rotate △DEF 90° about point O.

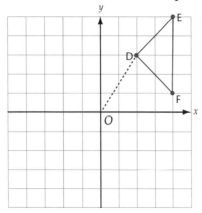 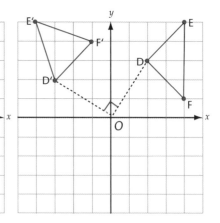

1. Sketch a line from point D to the origin.

2. Measure a 90° angle, and sketch D'O so that D'O = DO.

3. Repeat steps 1 and 2 for points E and F

Exercises

Does each figure have rotational symmetry?

1.

2.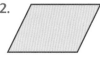

3.

4.

Rotate each figure below 90° about point O.

5.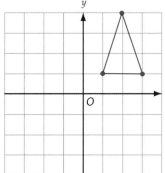

6.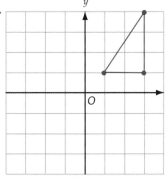

7.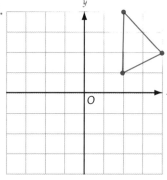

Problem SOLVING

8. Name two letters of the alphabet that have rotational symmetry.

9. Describe an object in your house that has rotational symmetry. Explain how it shows rotational symmetry.

10. Is a rotation of 180° the same as a reflection about the *x*-axis? Give an example to support your answer.

Mid-Chapter REVIEW

On graph paper, draw coordinate axes. Then graph each ordered pair. Label each point with the given letter.

1. A(0, -3)

2. B(2, -4)

3. C(-4, -1)

4. D(2, 5)

Use the triangle to the right to solve problems 5–6.

5. Translate the triangle 4 units down and 2 units right.

6. Reflect the triangle over the *y*-axis.

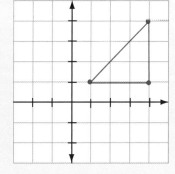

Objective: to dilate polygons on a coordinate plane

Exploration Exercise

1. Draw △ABC A(1, 1), B(2, 4), and C(4, 1).

2. Multiply each coordinate by 2.

3. Graph the new coordinates. This is △A′B′C′.

4. What do you notice about the two triangles?

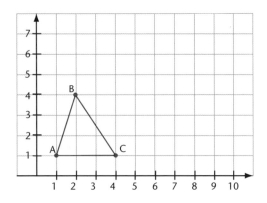

A **dilation** is a transformation that makes a figure larger or smaller but does not affect the shape of the figure. The dilation image is similar to the original figure.

In the exercise above, △A′B′C′ is two times as large as △ABC. It is enlarged by a scale factor of 2. A **scale factor** is the ratio found by comparing the distances from the center of dilation to the original image's center.

Examples

A. Graph the dilation of the image below with a scale factor of 3.

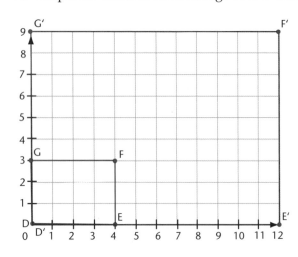

■ Step 1: Multiply each coordinate by 3.

D(0, 0) ⟶ (3 • 0, 3 • 0) ⟶ D′(0, 0)

E(4, 0) ⟶ (3 • 4, 3 • 0) ⟶ E′(12, 0)

F(4, 3) ⟶ (3 • 4, 3 • 3) ⟶ F′(12, 9)

G(0, 3) ⟶ (3 • 0, 3 • 3) ⟶ G′(0, 9)

■ Step 2: Plot the new points and connect.

Rectangle D′E′F′G′ is three times as large as rectangle DEFG.

B. Graph the dilation of the image below with a scale factor of $\frac{1}{2}$.

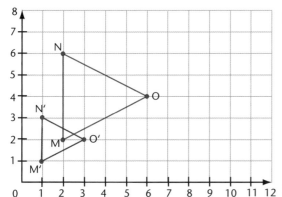

■ Step 1: Multiply each coordinate by $\frac{1}{2}$.

$$M(2, 2) \longrightarrow (\tfrac{1}{2} \cdot 2, \tfrac{1}{2} \cdot 2) \longrightarrow M'(1, 1)$$

$$N(2, 6) \longrightarrow (\tfrac{1}{2} \cdot 2, \tfrac{1}{2} \cdot 6) \longrightarrow N'(1, 3)$$

$$O(6, 4) \longrightarrow (\tfrac{1}{2} \cdot 6, \tfrac{1}{2} \cdot 4) \longrightarrow O'(3, 2)$$

■ Step 2: Plot the new points and connect.

$\triangle M'N'O'$ is half the size of $\triangle MNO$.

Exercises

1. Graph the dilation with a scale factor of 4 of $\triangle XYZ$.

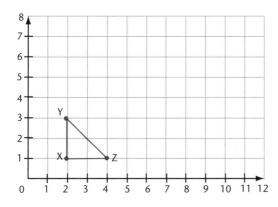

2. Graph the dilation with a scale factor of $\frac{1}{2}$ of parallelogram RSTU.

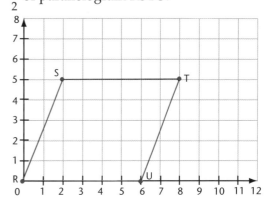

3. Draw a triangle that has vertices at A(-1, 1), B(3, -2), and C(-2, -3). Dilate the triangle with a scale factor of 3. Draw a new triangle and label the coordinates.

Problem SOLVING

4. A 35-mm negative is 25 mm by 34 mm. A print is made that is enlarged by a scale factor of 3. What are the dimensions of the new print?

Constructed RESPONSE

5. A triangle with the coordinates A(2, 1), B(4, 4), and C(5, 2) is dilated by a scale factor of -2.

   a. Draw the new triangle and label the coordinates.

   b. As well as being dilated, what other transformation occurred? Explain.

Mr. Clipper's Backyard

Mr. Clipper has a backyard that is 25 meters long and 10 meters wide. The paths that Mr. Clipper's lawn mower cuts are 1 meter wide. If Mr. Clipper mows his lawn in the manner shown, how far will he have walked when he is finished?

Extension

Suppose the mower cuts a path 0.5 meters wide. How far will Mr. Clipper walk?

Cumulative Review

Compute.

1. 5.24
+ 2.17

2. 27.37
+ 9.8

3. 34.62
− 17.54

4. 760.41
− 92.66

5. 26.3
0.97
+ 4.983

6. $0.5\overline{)4.95}$

7. $3.4\overline{)2.38}$

8. $16\overline{)40}$

9. $2.4\overline{)27.6}$

10. $9.6\overline{)0.24}$

11. $2\frac{2}{5} + 6\frac{7}{10}$

12. $5\frac{7}{9} - 3\frac{1}{3}$

13. $1\frac{1}{2} \times 2\frac{5}{6}$

14. $2\frac{1}{4} \div 2\frac{2}{3}$

Write each fraction as a percent.

15. $\frac{1}{2}$

16. $\frac{8}{10}$

17. $\frac{2}{3}$

18. $\frac{5}{8}$

19. $\frac{3}{5}$

Solve each equation.

20. $n - 6.2 = 14.8$

21. $15t = 22.5$

22. $\frac{r}{0.3} = 165$

23. $x + \text{-}5 = \text{-}3$

24. $\text{-}3y = \text{-}24$

25. $z - 3 = \text{-}4$

Solve.

26. What number is 63% of 22?

27. What percent of 80 is 8?

28. 66 is 25% of what number?

29. 4.2% of 90 is what number?

Compute.

30. $3 + \text{-}1$

31. $\text{-}7 + \text{-}2$

32. $7 + \text{-}13$

33. $6 - \text{-}3$

34. $\text{-}9 - 5$

35. $4 - 9$

36. $\text{-}8 \times \text{-}4$

37. $\text{-}6 \times 6$

38. $3 \times \text{-}9$

39. $\text{-}81 \div \text{-}9$

40. $\text{-}42 \div 7$

41. $\text{-}56 \div \text{-}7$

Solve. Use 3.14 for π.

42. Find the volume of a pyramid whose base is 6 ft^2 and height is 5 ft.

43. Find the volume of the cylinder.

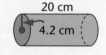

20 cm

4.2 cm

44. The rainfall in each of the last 5 years, in inches, was 44.2, 40.6, 41.2, 45.6, and 39. Find the mean yearly rainfall to the nearest tenth of an inch.

45. Carpet for a rectangular living room costs $17.50 a square yard. If the room is 18 feet by 15 feet, find the cost of carpet for the entire room.

Objective: to graph relations

Marcus walks each day to be more physically active. The distance he travels in 3 hours depends on how fast he is going (his rate). Marcus keeps a table showing his rate and distance.

In Marcus' chart the numbers 2 and 6, 3 and 9, and 4 and 12 are paired. These pairs are examples of a **relation**.

A relation is a set of ordered pairs. A relation can be shown by a table, a set of ordered pairs, or a graph.

Rate (mph)	Distance (mi)
2	6
3	9
4	12

Ordered Pairs
(2, 6)
(3, 9)
(4, 12)

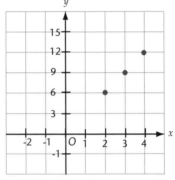

The first coordinates of the ordered pairs above are 2, 3, and 4. These values are the **domain** of the relation. The domain is the set of first coordinates of the ordered pairs of a relation.

The second coordinates of the ordered pairs above are 6, 9, and 12. These values are the **range** of the relation. The range is the set of second coordinates of the ordered pairs of a relation.

The above relation is a **function**. A function is a special relation in which exactly one member of the domain is matched with an element of the range. All functions are relations, but not all relations are functions.

Example

Copy and complete the function table. State the domain and range.

x	x + 5	y
0	0 + 5	5
1		
2		
3		

▷ To complete the function table, substitute the x-values into the function and simplify.

The domain of the function is (0, 1, 2, 3). The range of the function is (5, 6, 7, 8).

x	x + 5	y
0	0 + 5	5
1	1 + 5	6
2	2 + 5	7
3	3 + 5	8

·······························

State the domain and range of each relation. State whether each relation is a function.

1. {(0, 2), (1, -2), (2, 4)}

2. {(-4, 2), (-2, 0), (0, 2), (2, 4)}

3. {(-3, 1), (-2, 0), (-1, 1), (0, 2)}

4. {(-3, 0), (-2, -5), (-2, 6), (3, 7), (0, -17)}

State the relation shown by each graph as a set of ordered pairs. Then state the domain and range of each relation.

5.
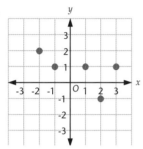

6.
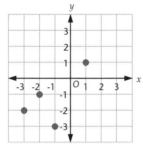

7.
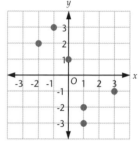

Copy and complete each chart for the given function. State the domain and range of each function. Graph each function.

8.

x	3x – 4	y
-2	3(■) – 4	
0	3(■) – 4	
2	3(■) – 4	
3	3(■) – 4	

9.

x	-2x	y
-3		
-1		
0		
2		

10.

x	$\frac{1}{2}x + 1$	y
-2		
0		
2		
4		

·····································

11. The number of times that a cricket chirps per minute n depends on the temperature t in degrees Fahrenheit. The function is $n = 4(t – 40)$. Choose five values for t, and make a function table.

12. Write five ordered pairs in which the second coordinate is twice the first coordinate. Graph the relation.

·····································

A jar contains 6 red marbles, 5 green marbles, and 9 yellow marbles. When a marble is picked, it is *not* replaced. Find each probability.

13. P(red, red)

14. P(yellow, green)

15. P(red, yellow, green)

Objective: to graph functions

Some of the solutions of $y = 2x + 3$ are shown in the table. The solutions can also be shown by a graph.

Graph the equation $y = 2x + 3$.

Step 1	Step 2	Step 3
Choose at least four values for *x*, and find the corresponding values for *y*.	Graph the ordered pairs.	Use a straightedge to draw a line through the points.

Step 1

$$y = 2x + 3$$

x	2x + 3	y	(x, y)
-2	2(-2) + 3	-1	(-2, -1)
-1	2(-1) + 3	1	(-1, 1)
0	2(0) + 3	3	(0, 3)
1	2(1) + 3	5	(1, 5)

The coordinates of any point on the line will satisfy the equation. The equation above is a **linear equation** because the graph is a straight line.

Another Example

Copy and complete the table. Then graph the equation.

$$y = x - 4$$

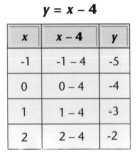

x	x – 4	y
-1	-1 – 4	-5
0	0 – 4	-4
1	1 – 4	-3
2	2 – 4	-2

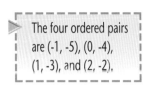

The four ordered pairs are (-1, -5), (0, -4), (1, -3), and (2, -2).

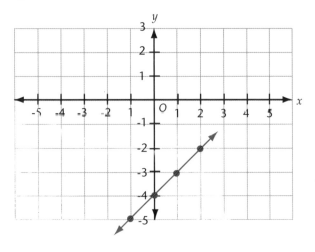

....

Make a table using four values for x. Graph each equation on graph paper. Write the equation on the graph.

1. $y = 2x$
2. $y = \frac{1}{2}x$
3. $y = x$
4. $y = -3x$

5. $y = -4x$
6. $y = -\frac{1}{3}x$
7. $y = x + 5$
8. $y = x - 6$

9. $y = x - 2$
10. $y = 3x - 1$
★11. $y - x = 4$
★12. $2x + 3y = 1$

Problem SOLVING ....

13. Stephanie earns $4.00 per hour at her job. Write an equation that shows the relationship between the hours worked and money earned. Graph the equation. How much money will she earn after working 8 hours?

★14. Not all equations are linear. Graph $y = x^2 + 1$ on graph paper. Explain the differences between this graph and others in this lesson.

Mind BUILDER

Graphing Two Functions

When two lines cross, the point where they cross is their intersection.

y = 2x + 1	
x	**y**
0	1
1	3
2	5
3	7

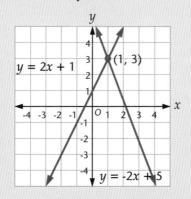

y = -2x + 5	
x	**y**
0	5
1	3
2	1
3	-1

Notice that the graphs intersect at (1, 3). Since this point lies on the graph of each equation, it follows that the ordered pair (1, 3) satisfies both $y = 2x + 1$ and $y = -2x + 5$.

Graph each pair of equations on the same coordinate system. Then label their point of intersection with an ordered pair.

1. $y = x + 5$
   $y = -x + 5$

2. $y = 3x - 1$
   $y = -2x + 4$

3. $y = \frac{1}{2}x + 4$
   $y = 4x - 3$

Objective: to find the slope of lines

The graph to the right shows the amount of money Kelly earns when she baby-sits. Kelly is paid $3 an hour. In the equation $y = 3x$, x is the number of hours and y is the amount of money Kelly earns. We can find the **slope** of the line by looking at the rise and the run or by looking at the equation.

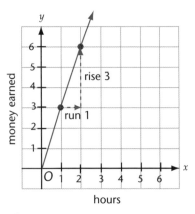

$$\text{Slope} = \frac{\text{rise}}{\text{run}} = \frac{\text{change in } y}{\text{change in } x} = \frac{3}{1} = 3$$

The equation of a line is $y = mx + b$, where m is the slope and b is the y-intercept, where the line crosses the y-axis.

There are three ways to find the slope of a line: from the graph, from the equation, and from two points that pass through the line.

Example

Find the slope of the line that passes through the points (-2, 3) and (-1, 1). Graph the line.

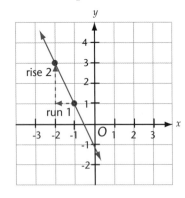

$$\text{Slope} = \frac{\text{rise}}{\text{run}} = -\frac{2}{1} = -2$$

> A line with a positive slope rises from left to right. A line with a negative slope falls from left to right.

The slope of the equation is -2. The slope of the line is negative.

You can also look at the equation to find the slope.

The equation of the line is $y = -2x - 1$.

From the equation, we can see that the slope is -2.

State whether each line has a positive or negative slope.

1.

2.

3.

Exercises

Find the slope of the line that passes through each given pair of points.

1.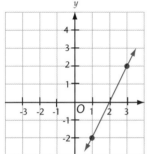

2.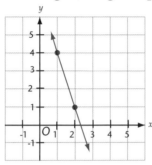

3.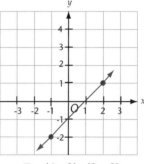

4. (5, 7), (3, 1) 5. (-2, 4), (3, -1) 6. (0, 3), (2, 4) 7. (6, -2), (3, -3)

8. (4, 0), (1, 3) 9. (-5, 9), (4, 3) 10. (-1, 2), (1, -1) 11. (3, 3), (4, 5)

Problem SOLVING

12. Katie pays $4.00 a month for her phone bill and is charged $0.50 a minute for airtime. The equation that represents this situation is $y = \frac{1}{2}x + 4$, where x is the number of minutes. Graph the function. What is the slope of the function?

13. A ladder rests against a wall 20 feet up the wall. The foot of the ladder is 12 feet from the base of the wall. What is the slope of the ladder?

14. A driveway has a slope of $\frac{1}{8}$. The street is 40 feet from the garage door. If the driveway slopes downward, how much lower than the street is the garage door?

Test PREP

15. What is the slope of the line that goes through (6, 5) and (3, 1)?

   a. $\frac{3}{4}$ b. $-\frac{3}{4}$ c. $\frac{4}{3}$ d. $-\frac{4}{3}$

16. The slope of the line that goes through (-3, -5) and (-4, -6) is _____.

   a. positive   b. negative   c. zero   d. none of the above

Objective: to solve problems by finding a pattern

Tennis balls are sold in cans of three. You can make a table to show the relationship between the number of cans and the number of tennis balls. Use x for the number of cans and y for the number of tennis balls.

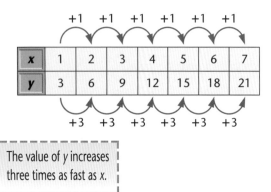

The value of y increases three times as fast as x.

This relation can be shown as an equation. Since y is always three times x, the equation is $y = 3x$.

Another Example

Find the pattern in the table. Describe it using an equation.

	+1	+1	+1	+1	+1	+1
x	1	2	3	4	5	6	7
y	2	5	8	11	14	17	20
	+3	+3	+3	+3	+3	+3

Notice that as x increases by 1, y increases again by 3.

However, $y = 3x$ does not describe this relation. The x-value 1 is paired with the y-value 2 instead of 3. Since 2 is 1 less than 3, try subtracting 1 from $3x$. That is, try $y = 3x - 1$.

If $x = 3$ and $y = 3x - 1$

then $\quad y = 3(3) - 1$

$\qquad\quad y = 8$ ✔

If $x = 6$ and $y = 3x - 1$

then $\quad y = 3(6) - 1$

$\qquad\quad y = 17$ ✔ Check against the table.

The relation in the table is shown by the equation $y = 3x - 1$.

Find the missing terms in each pattern.

1. 7, 9, 11, 13, ■, ■, ■
2. 12, ■, ■, 30, 36, ■
3. 15, 10, 5, 0, ■, ■, ■
4. -8, -13, -18, -23, ■, ■, ■
5. 11, 18, 25, 32, ■, ■, ■
6. 1, 2, 4, 8, ■, ■, ■
7. $2, 1, \frac{1}{2}, \frac{1}{4},$ ■, ■, ■
8. 1, 1, 2, 3, 5, 8, ■, ■, ■

Exercises ·······································

Copy and complete each table. Then write an equation.

1.

x	1	2	3	4	5	6	7
y	5	10	15	■	25	30	■

2.

x	1	2	3	4	5	6	10
y	5	7	9	11	■	■	■

3.

r	-3	-2	-1	0	1	2	8
s	■	-7	■	-1	2	5	■

4.

m	0	1	2	3	5	9	15
n	2	5	8	■	■	29	■

5.

x	3	4	5	6	7	8	15
y	11	15	19	■	■	31	■

6.

a	-2	-1	0	1	2	5	7
b	-11	-9	-7	-5	■	■	■

Solve ·······································

7. Last week, the total sales at a small store were $4,300. This week, the sales were 25% less. What were the sales this week?

8. What happens to the perimeter and area of a rectangle when the length and width are tripled? What happens when the length and width are quadrupled?

9. You fold a square piece of paper in thirds and create 3 rectangles when you open it up again. How many rectangles will you create if you fold the paper in thirds 4 times?

MiXeD REVIEW ·······························

Write each percent as a decimal and as a fraction in simplest form.

10. 15%
11. 38%
12. 6%
13. $66\frac{2}{3}\%$
14. 8.5%

Write each fraction as a decimal and as a percent.

15. $\frac{3}{5}$
16. $\frac{11}{20}$
17. $\frac{27}{10}$
18. $\frac{5}{12}$
19. $\frac{1}{3}$

Language and Concepts

Choose the letter of the correct term to complete each statement.

1. In a(n) _____, the shape of the original figure is not changed but the size is.

2. In the coordinate plane, the axes intersect at the _____.

3. A(n) _____ is a special relation in which exactly one member of the domain is matched with an element of the range.

4. A(n) _____ turns a figure about a fixed point.

5. Sliding every point on a polygon the same distance and in the same direction is a(n) _____.

6. The _____ has two perpendicular number lines.

7. A(n) _____ is a flip with respect to an axis of the coordinate plane.

8. The ratio found by comparing the distances from the center of dilation to the original image's center is the _____.

9. An equation whose graph is a straight line is a(n) _____.

10. The _____ of a line is the rise over the run.

a. coordinate plane

b. dilation

c. function

d. linear equation

e. origin

f. reflection

g. rotation

h. scale factor

i. slope

j. translation

Skills and Problem Solving

On graph paper, draw coordinate axes. Then graph each ordered pair. Label each point with the given letter. Section 12.1

11. A(1, 4)　　　　12. B(-2, 3)　　　　13. C(5, -2)　　　　14. D(-4, -3)

Use the triangle to the right to complete each transformation. Sections 12.3–12.5

15. Translate the triangle 3 units left and 2 units up.

16. Reflect the triangle about the *x*-axis.

17. Rotate the figure 180° about the origin *O*.

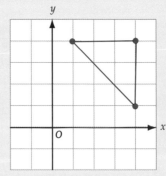

Use the triangle below to solve problem 18. Section 12.6

18. Dilate the triangle with a scale factor of 2 about the origin.

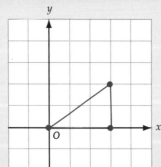

State the relation shown by each table or graph as a set of ordered pairs. Then state the domain and range of each relation. Section 12.7

19.

x	y
-1	3
0	-2
$\frac{1}{2}$	-4
1	-6

20.

x	y
4	0
6	1
8	2
10	3

21.

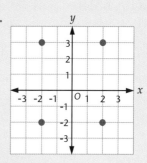

Graph each equation. Write the equation on each graph. Section 12.8

22. $y = x + 3$ 23. $y = -4x$ 24. $y = 2x - 1$

Find the slope of the line that passes through each pair of points. Section 12.9

25. $(5, 3), (2, 1)$ 26. $(-4, 6), (2, 0)$ 27. $(-2, -3), (-5, -7)$

Copy and complete each table. Then write an equation. Section 12.10

28.

x	1	2	3	5	7	10
y	1	4	7	13	■	■

29.

a	-3	-2	-1	0	1	2	3
b	■	7	■	■	1	-1	-3

John works part-time in a store that sells stereo equipment. His base salary is $20 per week. He also receives a commission of 5% on all sales. Use the graph to solve problems 30–36. Section 12.2

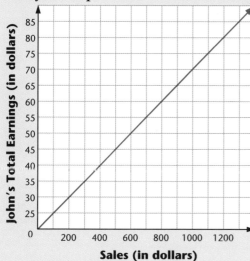

Find John's total earnings for each sales amount.

30. $100   31. $400

32. $800   33. $950

34. John wants total earnings of $45 this week. How much must his sales be?

35. John wants total earnings of $55 next week. How much must his sales be?

36. John wants total earnings of $80 next week. How much must his sales be?

Chapter 12 Test

Find the ordered pair for each point on the coordinate plane at the right.

1. M   2. N   3. O   4. P

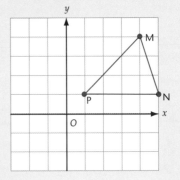

Use the triangle to the right to complete each transformation.

5. Reflect over the y-axis.

6. Translate 4 units left and 3 units down.

7. Rotate the triangle 90° about point O.

8. Dilate the triangle with a scale factor of $\frac{1}{2}$.

State the relation shown by each table or graph as a set of ordered pairs. Then state the domain and range of each relation. State whether the relation is a function.

9.

x	y
-5	5
-2	2
-1	1
0	0

10.

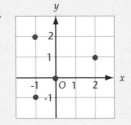

Graph each equation. Write the equation on the graph.

11. $y = x - 4$ 12. $y = -2x + 5$ 13. $y + 3x = 10$

Find the slope of the line that passes through each pair of points.

14. (6, 4), (3, 1)   15. (-7, -2), (5, -3)

Use the following graph to solve problems 16–20.

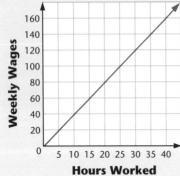

16. What wages are earned when 20 hours are worked?

17. What wages are earned when 35 hours are worked?

18. How many hours are worked to earn $60?

19. How many hours are worked to earn $130?

20. Write an equation that describes the relationship between the hours worked (x) and the weekly wages (y). Explain why this equation describes the relationship.

Other Graphs

Different kinds of graphs can be used to describe events. This graph shows the height of a football above the ground from the time the ball was snapped for a field goal attempt.

Over which time periods did these events occur?

1. The holder received the snap.

2. The ball was increasing in height.

3. The ball was kicked.

4. The ball lands in the stands behind the goal posts.

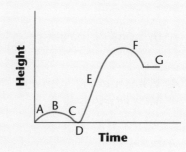

Notice that there are no breaks in the curve because it is possible to have fractional units of both time and height.

This graph shows one team's score during the course of a football game. Give the letter that corresponds to the time these events occurred. The closed circles mean the value is included. The open circles mean the values are not included.

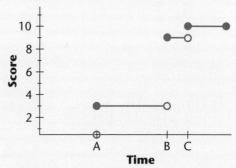

5. The team scored a touchdown (worth 6 points).

6. The team kicked the extra point.

7. The team kicked a field goal (worth 3 points).

8. The team scored its first points.

9. Copy and complete the graph at the right to show the price a fan would have to pay to purchase tickets for a football game. Each ticket costs $10.00. The dots on the graph should not be connected because it is impossible to buy a fractional number of tickets or to pay a fractional value for those tickets.

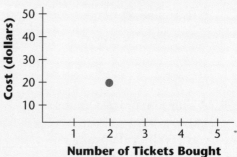

Sketch a graph representing each situation.

10. A call to London, England, costs $1.78 for the first minute and $1.00 for each additional minute. Fractions of a minute are charged as an entire minute.

11. The speed of a skier changes as she goes up the mountain on a lift, waits her turn, and skis down the mountain.

Cumulative Test

1. Which point is not on the graph of $x \geq 5$?
   a. 5
   b. 6
   c. 7
   d. none of the above

2. Solve. $y - 3 = -4$
   a. -7
   b. -1
   c. 1
   d. 7

3. $4 + 8 \cdot 2 \div 4 = $ _____
   a. 5
   b. 6
   c. 8
   d. none of the above

4. What number added to 10 is equal to 4?
   a. -14
   b. -6
   c. 6
   d. 14

5. Find 16% of 320.
   a. 0.512
   b. 5.12
   c. 51.2
   d. 512

6. The ratio of boys to girls is 4 to 3. There are 15 girls. How many boys are there?
   a. 12
   b. 15
   c. 20
   d. 24

7. How is $\triangle ABC$ related to $\triangle DEF$?
   a. dilation
   b. reflection
   c. translation
   d. none of the above

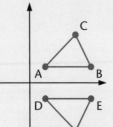

8. A dress originally priced at $65.50 is on sale at a 20% discount. What is the sale price?
   a. $13.10
   b. $52.40
   c. $58.95
   d. $78.60

9. A diagram of the Dunn's patio is shown at the right. Which diagram shows the easiest way to find the area of the patio?

   a. 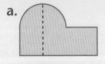   b.

   c.   d. none of the above

10. Which point on the coordinate grid is the graph of the ordered pair (0, -2)?

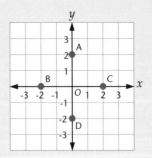

   a. A   b. B
   c. C   d. none of the above

Appendix

Mathematical Symbols

$=$	is equal to
$\neq$	is not equal to
$>$	is greater than
$<$	is less than
$\geq$	is greater than or equal to
$\leq$	is less than or equal to
$\approx$	is approximately equal to
$\overleftrightarrow{AB}$	line AB
$\overline{AB}$	line segment AB
$\overrightarrow{AB}$	ray AB
$\angle$	angle
$\perp$	is perpendicular to
$\parallel$	is parallel to
$\cong$	is congruent to
$\sim$	is similar to
$^\circ$	degrees
$\sqrt{}$	square root
π	pi
$4:3$	ratio of 4 to 3
$\%$	percent

Formulas

$A = l \times w$	area of a rectangle
$A = b \times h$	area of a parallelogram
$A = \frac{1}{2} \times b \times h$	area of a triangle
$C = \pi \times d$	circumference of a circle
$A = \pi \times r^2$	area of a circle
$V = l \times w \times h$	volume of a rectangular prism
$V = \pi \times r^2 \times h$	volume of a cylinder
$V = \frac{1}{3} \times \pi \times r^2 \times h$	volume of a cone
$V = \frac{1}{3} \times l \times w \times h$	volume of a pyramid
$F = \frac{9}{5} \times C + 32$	changing Celsius to Fahrenheit
$C = \frac{5}{9} \times (F - 32)$	changing Fahrenheit to Celsius
$I = p \times r \times t$	interest
$S = 2lw + 2lh + 2wh$	surface area of a prism
$S = 2\pi rh + 2\pi r^2$	surface area of a cylinder
$S = \pi r^2 + \pi rs$	surface area of a cone

Metric System of Measurement

Length   1 centimeter (cm) = 10 millimeters (mm)

   1 meter (m) = 100 centimeters or 1,000 millimeters

   1 kilometer (km) = 1,000 meters

Mass   1 gram (g) = 1,000 milligrams (mg)

   1 kilogram (kg) = 1,000 grams

   1 metric ton (t) = 1,000 kilograms

Capacity   1 liter (L) = 1,000 milliliters (mL)

   1 kiloliter (kL) = 1,000 liters

Customary System of Measurement

Length   1 foot (ft) = 12 inches (in.)

   1 yard (yd) = 3 feet or 36 inches

   1 mile (mi) = 1,760 yards or 5,280 feet

Weight   1 pound (lb) = 16 ounces (oz)

   1 ton = 2,000 pounds

Capacity   1 cup (c) = 8 fluid ounces (fl oz)

   1 pint (pt) = 2 cups

   1 quart (qt) = 2 pints

   1 gallon (gal) = 4 quarts

Glossary

A

absolute value **1.1** The number of units a number is from 0 on the number line. For example, the absolute value of -3 is 3.

acute angle **7.1** An angle that measures between 0° and 90°.

acute triangle **7.7** A triangle that has all acute angles.

addition property of equality **5.3** If a number is added to each side of an equation, the new equation has the same solution.

$$t - 8 = 13$$
$$t - 8 + 8 = 13 + 8$$
$$t = 21$$

adjacent angles **7.2** Two angles that share a vertex, a side, and do not overlap. $\angle ROS$ and $\angle SOT$ are adjacent.

algebraic expression **1.7** An expression that contains at least one variable.

angle **7.1** Two rays with a common endpoint, such as $\angle ABC$.

arc **7.5** A part of a circle.

area **8.2** The number of square units that cover the surface.

associative property of addition **1.8** The way in which addends are grouped does not change their sum.

$$5 + (6 + 7) = (5 + 6) + 7$$

associative property of multiplication **1.8** The way in which factors are grouped does not change their product.

$$(2 \times 3) \times 4 = 2 \times (3 \times 4)$$

B

bar graph **11.5** A way to represent data using horizontal and vertical bars to represent quantities.

base (of an exponent) **1.4** The number that is used as a factor. In 10^2, the base is 10.

$$10^2 = 10 \times 10$$

base (of a percent) **6.9** The number to which another number, called the percentage, is compared. See **percent proportion.**

bisect **7.5** To separate into two congruent parts.

box-and-whisker plot **11.4** A way to visualize how data are arranged. A box is drawn around the quartile values, and whiskers are extended from each quartile to the extreme data points.

C

center of rotation **12.5** A fixed point a figure rotates around.

circumference **8.6** The distance around a circle.

cluster **11.2** An area on a line plot which seems to contain many numbers in the data set.

coefficient **5.2** The number in front of a variable in a term.

combination **10.5** An arrangement in which order is not important.

common factor **3.2** A number that is a factor of two or more given whole numbers. Common factors of 24 and 30 are 1, 2, 3, and 6.

common multiple 3.3 A number that is a multiple of two or more given whole numbers. Some common multiples of 8 and 12 are 0, 24, 48, and 72.

commutative property of addition 1.8 The order in which addends are added does not change the sum.

$$8 + 9 = 9 + 8$$

commutative property of multiplication 1.8 The order in which factors are multiplied does not change the product.

$$5 \times 6 = 6 \times 5$$

compass 7.4 An A-shaped instrument used to draw circles or parts of circles.

complementary angles 7.2 Two angles are complementary if the sum of their degree measures is 90. $\angle$CFD and $\angle$DFE are complementary.

complementary events 10.1 Two events that include all possible outcomes.

composite number 3.1 A number that has more than two factors.

compound event 10.8 Consists of two or more simple events.

cone 9.1 A solid figure with a circular base and one vertex.

congruent figures 7.10 Figures that have the same size and shape.

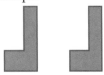

constant 5.2 A term that does not contain a variable.

construction 7.4 A drawing made with a straightedge and compass.

coordinate 12.1 A coordinate of a point is a number on a number line that corresponds to it.

coordinate plane 12.1 The number plane formed by two perpendicular number lines, called *axes*.

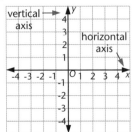

corresponding parts 7.10 The parts of two figures that match.

cube 7.11 A three-dimensional figure where all the faces are equal.

cylinder 9.1 A solid figure that has two parallel congruent circular bases.

D

degree 7.1 A unit for measuring angles. The angle below measures 10°.

dependent events 10.8 Events that affect each other.

diameter 8.6 A line segment through the center of the circle with endpoints on the circle.

dilation 12.6 A transformation which effects the size but not the shape of a figure.

discount 6.10 An amount subtracted from the regular price.

distributive property 1.9 The product of a number and sum is equal to the sum of the products.

$$3 \times (5 + 6) = (3 \times 5) + (3 \times 6)$$

division property of equality 5.4 If each side of an equation is divided by the same number, the new equation has the same solution.

$$7p = 63$$
$$\frac{7p}{7} = \frac{63}{7}$$
$$p = 9$$

domain (of a relation) 12.7 The set of first coordinates of the ordered pairs of a relation.

E

edge 9.1 The intersection of the two faces in a three-dimensional figure.

equation 1.10 A mathematical sentence that contains an equals sign.

$$5 \times 4 = 20 \quad y - 5 = 9$$

equilateral triangle 7.7 A triangle that has three congruent sides. An equilateral triangle is another name for a *regular* triangle.

equivalent 2.1 Two or more numerals are equivalent if they name the same number.

equivalent decimals: 0.2, 0.20, 0.200
equivalent fractions: $\frac{3}{4}, \frac{6}{8}, \frac{9}{12}$

equivalent equation 5.3 A balanced equation, both sides are equal to each other.

error of measurement 8.1 The difference between the true length and the measured length.

estimate 2.2 To find an approximate answer.

event 10.1 A specific outcome or type of outcome.

experimental probability 10.6 The probability of an event occurring based on the relative frequency of the event during an experiment.

exponent 1.4 A number used to tell how many times the base is used as a factor. In 10^2, the exponent is 2.

F

face 9.1 The polygon that makes up the solid.

factor (of a number) 3.2 Any one of two or more numbers whose product is a given number. Since $5 \times 7 = 35$, the factors of 35 are 5 and 7. When you divide a whole number by one of its factors, the remainder is 0.

first coordinate 12.1 The first number of an ordered pair. The first coordinate is a number on the horizontal axis.

frequency table 11.2 A table for organizing numbers of items in a set of data. The frequency column gives the number of times each number or item occurs.

front-end estimation 2.2 A form of estimation where you add the front-end digits and estimate the sum of the remaining digits.

function 12.7 A relation in which exactly one member of the domain is matched with an element of the range.

fundamental counting principle 10.3 It is used to find the total number of possible outcomes of an event.

G

greatest common factor (GCF) 3.2 The greatest whole number that is a factor of two or more given whole numbers. For example, the GCF of 16 and 24 is 8.

H

histogram 11.5 A graph showing how data are distributed.

hypotenuse 8.9 The side of a right triangle opposite the right angle.

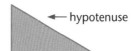

I

identity property of addition **1.8** When zero is added to a number, the sum is that number.

identity property of multiplication **1.8** When a number is multiplied by one, the product is that number.

improper fraction **4.4** A fraction which has a numerator greater than or equal to its denominator.

$$\frac{18}{4} \quad \frac{3}{2} \quad \frac{8}{8}$$

independent events **10.8** Events that do not affect each other.

inequality **5.7** A mathematical statement used to compare quantities.

$$y > 6 \qquad x < 3$$

integers **1.1** The whole numbers and their opposites.

$$\dots, -4, -3, -2, -1, 0, 1, 2, 3, 4, \dots$$

interest **6.11** The principal times the interest rate times the time, given in years.

inverse property of addition **1.8** When a number is added to its opposite, the sum is zero.

inverse property of multiplication **1.8** When a number is multiplied by its reciprocal, the product is one.

irregular figure **8.7** A figure made of triangles, rectangles, circles, and other two-dimensional figures.

isosceles triangle **7.7** A triangle that has two congruent sides.

L

least common denominator **3.7** The least common multiple of the denominators of two or more fractions. The least common denominator of $\frac{1}{6}$ and $\frac{2}{9}$ is 18.

least common multiple (LCM) **3.3** The least whole number other than zero that is a multiple of two or more numbers. For example, the LCM of 18 and 4 is 36.

legs (of a right triangle) **8.9** The two sides of a right triangle which form the right angle.

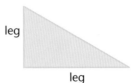

like terms **5.2** Terms that have identical variable parts.

line plot **11.2** A picture of information on a number line. An **x** is often used to indicate the occurrence of a number.

linear equation **12.8** An equation whose graph is a straight line.

lower quartile **11.4** The median of the lower half of data.

M

mean **11.1** The number each member of a set would be if the members were all the same. The mean is found by dividing the sum of the members by the number of addends.

measures of central tendency **11.1** Numbers that represent the center of a data set.

median **11.1** The middle number in an ordered set of data. When there are two middle numbers, the median is the mean of those two numbers.

metric system **2.7** A measurement system that measures length in millimeters, centimeters, meters, or kilometers; capacity in liters or milliliters; and mass in grams or kilograms.

mode **11.1** The number or item that appears most often in a set of data. Some sets of data have no mode or more than one mode.

multiples (of a number) 3.3 Numbers that have the given number as a factor. The multiples are found by multiplying the number by 0, 1, 2, 3, 4, and so on. The multiples of 4 are 0, 4, 8, 12, 16, and so on.

multiplication property of equality 5.4 If each side of an equation is multiplied by the same number, the new equation has the same solution.

$$\frac{x}{8} = 9$$
$$\frac{x}{8} \times 8 = 9 \times 8$$
$$x = 72$$

N

negative integer 1.1 The opposite of a whole number.

O

obtuse angle 7.1 An angle that measures between 90° and 180°.

obtuse triangle 7.7 A triangle that has an obtuse angle.

opposites 1.1 Two numbers that are the same distance from 0 on the number line. For example, 7 and -7 are opposites. The sum of a number and its opposite is 0.

ordered pair 12.1 A pair of numbers in a specific order, such as (4, 3) or (-1, 5). Ordered pairs are graphed on the coordinate plane.

origin 12.1 The point in the coordinate plane where the axes intersect. The ordered pair for the origin is (0, 0).

origin

outlier 11.2 A number much higher or lower than the rest of the numbers in the data set.

P

parallel lines 7.3 Lines in the same plane that do not intersect.

parallelogram 7.8 A quadrilateral with two pairs of parallel sides and opposite sides and angles congruent.

pentagon 7.9 A polygon with five sides.

percent 3.6 A ratio that compares a number to 100. Percent means hundredth. The symbol % indicates percent.

$$23\% = \frac{23}{100} = 0.23$$

percent proportion 6.9 A number that is compared to another number, called the base (B). The rate (r) is a percent.

$$\frac{P}{B} = \frac{r}{100}$$

perfect square 8.8 A rational number whose square root is a rational number. For example, 25, 6.25, and $\frac{1}{9}$ are perfect squares.

perimeter 8.2 The distance around a polygon.

permutation 10.4 An arrangement in which order is important.

perpendicular lines 7.3 Lines that intersect to form right angles.

point 12.1 An exact location in space. It is represented by a dot.

polygon 7.9 A simple, closed figure formed by line segments that are all in one plane and meet only at their endpoints.

positive integer 1.1 A whole number.

power 1.7 A number that can be expressed using an exponent.

prime factorization 3.1 A way to express a composite number as a product of prime numbers. For example, the prime factorization of 60 is $2 \times 2 \times 3 \times 5$.

prime number 3.1 A whole number that has exactly two factors—itself and 1.

principal 6.11 The amount of money you deposit in a savings account or the amount of the unpaid balance of a loan.

prism 9.1 A solid figure that has two parallel congruent sides, called *bases*.

probability 10.1 The ratio of the number of ways an event can occur to the number of possible outcomes.

proportion 6.3 An equation that states that two ratios are equivalent.

$$\frac{3}{8} = \frac{12}{32}$$

protractor 7.1 An instrument used to measure angles.

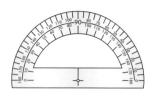

pyramid 9.1 A solid figure in which all the faces, except one, intersect at a point called the vertex. The face that does not intersect at the vertex is called the base.

Pythagorean theorem 8.9 It describes the relationship that exists among the sides of a right triangle. In any right triangle, the square of the length of the hypotenuse is equal to the sum of the squares of the lengths of the other two sides.

Q

quadrilateral 7.8 A polygon with four sides.

quartiles 11.4 The values that separate the data into four parts.

R

radius 8.6 A line segment from the center of the circle to any point on the circle.

range 11.1 The difference between the greatest number and the least number in a set of data.

range (of a relation) 12.7 The set of second coordinates of the ordered pairs of a relation.

rate 6.2 A ratio of two measurements having different units. Examples of rates are $\frac{5 \text{ km}}{2 \text{ min}}$ and 8 mi/h.

ratio 6.1 A comparison of two numbers by division. The ratio of 1 to 3 may be stated as 1 out of 3, 1:3, or $\frac{1}{3}$.

rational number 3.7 Any number that can be expressed as the quotient of two integers, where the divisor is not 0.

$$2.3 = \frac{23}{10} \qquad 5\frac{1}{2} = \frac{11}{2} \qquad -2 = \frac{-2}{1}$$

ray 7.1 Begins at one point, the endpoint, and continues forever in one direction.

reciprocals 4.5 Two numbers whose product is 1. Since $\frac{2}{3} \times \frac{3}{2} = 1$, $\frac{2}{3}$ and $\frac{3}{2}$ are reciprocals of each other.

rectangle 7.8 A parallelogram with all angles congruent.

reflection 12.4 A transformation that is a flip with respect to an axis of the coordinate plane.

regular polygon 7.8 A polygon that has all sides congruent and all angles congruent.

relation 12.7 A set of ordered pairs.

relative error 8.1 The greatest possible error divided by the measured value.

relatively prime numbers 3.2 Two or more nonzero numbers whose greatest common factor is 1.

repeating decimal 3.4 A fraction for which the division of the numerator by the denominator of the fraction yields a quotient in which the digits repeat without end. The fraction $\frac{1}{3}$ can be expressed by a repeating decimal.

$$0.333\ldots = 0.\overline{3}$$

rhombus 7.8 A parallelogram with all sides congruent.

right angle 7.1 An angle that measures 90°.

right triangle 7.7 A triangle that has a right angle.

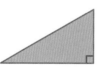

rotation 12.5 The movement of a figure around a fixed point.

rotational symmetry 12.5 When a figure can be rotated 180° or less about its center and line back up with itself.

S

sales tax 6.10 An amount of money that a store charges in addition to the purchase price.

sample 10.7 A small group chosen at random from a larger group. Predictions about the larger group are made by studying the sample.

sample space 10.1 A listing of all possible outcomes of an experiment.

scale drawing 6.5 A representation of something that is too large or too small to be shown in actual size. The scale is the ratio of the scale distance to the actual distance.

scale factor 12.6 The ratio found by comparing the distances from the center of dilation to the original image's center.

scalene triangle 7.7 A triangle that has no congruent sides.

scientific notation 2.6 A way of expressing a number as the product of a factor and a power of 10. The factor must be 1 or greater but less than 10.

$$835,400 = 8.354 \times 10^5$$

second coordinate 12.1 The second number of an ordered pair. The second coordinate is a number on the vertical axis.

similar figures 7.10 Figures that have the same shape but differ in size.

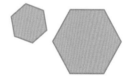

simulation 10.9 To solve a problem by acting it out.

skew lines 7.3 Lines in different planes that neither intersect nor are parallel.

slope 12.9 The ratio of the vertical distance to the horizontal distance.

solid 9.1 A three-dimensional figure that has length, width, and depth.

solution set 5.8 The set of all replacements for the variable that makes the inequality true.

sphere 9.1 A solid with all points the same direction from a given point called the center.

square 7.8 A
parallelogram with
all sides congruent
and all angles congruent.

square root (of a number) 8.8 The opposite of
squaring a number. The symbol for square root
is $\sqrt{}$.

standard form (of a number) 1.4 The simplest
place-value form. The standard form for one
hundred ninety-one is 191.

statistics 11.7 Ways to gather data, graph
data, and make conclusions based on the data.

stem-and-leaf plot 11.3 A way to organize data
that displays all numbers in the data set by
place value. Numbers in the data set are ordered
when a stem-and-leaf plot is completed.

Stem	Leaf
2	1 1 3 8
3	0 2 4 5 5 5
4	3 5 7 7
5	1

2|1 = 21

straight angle 7.1 An angle that measures
180°.

straightedge 7.4 Any object that can be used
to draw a straight line.

subtraction property of equality 5.3 If a
number is subtracted from each side of an
equation, the new equation has the same
solution.

$$k + 3 = 12$$
$$k + 3 - 3 = 12 - 3$$
$$k = 9$$

supplementary angles 7.2 Two angles are
supplementary if the sum of their degree
measures is 180. ∠WYZ and ∠ZYX are
supplementary.

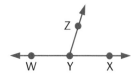

surface area 9.2 The sum of the all of the faces
of a solid.

T

terminating decimal 3.4 A fraction for which
the division of the numerator by the
denominator of the fraction has a last
remainder of 0. The fraction $\frac{1}{5}$ can be expressed
by the terminating decimal 0.2.

term 5.2 A number or variable or a product or
quotient of numbers or variables.

theoretical probability 10.6 The quotient of
the number of ways an event can occur and the
number of possible outcomes.

translation 12.3 A transformation that is a
slide along one of the axes of the coordinate
plane.

transversal 7.3 A line that intersects a set of
parallel lines.

trapezoid 7.8 A quadrilateral with exactly one
pair of parallel sides.

tree diagram 10.2 A diagram that uses
branches to show all possible outcomes.

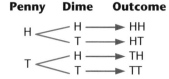

triangle 7.7 A polygon with three sides.

U

unit rate 6.2 A rate with a denominator of 1.

$$\frac{8 \text{ km}}{1 \text{ h}} = 8 \text{ km/h}$$

upper quartile 11.4 The median of the upper
half of data.

V

variable 1.5 A symbol, usually a letter, that is used to stand for an unspecified number. In the open sentence $x + 8 = 15$ the variable is x.

Venn diagram 7.6 Overlapping circles enclosed in a rectangle that show how objects are classified.

vertex (in a solid) 9.1 The point where the edges of a three-dimensional figure intersect.

vertex (of an angle) 7.1 The common endpoint of the two rays that form an angle.

← vertex

vertical angles 7.2 Two angles that are opposite each other and are formed by two intersecting lines.

volume 9.4 The amount of space that a solid figure contains. It is measured in cubic units, such as cubic inches (in.^{3}) or cubic centimeters (cm^3).

Index